★ AMERICA'S FAILING EMPIRE ★

AMERICA'S RECENT PAST

This new and exciting series charts the most recent historical developments that have shaped America and the world. While the study of history generally concentrates on the distant past, where there are established works and perspectives shaped by several generations of historians, this series tackles new questions and issues. Each book in the series provides a concise and engaging overview of specific events and historical trends of the late twentieth century and beyond. Authors present sustained historical arguments about particular problems in recent American history, to give students an immediate historical grasp of current events and to stimulate general readers interested in contemporary topics and issues.

AMERICA'S FAILING EMPIRE:

U.S. FOREIGN RELATIONS SINCE THE COLD WAR

Warren I. Cohen

Blackwell Publishing

BLACKWELL PUBLISHING
350 Main Street, Malden, MA 02148-5020, USA
9600 Garsington Road, Oxford OX4 2DQ, UK
550 Swanston Street, Carlton, Victoria 3053, Australia

First published 2005 by Blackwell Publishing Ltd

2   2006

Library of Congress Cataloging-in-Publication Data

Cohen, Warren I.
America's failing empire : U.S. foreign relations since the Cold War / Warren
I. Cohen.
    p. cm. – (America's recent past ; 1)
Includes bibliographical references and index.
ISBN-13: 978-1-4051-1426-4 (hardback : alk. paper)
ISBN-10: 1-4051-1426-6 (hard cover : alk. paper)
ISBN-13: 978-1-4051-1427-1 (pbk. : alk. paper)
ISBN-10: 1-4051-1427-4 (pbk. : alk. paper)
1. United States–Foreign relations–1989– I. Title. II. Series.

E840.C45 2005
327.73′009′049–dc22   2004027276

A catalogue record for this title is available from the British Library.

Set in 10/12.5 pt Sabon
by SNP Best-set Typesetter Ltd, Hong Kong
Printed and bound in the United Kingdom
by TJ International Ltd, Padstow, Cornwall

The publisher's policy is to use permanent paper from mills that operate a sustainable
forestry policy, and which has been manufactured from pulp processed using acid-free and
elementary chlorine-free practices. Furthermore, the publisher ensures that the text paper
and cover board used have met acceptable environmental accreditation standards.

For further information on
Blackwell Publishing, visit our website:
www.blackwellpublishing.com

FOR MY CHILDREN,

GEOFF AND ANNE

AND MY GRANDCHILDREN,

GRACE AND TESS

AASE MARIE AND MIRIAM,

ALL OF WHOM

WOULD HAVE MADE MY FATHER,

MURRAY COHEN (1909–63),

VERY PROUD

CONTENTS

Acknowledgments

First, I am grateful to Ron Edsforth for inviting me to contribute a volume to his series. Many years ago, when Ron was enrolled in my seminars at Michigan State University, I realized I was learning at least as much from him as he was from me. I was reminded of that fact by his critique of the first draft of this book. I remembered also how gentle he was in redirecting the errant thought of his classmates. I am not surprised to discover that he is a superb editor.

I am also grateful to Nancy Bernkopf Tucker, who put aside her own manuscript on several occasions to comment on mine, allowing herself to fall further behind in the race to see which of us will write more books. Nancy, too, has taught me a great deal and saved me from many errors – including a few of a scholarly nature – in the 17 years we've been together.

My friend and colleague, John Jeffries, was my third reader. No one knows recent American history better than John. Although he sometimes despairs of my analyses, he, too, has been gentle in his efforts to nudge me in the right direction.

I did not ask Jim Mann to read this manuscript, but I have benefited enormously from his writings, most obviously his magnificent *Rise of the Vulcans*, and the many conversations we have had about American foreign policy over the last decade.

Finally, I would like to thank Peter Stothard, editor of the *Times Literary Supplement*, and Steve Wasserman, Book Review editor of the *Los Angeles Times*, for sending me so many fascinating books to read. Working on those reviews proved to be wonderful preparation for writing this volume.

INTRODUCTION:
THE COLD WAR AS HISTORY, 1945–89

In 1989, Mikhail Gorbachev, the last leader of the Soviet Union, signaled to the world that he was withdrawing Moscow from the confrontation with the United States, generally known as the Cold War. For more than 40 years, the two great empires had competed to make the world safe for their respective visions. What had begun as a familiar great power contest in an anarchic world had become an ideological crusade as well, perceived on both sides as a struggle between liberal democracy and communism. Now Gorbachev had concluded that his nation could no longer afford the effort. The Soviet Union was on the brink of collapse and his only hope of revitalizing it was to surrender its sphere of influence in Eastern Europe, reduce military spending, and end subsidies to its friends around the world. The Cold War was over. Among American leaders, a profound and persistent suspicion of Soviet motives would slowly give way to a sense of having triumphed in an epic struggle.

When World War II ended in 1945, the men who had led the United States to victory were determined to do whatever was necessary to protect the interests and security of their country. They concluded that Americans, their values, and their friends abroad would be safe only if American power, economic, political, and military, was sufficient to deter any potential transgressor. Although there were many bumps along the way, the decisions Gorbachev made in 1989 indicated that the "wise men" of 1940's Washington had been successful.

The economic dominance of the United States had been assured by the international economic regime created at the Bretton Woods Conference of 1944. Meeting in New Hampshire in July of that year, the representatives of 44 nations agreed to the outline of a postwar monetary regime. The principal goal of the conference was the creation of mechanisms for assuring stable exchange rates to facilitate the expansion of international trade. To that end the participants created the International Monetary Fund (IMF), designed to provide member nations with assistance whenever their balance of payments (the balance between funds coming in through exports, services, tourism, remissions, etc., and funds expended for imports, overseas travel, and investments by one's nationals) was in deficit. They also created a bank for reconstruction and development which came to be known as the World Bank to provide or guarantee loans private bankers might find unattractive. In addition, beyond the scope of the conference, the American planners envisioned an international trade organization (initially the General Agreement on Tariffs and Trade (GATT) and subsequently the World Trade Organization (WTO), that would gradually eliminate restrictive trade practices.

The United States, as the wealthiest nation in the world, with an economy that had rebounded from the Great Depression and manifested extraordinary productivity during the war, would provide much of the funding required by these institutions – and maintain a commensurate degree of control over their operations. There was never any doubt, anywhere in the world, that the Bretton Woods system was designed to serve the long-term interests of the United States. In a willing suspension of disbelief, the leaders of other nations accepted the idea that what was good for America would be good for the world; that the world would benefit from the responsible and generous position to which the United States had committed itself.

Politically, American leaders expected to exercise influence through the United Nations. They were of a generation that had been taught that the failure of the United States to join the League of Nations after World War I had invited Japanese, Italian, and German aggression in the 1930s. They would not repeat that mistake. The United States would join the new international organization. Washington – and the other four permanent members of the UN Security Council – would be able to veto substantive (as opposed to procedural) measures of the Security Council guaranteeing that the UN could never take effective action against American interests. In the 1940s, however, it seemed highly unlikely that the UN would ever oppose the United States when so many of its members were dependent upon American largesse. Ostensibly an organization for collective security, American leaders perceived it as an instrument of American foreign policy. The validity of that perception did not come into question until the 1960s – and then in large part because of the great expansion of membership as the decolonization process created new independent states.

In the course of World War II, the United States had constructed an enormously powerful military machine and the admirals and generals who ran it were loath to dismantle it. American troops had conquered scores of Pacific islands once controlled by the Japanese. The U.S. Navy had no intention of surrendering any of these. They would become part of the new empire, the fortified positions that would make the Pacific an American lake. In Japan, in Europe, and in the Middle East, during and after the war, the American military gained control of the bases that the men in Washington perceived as vital to assuring the dominance of the United States in the parts of the world that they considered critical. There was nothing sinister about their efforts: they were charged with assuring the security of the nation and facilitating the expansion of its influence and they acted as they deemed necessary to meet their responsibilities.

The principal obstacle to ensuring American predominance in the immediate postwar era was the unwillingness of most of the American people and their elected representatives in Congress to make any further sacrifices. After the Japanese surrender in August, 1945, they saw no need to keep their fathers, brothers, and sons overseas, or even in uniform. The threat from Germany and Japan had been eliminated.

They demanded and won an extraordinarily rapid demobilization of the armed forces. The United States had joined the United Nations. It had a monopoly of nuclear weapons. Surely it no longer needed its military. The popular attitude toward taxes was comparable. The people had tightened their belts to pay for the war. Now they wanted to spend their money on all the goods they had done without. Shrewd politicians were quick to promise tax cuts.

In this context, admirals determined to maintain a two-ocean navy, and air force generals eager for a postwar role, scanned the horizon for danger – and the Soviet Union was the obvious candidate. Only months after General Douglas MacArthur accepted the Japanese surrender in Tokyo Bay, Washington buzzed with concerns over the Soviet threat.

With the access to Soviet archives gained after the Soviet collapse, there can no longer be any doubt of Josef Stalin's hostile intentions toward the West. American leaders who were troubled by Soviet actions in Eastern Europe and worried about possible conflict with the Soviet Union were unquestionably perceptive. But they also knew that the Soviets did not pose an imminent threat to the United States or its friends in Western Europe. The Red Army was not coming, at least not any time soon.

The challenge to those who led the country in the late 1940s – Harry Truman, George Marshall, Dean Acheson – was to persuade the American people and the Congress to make immediate sacrifices to stave off a danger that *might* emerge five or ten years down the line. The United States would have to reconstitute its military power and project it all over the world to assure American dominance – and, presumably, world peace. Only an American imperium, a Pax Americana, would protect the best interests of humankind – and that would cost billions of dollars, taxpayers' dollars.

Acheson proved equal to the challenge. He explained to a Congress elected with a mandate to cut government spending and taxes that the Soviet Union had embarked on a course of conquest, beginning with Greece and Turkey, then the rest of the Middle East, spreading its influence like the rot in a barrel of apples across Africa, South Asia, Europe – and tomorrow the world. Stalin could be stopped, but only by the United States, and only if Congress recognized the danger and appropriated the funds the government needed to save what came to be known as the "free world."

The elected representatives of the American people gave the government what it wanted. They funded aid to Greece and Turkey to help "free peoples" resist communist pressures. They passed the European Recovery Act – the Marshall Plan – to facilitate the reconstruction of Western European economies, a prerequisite to implementation of the Bretton Woods system. Wisely, the United States allowed the Europeans to design their recovery program rather than imposing one made in Washington. American dollars and American military advisers began to move into distant regions. The new American mission to control as much of the world as possible to contain the evil of Soviet communism was under way.

The British and other Europeans closer to Soviet forces did not have to be persuaded of the threat. Indeed, the British had feared the Americans were insufficiently concerned. Several European leaders urged the United States to post troops in Western Europe and to forge the alliance that emerged as the North Atlantic Treaty Organization (NATO). A prominent Norwegian scholar called it "empire by invitation." Most Europeans were prepared to accept the idea that an American presence would be benign.

Acheson and his staff also concluded, after a study known as NSC-68 which was presented to the president early in 1950, that the American military budget would have to be tripled to build the kind of force that could counter the Soviets or their proxies anywhere they probed. Truman thought it ludicrous, politically suicidal – and unnecessary. But Stalin rescued the plan when he enabled Kim Il Sung's North Korean army to attack South Korea in June 1950. The nature and imminence of the Soviet threat appeared obvious, and in the process of leading those forces repelling the North Koreans – and the Chinese Communists who came to their defense – the United States began a major military build-up. When the war ended,

40,000 American troops remained in Korea to deter a future attack. Based in Korea, Japan, Taiwan, the Philippines, and on a long string of Pacific islands, American troops attempted to halt the spread of Soviet influence in the region.

There was one other part of the world that became enormously important to the United States after World War II: the Middle East. Historically, Americans had not perceived any vital interest in the area. The United States was, after all, a net exporter of oil until the 1950s. But an assured flow of oil at a reasonable price was essential not only to American military and industrial power, but to that of its friends and allies as well. The oil of the Middle East was a vital ingredient of the international economic system Washington advocated – and American oil companies were eager to have access to it. A symbiotic relationship developed between the United States and Saudi Arabia, possessor of the world's largest petroleum reserves. The Saudis kept the oil flowing and the Americans offered protection from radical Arab states, such as the Egypt of Gamal Abdel Nasser or the Iraq of Saddam Hussein. Control of the Persian Gulf, through which much of the world's oil traveled, came to be viewed as a vital American interest.

Although access to oil was the principal concern of the United States in the Middle East, a second concern – for the well-being of the state of Israel – greatly complicated American involvement in the region. After World War II, many European Jews who survived the Holocaust, victims of the world's earlier indifference and persecution, were allowed to migrate to Palestine and promised a homeland there. The return of the Jews to their ancient land displaced thousands of Palestinian Arabs who did not move aside voluntarily. The Palestinians and their Arab neighbors fought war after war against the Israelis and both sides manipulated the superpowers to obtain aid for their respective causes. Truman, contrary to the advice of his secretaries of state and defense who were fearful of antagonizing the Arab world, had been quick to recognize Israel when it declared its existence in May, 1948. His domestic political advisers thought it urgent to lock-in the pro-Zionist vote before the November election. The Eisenhower administration attempted to remain aloof from the Arab-Israeli conflict, but in the 1960s, as the Soviets aided several Arab countries, the United States became Israel's principal backer and *de facto* ally. Increasingly hostility toward the Jewish state among Arabs and other Muslims was directed toward the United States as well.

As the confrontation with the Soviet Union and its allies developed, the United States retreated from its historic opposition to colonialism. This was most apparent in East Asia, where American aid to metropolitan France and the Netherlands facilitated efforts by those countries to reimpose their control over Indochina and the East Indies. Revolutionaries in both colonies had hoped for American support, quoting Washington, Jefferson, Lincoln, or Wilson in their appeals for self-determination. But American leaders were reluctant to antagonize their European allies and fearful of communist influence in the independence movements. They pressured the Dutch to withdraw only after becoming convinced that non-communist nationalists would control a free Indonesia – and that continued warfare played into the hands of Indonesian communists. In Indochina, the Americans muted their criticism of the French early, began aiding them in May, 1950, and ultimately supplanted them in the mid-1950s. After all, Ho Chi Minh, the Vietnamese leader of the struggle against France, was a communist.

Similarly, Washington withheld criticism of Belgian and Portuguese imperialism in Africa. American actions failed to match the traditional anti-imperialist rhetoric that had fired the imagination of so many of the colonized peoples of the world. And among the peoples of what came to be called the Third World, mostly nations aligned with neither the Americans nor the Soviets, the United States began to be perceived as the power that allowed for the persistence of colonialism, that propped up the European imperialists who oppressed them.

America also ceased to be viewed as the beacon of democracy – although the American people stubbornly held to that image of their country. Commitment to democratic norms and respect for human rights no longer seemed an important criterion for obtaining support. Virtually any regime that espoused anticommunism, however abhorrent its government, could count on American military and economic assistance – Francisco Franco in Spain, Antonio Salazar in Portugal, the Colonels in Greece, the House of Saud in Saudi Arabia, the Shah of Iran, Muhammad Zia-ul Haq in Pakistan, Chiang Kai-shek in China and Taiwan, Syngman Rhee, Park Chung Hee, and Chun Doo Hwan in Korea, Suharto in Indonesia, Joseph Mobutu in the Congo, Augusto Pinochet in Chile, to name a few.

Earlier in its history, the United States had not hesitated to intervene in the internal affairs of Mexico and various states in Central America and the Caribbean whenever the men in Washington considered their country's strategic or economic interests at stake. Sometimes they perceived themselves as merely giving lessons in good government. In the context of the Cold War, this practice was extended across the globe.

As early as 1948, the United States secretly poured funds into Italy to support candidates it preferred in a democratic election. In the 1950s, it removed suspect leaders in Iran and Guatemala and tried unsuccessfully to do the same in Indonesia and Laos. It installed a government of its choosing in Vietnam and encouraged a coup against it in 1963 when it no longer behaved to Washington's satisfaction. Efforts to overthrow Fidel Castro in Cuba failed, despite subcontracting his planned assassination to the Mafia, but the United States moved quickly to prevent alleged Castro supporters from taking control in the Dominican Republic in 1965. It conspired to bring down the democratically elected government of Salvatore Allende in Chile. In each instance, American presidents – Truman, Dwight Eisenhower, John F. Kennedy, Lyndon Johnson, and Richard Nixon – acted to preserve or enhance the security of the empire, with little cost in American lives and with minimal awareness among the American people.

Intervention in Vietnam proved to be a very different story. In 1954, the Viet Minh, led by Ho Chi Minh, forced the French to withdraw from Indochina. As part of the Geneva Agreements that halted the fighting, Vietnam was divided *temporarily* at the 19th parallel to permit the opposing forces to disengage. The country was to be reunified after an election in 1956 in which Ho was the overwhelming favorite to win popular support. Eisenhower described him as the George Washington of his people. Unwilling to allow the communists to gain control of the entire country, Eisenhower intervened to prevent the election. The United States had claimed success in containing Soviet influence in Europe. American leaders were determined to do as well fighting the Cold War in Asia, where the principal communist threat appeared to come from Moscow's Beijing ally. The Chinese had aided Ho in his struggle against the French and were assumed to have great influence over his government. Eisenhower described Vietnam as the first in a set of potentially falling dominoes in Southeast Asia. He and his advisers chose to draw the line at the 19th parallel, south of which communism would not be permitted to spread. The United States attempted to create a separate state out of southern Vietnam and supported Ngo Dinh Diem, a prominent anticommunist nationalist to head its government.

The attempt to create a nation in southern Vietnam failed miserably. Unable to accomplish its goal of establishing a viable anticommunist regime through financial and technical assistance, Washington, beginning with the Kennedy administration, turned the assignment over to its military with traumatic results. To the astonishment and horror of the American public, the deployment of more than 500,000 American troops by President Johnson and the use of all sorts of advanced military technology, did not suffice to win the day. The mighty United States was defeated by a Third World people unwilling to yield to overwhelming power, and prepared to pay any price to assure its independence.

Worst of all, from the perspective of American leaders, more than 50,000 young Americans died fighting in Vietnam. The public support for the war eroded and increasing numbers of Americans became convinced that maintaining such imperial outposts was not worth the cost – a feeling intensified by the impact of the war's financing on the nation's economy.

The so-called Vietnam syndrome put a brake on American interventionism in distant lands for a few years. After withdrawing ignominiously from Vietnam in 1973, empire building seemed to lose momentum. Activities that required large-scale American military forces were out of the question; so, too, were costly covert operations employing local troops or mercenaries, as in Angola. Congress asserted itself against the White House, against the "imperial presidency," insisting that the urge to expand the influence of the United States was not contributing to the security or well-being of the American people. There were few advocates of isolationism, but there was a widespread feeling that the nation had over-reached itself, that the foreign policy elite, the "best and the brightest," had led the country astray. The crusade against communism faltered.

Indeed, for a few years in the early 1970s, as the United States extricated itself from Vietnam, the question of whether the containment of communism was the ultimate purpose of American foreign policy seemed worthy of debate. Richard Nixon and Henry Kissinger, pursuing a policy of *détente*, had ended decades of hostility between the United States and the People's Republic of China. They had both traveled to Beijing to court Mao Zedong, the Chinese Communist leader responsible for the deaths of tens of millions of his own people. Their goal was not to persuade him to improve his government's performance in human rights, but rather to align his nation with the United States against their common Soviet adversary. Meeting with a significant degree of success, they used the rapprochement with China as a lever with which to win the moderation of Soviet behavior. For a few years, Cold War tensions eased. However fleeting, it seemed that this was the triumph of Nixon/Kissinger *Realpolitik* over ideology.

Unfortunately, the Soviet leader, Leonid Brezhnev, had no intention of ending the competition with the United States in the Third World. He certainly had no intention of surrendering any influence the Soviet Union had gained since the end of World War II. In 1968, when Soviet-backed forces crushed a Czech communist government planning to create a multiparty system, he had claimed the right to intervene to preserve "socialist" regimes – the "Brezhnev Doctrine." The doctrine was still very much in force a decade later when the communist government of Afghanistan verged on collapse. In marched the Red Army to the rescue, horrifying the men and women in Washington who had visions of ending the Cold War. President

Jimmy Carter had normalized relations with China, his secretary of state, Cyrus Vance, was working frantically to strengthen *détente* with the Soviets, and Carter had dreamt of being remembered for efforts worldwide on behalf of human rights. Hyperbolically, he pronounced the Soviet invasion of Afghanistan to be the gravest danger to world peace since World War II and began a new arms buildup in the United States. A new era of confrontation between the two great empires began.

The Soviets were shocked by the forcefulness of Carter's response and went on the defensive in the court of world opinion. Their war in Afghanistan gradually drained resources from their already seriously troubled economy. Their army, no matter how brutally it performed, could not crush Afghan guerrilla forces, supplied primarily by the United States and China, with enormously important assistance from Pakistan. From across the Muslim world, *jihadis* traveled to Afghanistan to fight alongside the local *mujahadin* against the Soviet infidels. By the mid-1980s, American Green Berets were slipping into Afghanistan to train anti-Soviet forces in the use of shoulder launched Stinger antiaircraft missiles to take out Soviet helicopters. The Soviets had met their own Vietnam and their economy proved far less resilient than that of the Americans. Moscow could no longer bear the cost of empire.

Throughout the confrontation with the Soviet Union, the men and women who directed the course of American foreign policy perceived the United States as the leader and protector of friendly states across the globe. Few, if any, among them thought of their country as an imperial power dominating half the world, controlling the destinies of billions of people. Friendly nations were allies, not subjects. In theory, major decisions were made in consultation. Leaders of allied states were not puppets. Washington could not dictate to Charles de Gaulle, the haughty French president who withdrew his forces from NATO command, or to Park Chung Hee, the Korean general who seized power in Seoul, or to Ferdinand Marcos, who decided to end democracy in the Philippines. Japan could not be forced to open its markets to American goods and services.

But no American leader in the Cold War era doubted that the United States was the dominant power in the noncommunist world; that all major decisions would be made in Washington. The commitment to consulting with friends and allies was genuine and generally respected, but the Americans were always prepared to act unilaterally. There were no important instances when arguments from other states stopped the United States from doing what its policymakers thought necessary. In the case of Korea in 1950, the United States won the support of a compliant UN, fought the war under the UN flag, but provided the military leadership, controlled the military decisions, and provided the largest number of foreign troops participating. On that occasion, it obtained key support from Great Britain and significant support from several other UN member states. In Vietnam, however, American allies were far less willing to join the fray. Much of the little outside support was bought and paid for, as, for example, the Korean contingent, funded entirely by the United States.

The unsuccessful war to prevent a communist victory over all of Vietnam was overwhelmingly an American war, directed, financed, fought, and lost by Americans. Increasingly in the 1980s, American interventions found little or no support from the nation's friends as it sent troops to Lebanon and Grenada, planes against Qaddafi's Libya, and aid to the contras in Nicaragua.

As the Cold War wound down in the mid-1980s, largely as a result of Gorbachev's recognition of the internal rot in the Soviet Union and its East European allies, the United States was also staggering. Many analysts wrote of its imminent decline. The Yale historian Paul Kennedy's *Rise and Fall of the Great Powers* (1987), stressing the danger of imperial "overstretch" became a bestseller. In particular, the American economy was in trouble. American industry was performing poorly, falling behind foreign competitors, specifically the Germans and Japanese, widely perceived as the real "winners" of the Cold War. The administration of Ronald Reagan had run up an enormous deficit in the federal budget, cutting taxes at the same time that it increased military spending. In the 1980s, the world's leading creditor nation since World War I became the world's leading debtor nation.

There were other problems as well. The United Nations was no longer an instrument of American foreign policy. Third World countries, usually supported by the Soviets and their allies, had turned the organization against the United States. The UN could do little harm to American interests, thanks to the veto, but as a platform for opposition to those interests and to American values, it was now perceived in Washington as an irritant rather than an asset. Congress began withholding American dues to the UN, hindering some of its operations.

The brightest spot remaining was military power. No nation, not even the Soviet Union, could match American military power. American military technology, specifically the design of so-called "smart" weapons that could home in on selected targets, was intimidating. Only the Soviet Union, with its huge conventional forces, its missiles and its nuclear weapons, could deter the United States from using its power when and where it pleased.

If the Cold War did end, what new course might American policymakers choose? Most of the international economic system the United States had created at Bretton Woods – the IMF, the World Bank, GATT – remained in place. By 1989, even the People's Republic of China was eager to play a part in it, working toward a market economy "with Chinese characteristics," attracting foreign capital and expanding its international trade exponentially. The Soviet model, the command economy, was discredited. If a future administration in Washington could get the deficit under control, if American industry could recover its competitiveness – very big "ifs," indeed – the United States could continue to lead if not dominate the international economic system.

And if the Soviet Union chose to play a more constructive role in the world, perhaps even to collaborate with the United States in shaping a new world order, America's political leadership might be retained. The United Nations might once again be responsive to Washington's influence and vision.

A world freed of superpower confrontation might be a world without war, a world in which Americans did not have to send their children to fight and die in distant lands. The arms race between the United States and the Soviet Union would end and defense spending could be cut sharply. American taxpayers' dollars could be used for education, and the environment, and health care. More attention might be paid to the problems created by globalization – the widening gap between rich and poor nations, the spread of diseases such as AIDS, Ebola, West Nile, and SARS, the opportunities open borders provide for terrorists and drug traffickers. Nongovernmental organizations struggling to improve human rights performance around the world, to rid the earth of landmines, to find peaceful solutions to conflicts large and small, to protect the environment might have a greater chance for success.

But first the Cold War would actually have to end – and George H.W. Bush, the man who succeeded Reagan as president of the United States, would have to work with Gorbachev to end it peacefully. Then the Bush administration would have to decide how that tremendous military power of the United States would be used, if at all. Most of all, Bush and his advisers would have to choose a new course in foreign policy if containment of the Soviet Union, the overarching aim of American policy for more than four decades, was no longer necessary.

1

THE END OF THE COLD WAR
INTERNATIONAL SYSTEM

In November 1988, the American people elected as their new president a man very different from their beloved Ronald Reagan. Whereas Reagan, long-time actor, sometime voice of General Electric, and two-term governor of California entered the White House with no experience in international affairs, George Herbert Walker Bush was one of the most experienced and best qualified presidents ever called upon to oversee the foreign policy of the United States. He had served as ambassador to the United Nations, head of the liaison office in Beijing, and director of the Central Intelligence Agency. As Reagan's vice president for eight years he had remained deeply engaged in international issues, perhaps more than the president.

Reagan had had a few big ideas – build-up American military power, protect the country against nuclear attack, defeat communism – but notoriously left details to his subordinates. Briefings generally bored him and he often fell asleep as his aides debated issues. In his last years, he may have been slipping into the dread grip of the Alzheimer's disease that subsequently ravaged his mind. Bush was less ideological and widely perceived as pragmatic – a problem solver. Philosophically, he was closer to the *Realpolitik* of Henry Kissinger than to the ideological purity demanded by conservative Republicans. His work style was radically different from Reagan's. On major policy issues he was in near constant contact with his national security adviser and secretary of state. On policy toward China, he was so deeply enmeshed in every detail that others involved joked that he had replaced the officer in charge of the China desk at the Department of State. In short, Bush was everything the foreign policy elite in the United States could have hoped for as the foundation of the Cold War system eroded.

In addition, Bush put together an able and experienced staff to assist him. Brent Scowcroft, his national security adviser, had served with distinction in the same capacity in the administration of Gerald Ford. Secretary of State James Baker had served as secretary of the treasury in the Reagan administration as well as White House chief of staff, and had proven to be a man who could maneuver exceptionally well at the cabinet level. His foreign policy experience was limited, but his diplomatic skills were not. As secretary of defense, Bush chose the highly regarded Richard Cheney, another skilled political operative who had served as chief of staff in the Ford White House and as a congressman from Wyoming. Robert Gates, a Soviet specialist, moved over from deputy national security adviser to director of the CIA. And Bush inherited the widely admired general, Colin Powell, as chairman of the Joint Chiefs of Staff. His appointees each assembled their own impressive teams, including figures such as Condoleezza Rice and Paul Wolfowitz, whose stature grew enormously in the years that followed.

The incoming Bush administration, promising as it was, had two major handicaps to overcome. First was the extraordinary deficit in the U.S. Treasury, the result of the combination of massive tax cuts and increased military spending during the Reagan presidency. In just eight years, Reagan's policies had changed the status of the United States from the world's leading creditor nation to the world's leading debtor, dependent on foreign investors to keep its economy afloat. There was not much leeway for funding foreign aid, overseas military adventures, or Reagan's dream of a Strategic Defense Initiative that would result in securing the nation against atomic attack. There was also, little money available for domestic needs, such as the rebuilding of decaying infrastructure or social welfare – had anyone in the administration been interested.

The second handicap Bush faced was the fact that the international stage had been seized by and was dominated by Mikhail Gorbachev. Throughout the late 1980s the dynamic Soviet leader, in a desperate attempt to resuscitate his country's economy, had pulled the fabric of the Cold War system apart, thread by thread. At home and abroad he was taking steps that gradually erased the terror that Stalin and his successors had instilled in the people of the Soviet Union and the threat to the security of the United States and its allies. Slowly the world awakened to the reality that the Cold War was over and Gorbachev was widely perceived as the man who had determined to end it. In 1990 he would be awarded the Nobel Peace Prize. Bush and his advisers searched in vain for a means to seize the initiative, to keep the American president from being completely overshadowed.

In December 1988, Gorbachev came to the United States, met with president-elect Bush, and delivered an extraordinary address before the General Assembly of the United Nations. He announced that he would reduce Soviet forces by 500,000 – *unilaterally* – and that he would eliminate units stationed in East Germany, Czechoslovakia, and Hungary. He ruled out the use of force to achieve Soviet goals and declared that the posture of Red Army units remaining in Eastern Europe would be shifted from offensive to defensive. He also spoke of the necessity of freedom of choice of political and economic systems for all nations, unintentionally clearing the way for the elimination of communist rule in Eastern Europe. As he explained to Bush, conditions in the Soviet Union allowed him no choice. His nation could not afford an empire.

As the Bush team took the reins of power in Washington, wariness best describes its approach to the Soviet Union. Bush was suspicious, uneasy about what he perceived as a Soviet propaganda campaign to divide the West. Scowcroft, Cheney, and Gates continued to fight the Cold War, convinced that Gorbachev was merely attempting to strengthen his country to enable it to compete more effectively against the United States. Cheney was most opposed to working with Gorbachev and resisted White House proposals for mutual force reductions in Europe. He brushed off *glasnost* (Gorbachev's efforts to open Soviet society) and *perestroika* (Gorbachev's program of political and economic reform) as mere cosmetic changes. Baker probably had the clearest sense of the meaning of the "new thinking" in the Soviet Union, of Gorbachev's determination to reform the Soviet state politically as well as economically and to end the Cold War, but his initial instinct seemed to be that of Bush's close personal friend and campaign manager: he wanted the spotlight on his man.

The Bush team decided on a two-pronged approach designed to counter Gorbachev both in the realm of public relations and in what most of them perceived as the continuing struggle for dominance in Europe. If Gorbachev was trying to undercut the United States with its allies, the Americans would encourage Eastern Europeans to loosen their ties to Moscow. And if Soviet troop reduction proposals were delighting Western Europe, Washington would counter with a major arms reduction plan of its own. Cheney attempted to kill the plan by stating publicly his conviction that Gorbachev would fail to change the Soviet Union and by insisting in internal debates that Gorbachev would be forced to make concessions without any by the United States. But, encouraged by Baker, Bush went ahead and the American proposal for mutual troop reductions presented at the May 1989 NATO meeting delighted the allies – and received a positive response from Gorbachev.

Baker and Bush became less and less suspicious of Gorbachev. Baker was very favorably impressed by Gorbachev's foreign minister, Eduard Shevardnadze, with whom he gradually developed an unusually close relationship of mutual trust. Gorbachev's acceptance of the American proposal, following his December paean to freedom of choice, was a clear signal that he did not intend to use the Red Army to protect unpopular communist regimes in Eastern Europe. It was beginning to be clear, at least to the two of them, that Gorbachev was for real. Events in Europe rapidly confirmed their perception.

And then, unexpectedly, the spotlight shifted to China. Throughout the 1980s, with only occasional reversals, Deng Xiaoping had directed economic and social reforms that opened his country to the outside world and loosened the ideological chains with which Mao had constricted the lives of the Chinese people. Many Americans came to imagine that China was on course to a market economy and democratic political institutions – that China, in the foreseeable future, would become a liberal democracy. In China, too, faculty and students at the universities, intellectuals dotted throughout the society – including Communist Party members – dared to call for political reforms. Intoxicated by the taste of freedom, they began to criticize the government. Most seemed troubled by corruption, the arbitrary use of power by officials, and the slow pace of reform. A few went further, demanding an end to the Party's monopoly on power and calling for political democracy.

In April 1989, following the death of Hu Yaobang, once considered Deng's heir apparent and believed to be sympathetic to political reform, Beijing student leaders organized a massive demonstration in Tiananmen Square, the heart of the city. Before long, tens of thousands of Chinese, workers as well as students and intellectuals, filled the Square, calling upon the government to end corruption and nepotism, take steps to improve the quality of the lives of students and ordinary people, and move toward democracy.

The Chinese government responded with surprising restraint. It allowed the growing mass of demonstrators to control the square through Hu's funeral and on through the month of May – when Mikhail Gorbachev paid a state visit to China. The student leaders were very much aware of the success of "people's power" in overthrowing dictatorship in the Philippines in 1986. Using similar techniques, they hoped to force the Communist Party to allow greater intellectual and political freedom and to become accountable to the people. Foreign journalists and photographers, in Beijing to cover Gorbachev, were captivated by the demonstrations and the widespread support the students were receiving from policemen, soldiers, and Communist Party cadres as well as workers and intellectuals. They gave the demonstrations extraordinary worldwide media coverage.

But Deng and the other aging veterans of the Chinese civil wars of the 1930s and 40s were angered by student demands that threatened their power and their vision of a socialist China. They were troubled greatly by the possibility of a coalition between industrial workers and the students, fearful of a reprise of a 1980 student-worker uprising in Poland. They wanted the demonstrators cleared out of Tiananmen Square, the movement crushed, and its leaders bloodied. They wanted the government to act ruthlessly, to use overwhelming force, to leave no doubt that the Communist Party would tolerate no challenge to its authority. On May 20, after a shake-up of the top leadership of the Party, Li Peng, the premier and long-time favorite of those who opposed reform, declared martial law and called troops into the city.

Dissatisfaction with the government was underscored when the citizens of Beijing obstructed the movement of the troops toward the Square. Leading military figures of the past circulated a letter arguing that the People's Liberation Army should not be used against the people. And for a few days it looked like the demonstrations might end peacefully as the students began to leave and some of the student leaders thought they had accomplished enough to declare victory and hope for a reasonable response. It was too late. Backed by Deng, Li labeled the demonstrators "counter-revolutionaries," perhaps the most negative term in the Party's lexicon, and ordered anti-American demonstrations to discredit the students by implying they were instruments of a foreign power.

On the night of June 3 and in the early morning hours of June 4, the People's Liberation Army (PLA) launched an assault on the people. The troops shot their way into Tiananmen Square, killing upwards of a thousand men and women, mostly in the western approaches to the Square. Thousands more were wounded and thousands more arrested, some of them beaten and summarily executed. Some of the savagery was caught on film by foreign cameramen and within hours it was shown on television screens all over the world – prompting protest demonstrations in Moscow and Hong Kong as well as Western Europe and the United States. The popular image of a China progressing toward liberal democracy vanished. The killing fields of Tiananmen left a stain the Communist Party of China could never erase.

In Washington, the president and his foreign policy team, like virtually all Americans, sympathized with the students and hoped for peaceful change in China. Nonetheless, they were still fighting the Cold War and perceived Chinese-American relations as strategically important. Immediately after the shooting started, Bush consulted former president Richard Nixon, who also stressed the value of the relationship he had begun in 1971, and urged him not to impose economic sanctions or to recall the American ambassador. Bush concluded that given the outrage that had spread across the United States – which he shared – he had to take punitive action. He suspended arms sales to China and broke off contacts with the PLA. Congress and the public demanded stronger action and, under pressure, the administration canceled a series of high-level visits, extended the visas of Chinese students in the United States, and promised to work to postpone Chinese applications for loans from international financial institutions.

Although he was trying to stay ahead of the avalanche of public hostility toward China, Bush feared driving the Chinese back into Soviet arms. He was determined to keep open the lines of communication with Beijing. After failing to establish direct contact with Deng by telephone, he succeeded in soliciting an agreement that the Chinese would receive an American mission. Three weeks after the Tiananmen massacres, despite a public declaration that the administration would have no high-level contact with China, the president sent Scowcroft, his national security adviser, and the deputy secretary of state on a secret mission to Beijing – secret, that is, from the American people. Their assignment was to assure Deng that Bush believed that friendly relations with China were a vital interest of the United States. They also requested that Deng make some appropriate gestures, such as ending public executions, releasing some demonstrators, allowing a prominent dissident scientist who had taken refuge in the American embassy to leave the country with his family, to make it possible for Bush to begin to lift or at minimum stave off further sanctions.

Deng and the other Chinese leaders treated the American emissaries on this occasion, on their second visit later in the year, and a subsequent mission led by Secretary of State Baker two years later, with utter contempt. They had no regrets about what had happened at Tiananmen. Li Peng even refused to allow the events to be called tragic, insisting the killings were a good thing. According to Deng, the Americans, by criticizing Chinese actions and imposing sanctions, had created the tensions. It was their problem to find a way out. He had done his share by deigning to receive Bush's representatives.

Bush succeeded in keeping the lines of communication with Beijing open, but won few concessions. Eventually Deng allowed the dissident scientist to leave China and several hundred lesser known prisoners were freed at least temporarily. International human rights organizations, such as Amnesty International, reported conditions were getting worse in China and Congress debated a litany of complaints against the Beijing regime and attempted unsuccessfully to impose trade sanctions. Outside of business interests eager to buy, sell, or invest in China, dissatisfaction with the administration's management of the relationship was widespread, especially after the secret Scowcroft mission became public knowledge. Bush was charged by liberals and conservatives with coddling dictators, of appeasing the "butchers of Beijing," a complaint that questioned his reputation for expertise in foreign affairs. Moreover, his fundamental assumption of the strategic importance of the relationship came to be doubted as the Soviet empire began to unravel in 1989. If there was no longer a Soviet threat, why did the United States need China? The People's Republic, which under Deng's reforms had seemed the most progressive of the communist states, suddenly seemed the most reactionary – the least likely to evolve into a society that shared the values of the American people.

At Tiananmen the Chinese had provided one possible response to demands for change. Across Eastern Europe a very different and exhilarating response occurred. In August 1989, understanding that the Soviets would not ride to its rescue, the Polish Communist government handed power over to the opposition Solidarity movement. For the first time, a Communist regime relinquished power peacefully. Soon afterward Hungary followed suit. As these states threw off the burden of communism, as the Warsaw alliance of the Soviet bloc crumbled, Gorbachev and his Red Army did nothing to interfere.

The German Democratic Republic would prove to be the critical test. Communist East Germany was the most powerful and the most important of the Soviet satellite states. What would happen if its people decided that they, too, had had enough of Communist rule? Would their leaders go peacefully – or choose the Chinese solution? Could Gorbachev accept the possibility of German reunification? Indeed, could any European country with equanimity accept the idea of a united Germany?

In the summer of 1989, thousands of East Germans fled to Hungary and Czechoslovakia, seeking access to the West. In the fall, after Hungary opened its border to Austria, tens of thousands of East Germans fled to the West through Hungary. Thousands more demonstrated at home, demanding change. By October, a badly shaken East German regime was threatening to follow the Chinese approach, but received no support from Moscow. Changes in the Communist leadership from hard-line Stalinists to admirers of Gorbachev did not satisfy the people. Demonstrations grew and the government ran before the crowds, trying desperately to satisfy their demands. Throughout the turmoil, Soviet troops remained in the barracks. On November 9, workers in East Berlin began the destruction of the Berlin Wall, hated symbol of the Cold War and of a divided Germany. Unless Gorbachev sent the Red Army into action, it was only a matter of time before East and West Germany would reunite.

Immediately after the Wall was breached, the longtime Communist dictator of Bulgaria resigned. In Czechoslovakia, Vaclav Havel's "Velvet Revolution" succeeded in taking control of the government. Only in Romania did the Communist government resist. There dictator Georgiou Ceausescu chose not to go quietly into the night – and was executed as a consequence. In Moscow, a Gorbachev spokesman remarked that the "Brezhnev Doctrine," used in the past to justify Soviet interventions to keep communist-bloc countries in line, had been replaced by the "Sinatra Doctrine:" the people of central and eastern Europe were free to do things their way.

In Washington there continued to be major resistance to the idea that the Cold War was over. Baker was urging Bush to meet with Gorbachev and present him with a list of American initiatives on a wide range of subjects including trade and arms control, Cuba, and Nicaragua. He wanted Bush to demonstrate recognition of Gorbachev's retreat and to offer programs to eliminate remaining tensions and support Gorbachev's reforms. Scowcroft and Cheney resisted, but Baker prevailed. Bush and Gorbachev met at Malta in December 1989 and Baker's strategy worked. Gorbachev liked what he heard and he and Bush established a good personal working relationship that helped them through some of the knotty problems that would emerge in the months ahead. Gorbachev insisted the Soviet Union no longer considered the United States an adversary – and even Scowcroft was persuaded the situation was promising.

Not long after he returned to the United States, Bush was distracted by an annoying situation that had developed in Panama. General Manuel Noriega, the Panamanian dictator, had been on the CIA payroll through much of the 1980s and the Agency resisted efforts by the State Department and the National Security Council to force him out – despite suspicions that he was a major drug trafficker and accusations of murder and money laundering. The State Department had urged military intervention to depose him, but the Joints Chiefs and Defense Department civilians had persuaded Reagan not to act. Aid to Panama was suspended, however, and the CIA took him off its payroll. Economic sanctions were attempted in 1988 to no avail.

Given events in Europe and Asia, the Bush administration had difficulty focusing on Panama, especially since the canal had lost much of its strategic significance by 1989. Closer to home, Noriega seemed less worthy of attention than Fidel Castro in Cuba or the Sandinistas in Nicaragua. Nonetheless, the administration tried to get rid of him by openly supporting his opponents. After he resorted to fraud to defeat the opposition in a May, 1989 election, it was readily apparent he could be removed only by force. The Organization of American States (OAS) denounced him, but was unable to persuade him to go. Bush chose to increase pressure by sending additional troops to the U.S.-controlled Canal Zone, but Cheney and the American military commander for the region – who was personally close to Noriega – undermined his efforts. Noriega became convinced the U.S. would not use force against him.

In October, without U.S. support, a coup attempt against Noriega failed and his men increased their harassment of Americans in Panama. It was clear that Noriega was not getting the message. In Washington, questions about Bush's resolve – what the media referred to as the "wimp factor" – began to emerge. Bush had never been popular with the Republican right and conservatives began to complain that Ronald Reagan would never have tolerated having Americans pushed around. In December, after Noriega's men murdered a marine officer, Powell and the Joint Chiefs were ready to send in the troops. Yes, there might be casualties, but the military foresaw casualties whether or not they attacked. Contemptuously, the Noriega-controlled Assembly declared war on the United States.

Shortly after midnight, December 20, 1989, Operation Just Cause, involving an invading force of 25,000, began. As Powell insisted, the Americans used overwhelming force and quickly defeated the Panama Defense Force with a minimum of casualties on both sides – although more than a hundred, perhaps several hundred, Panamanian civilians were killed. Unfortunately, Noriega slipped away and it took two more weeks to find him and take him into custody. More troubling was the failure of Bush's team to plan adequately for the reintroduction of a Panamanian civilian government. But the government that presumably would have won had the May election been fair was soon installed – and the American troops were out less than two months after they went in. Panama was undoubtedly better off without Noriega and Bush, no longer a wimp, could resume his pose as leader of the free world. Washington's unilateral decision to intervene was condemned, however, by both the OAS and the UN.

Once again, Bush was free to focus on the rapidly changing situation in Europe. In particular, events on the ground in Germany were moving faster than either Bush or Gorbachev had anticipated. Helmut Kohl, the West German leader, had no intention of allowing either the United States or the Soviet Union to impede his vision for the reunification of Germany; nor would he allow them to dictate the terms or the timing. In November 1989, while East German leaders still hoped to perpetuate two Germanys, Kohl, without consulting his allies, publicly offered a proposal for unification. Across Europe the prospect of a unified Germany, of German power revived, generated anxiety. Gorbachev warned Kohl to stop talking about reunification. On the other hand, Henry Kissinger warned Bush that German reunification was inevitable and that it would be a terrible mistake for the United States to be perceived by Germans as an obstacle.

The dilemma Bush faced was the perceived need to satisfy the Germans without undermining Gorbachev or provoking a harsh Soviet response to Kohl's plans. The British and French shared some of Gorbachev's concerns, as did most European leaders. They wanted to participate in any arrangements for German reunification. Baker argued that it was essential to involve the Soviets or risk antagonizing Gorbachev and braking the progress toward a new cooperative relationship. Scowcroft and Cheney argued for leaving the decision to the Germans, fearful that Gorbachev and Kohl might negotiate a deal to exclude Germany from NATO. Bush would not accept the idea of Germany outside NATO, but found Baker's argument convincing. Baker's staff then derived a clever formula, "2 + 4," that allowed the two Germanys to decide their own future in the presence of World War II's Big Four: France, Great Britain, the Soviet Union, and the United States. It would remain Kohl's show with Bush playing the critical supporting role, with a face-saving place at the table for the others. And it worked.

Initially, Gorbachev and Shevardnadze were adamant in their resistance to a unified Germany as a member of NATO. Not only the Soviet military, but the Soviet public as well would be appalled, conceivably rise up against them. But they had little leverage, negotiated arrangements with Kohl for financial assistance and a promise to keep NATO troops out the former East Germany – that angered the Bush team – and got out of the way. In October, 1990, the Cold War ended for the German people, who were formally reunited. Gorbachev's acceptance of a unified Germany remaining in NATO made a believer out of Scowcroft: he was prepared to concede that the Cold War was over. Cheney was probably the only one of consequence in the administration who was still not convinced.

For both the United States and the Soviet Union, the main arena of the Cold War had been central Europe. Both countries were leery of Germany. The stationing of large-scale American forces in West Germany had served not only to deter Soviet aggression, but also to contain the resurgence of German power. Similarly, the Soviets, their country having been invaded by the Germans in both World Wars, had a profound fear of a resurrected German *Reich*. Despite their rhetoric about working toward a unified Germany, both American and Soviet leaders had grown comfortable with its division. Now Germany was to be reunited *and* incorporated into NATO, a Soviet nightmare come true. It was a solution acceptable to most Americans and provided the best evidence that the contest had ended in their favor.

A major test of the new cooperative relationship between the United States and the Soviet Union came quickly. In 1980, Jimmy Carter had declared the Persian Gulf a vital interest of the United States, warning the Soviets to stand clear. The obvious American concern in the region was oil and Washington was determined to assure the free flow of oil to the United States and its allies. With the overthrow of their friend, the Shah of Iran, and the emergence of a hostile regime in Tehran 1979, the Americans were forced to contemplate a policy of dual containment – an attempt to keep either Iran or the Soviet-supported Iraq of Saddam Hussein from controlling the Gulf. Throughout the 1980s, Iraq and Iran fought a brutal war for dominance in the region and the Reagan administration found it expedient to tilt toward Iraq. The United States provided Iraq with export credits, covert military assistance, and intelligence while doing what it could to harass Iran. There was never any doubt that Saddam was a malevolent dictator, but Reagan's advisers were more fearful of Iran's Islamic fundamentalism and intense anti-Americanism than of Saddam's secular megalomania.

Bush intended to continue the approach of the Reagan administration, but relations between the United States and Iraq began to deteriorate not long after the end of the Iran-Iraq war in 1988. By the spring of 1990, Saddam was warned that his actions, especially his threats against Israel, were putting him on a collision course with the United States. In May, Washington suspended economic credits – to no avail. Saddam's rhetoric toward Israel and his other neighbors – Kuwait in particular – became increasingly belligerent. Calls for a shift in American policy toward Iraq were resisted in the National Security Council and Bush was unresponsive. The president was preoccupied with trouble that had erupted in the Baltic states where Soviet resistance to their quest for independence from the Soviet Union angered Americans of Estonian, Latvian, and Lithuanian origin – and threatened to derail progress toward Soviet-American cooperation.

In July, Iraqi forces began to mass along the Kuwaiti border. The consensus within the U.S. government and abroad was that Saddam was bluffing. Bush was unwilling to threaten him. There was no point in further alienating him if he really had no intention of invading Kuwait. The president chose not to warn Saddam of the consequences of aggression. On August 2, 1990, Iraqi forces swept across the border into Kuwait.

Although the fate of Kuwait was not a major concern of many Americans, Bush immediately condemned the invasion, froze Iraqi assets in the United States and prohibited trade. In Moscow, Secretary of State Baker and Soviet foreign minister Shevardnadze issued a joint statement condemning the aggression and calling on all nations to cut off arms supplies to Iraq. Military action by the United States was not contemplated and there was a widespread assumption that Saddam would take the slice of Kuwait's oil fields that he had long claimed – and go home. But the Iraqis stayed in Kuwait, deposed its government and were reportedly looting the country.

Bush became increasingly outraged by Iraqi actions and Saddam's refusal to pay heed to American admonitions. Several of his close advisers found him becoming emotional about the issue, likening Saddam to Hitler. Much like Harry Truman responding to the North Korean invasion of the South in 1950, Bush perceived an analogy to unchecked German and Japanese aggression in the 1930s: if not stopped now, acts of aggression would spread and the post-Cold War order would be anything but peaceful. He would do whatever was necessary to get Saddam out of Kuwait. America's response to Iraqi aggression would become a moral crusade, good versus evil.

Within the administration fear emerged that Saddam would go after Saudi Arabia as well as Kuwait, that he was intending to seize control of all of the oil resources of the Arabian Peninsula. There was rapid agreement among Bush and his advisers that Saudi Arabia would have to be protected. After gaining approval from the reluctant Saudis, Bush announced Operation Desert Shield: American forces would be sent to Saudi Arabia to deter an Iraqi attack. There was no consensus among Bush's advisers on any further military action, but the goals of U.S. policy were clear: secure Saudi Arabia and the Persian Gulf; liberate Kuwait; punish the aggressor.

The next step was to gain international support for economic sanctions against Iraq. The United States succeeded in having the United Nations Security Council vote an economic embargo against Iraq, winning the support of all the permanent members, including the Soviet Union and China. With luck the sanctions might suffice to persuade the Iraqis to withdraw from Kuwait. The American military buildup in the region, complete by mid-fall, would assure the security of Saudi Arabia and might demonstrate to Saddam that the United States was determined to see him retreat.

Weeks passed without any sign that the Iraqis intended to withdraw from Kuwait. The president grew impatient. Several of his advisers, including Colin Powell, chairman of the Joint Chiefs, urged him to let sanctions take their course. Bush, in a superb use of personal diplomacy, called around to the leaders of other nations to gain support for the military action that seemed to him inevitable. Given the Reagan deficits that had left the country unable to pay for the war itself, Bush had to obtain the financial backing he needed abroad. He won it from Germany and Japan, as well as the Saudis. He and his aides lobbied Congress, eager for Congressional endorsement. Congress proved more difficult. The Democrats, who controlled both houses, also wanted to give sanctions a chance. Some friends of Israel among the Democrats were more inclined to support tough measures against Saddam, given his threats against Israel, but Bush would need UN endorsement of the use of force to ensure the support of Congress. Secretary of Defense Cheney argued against seeking either UN or Congressional support, insisting the president needed neither. Bush, however, agreed with Baker's arguments for a UN-supported coalition rather than going to war alone.

Bush, Baker, and the American ambassador to the UN worked assiduously to gain support for a UN resolution permitting the use of force to liberate Iraq. British support was assured. British Prime Minister Margaret Thatcher was more militant than Bush, urging him on. The French were surprisingly easy to persuade, especially after it became clear that Baker had won Soviet backing. At one point he offered the Soviets a military role in return for their vote, but Cheney's Defense Department would have none of it. The American government had worked for too long to keep the Soviets out of the Gulf: this was no time to invite them in. Gorbachev wanted a multipower conference on Middle East issues, including Arab-Israeli relations – and was promised such a conference *after* the Iraqis were out of Kuwait. The Chinese, who hated to be isolated on the Security Council, were highly unlikely to veto the proposed resolution, but their abstention was purchased with an invitation for their foreign minister to visit Washington – a step back from the sanctions imposed after the Tiananmen massacres.

On November 29, 1990, the Security Council voted to allow members to use "all necessary means" to liberate Kuwait. Saddam was given until January 15, 1991 to withdraw. The several Arab leaders eager to be rid of Saddam had UN cover to join forces with the Americans. Bush now had a green light from the UN and it proved sufficient for him to get Congressional approval. After a harrowing six weeks of lobbying and debating and a fruitless last ditch meeting between Baker and the Iraqi foreign minister, the president won majority support for going to war.

The Soviets made several late efforts to head off American military action, but the men in Washington brushed them aside. Powell and his field commanders were given the overpowering force they demanded and the Iraqis never had a chance. At the suggestion of King Fahd of Saudi Arabia, Bush did not order the attack on January 15, assuming the Iraqis would be at their highest level of alert as time ran out. But two days later the air attacks began and they were, not surprisingly, devastating.

Probably the toughest diplomatic problem of the Gulf War was ensuring that the Israelis stayed out. Saddam shrewdly tried to turn the battle into an Arab-Israeli battle by launching Scud missiles against Israel. The Israelis were determined to retaliate, but the Americans understood that the Saudis in particular, but the Arabs generally, did not want to be perceived as allies of Israel against another Arab state. Holding the Israelis back as the Scuds landed in their cities took extraordinary effort and involved many promissory notes, but the price was deemed acceptable to accomplish the essential task of holding the anti-Saddam coalition together.

The air attack on Iraq lasted more than a month and included cruise missiles fired from naval vessels offshore and more than 94,000 sorties by coalition bombers. Although many of the weapons used were so-called "smart bombs" designed to hit specified targets, tens of thousands of Iraqi civilians were killed. The country's infrastructure was shattered. Iraqi military capabilities were greatly diminished, but Saddam continued to promise his people victory in "the mother of all battles."

By mid-February 1991, coalition troops numbered more than 500,000. On February 23, despite Soviet objections, they were ordered into action. Operation Desert Storm had begun. Within 48 hours, organized Iraqi resistance collapsed. Kuwait was liberated quickly, with minimal coalition casualties, and the routed Iraqi army fled north toward Baghdad. Unwilling to be perceived as massacring a defeated enemy, Bush called a halt to the fighting, but not before coalition forces had occupied parts of southern Iraq.

Bush and his advisers expected Saddam to be overthrown as a result of Iraq's devastating defeat and the suffering that he had brought upon his people and had no contingency plan for his survival. Military planning had also anticipated trapping and decimating his elite Republican Guard forces, but most of them escaped. The Americans were also unprepared for the Shiite uprising against Saddam in the south and the Kurdish uprising in the north. They hastily concluded that successful rebellions would fragment Iraq and allow Iranian domination of the Persian Gulf and its vital oil supplies. When Saddam moved to crush the rebellions, the Americans were slow to interfere. Too late to save the thousands killed by Saddam's forces, they established "no-fly" zones, to limit the mobility of government troops.

Briefly, the men in Washington contemplated their options. Saddam, the root cause of the crisis that had brought death and destruction to Kuwait and Iraq remained in power, claiming victory. He still had his programs to create weapons of mass destruction and there was no reason to assume that his regime's human rights abuses would abate. At home, however, the liberation of Kuwait was being cheered exuberantly. For Americans, the war was over and they had begun celebrating, greatly relieved that only 146 American lives were lost. There was little public interest in going on to Baghdad, in putting more American lives at risk. They were proud that the

United States had led an international force to throw back a brutal act of aggression. The war was perceived as a "good war," in which the Americans once again had acted in their preferred role as liberators riding to the rescue of a victimized people. The balance of power in the Gulf had been restored – and no hostile power controlled the region's precious oil. Bush feared that continuation of the war would shatter the coalition he and Baker had so carefully constructed. There was no UN mandate for an invasion of Iraq. The president decided to accept the bouquets and to bask in glory with his victorious military commanders. All of his advisers agreed. They just wanted to quit while they were ahead.

To those critics who argued that the job was not done until Saddam was removed from power, the administration had persuasive answers. The invasion of Iraq would have been costly in lives and treasure. Saddam could not easily be found. The United States would be forced to occupy Iraq for an indefinite time at a cost perhaps greater than the war itself. The military was ill-equipped for nation-building and opposed to "mission creep." The American public was satisfied and Bush's popularity soared.

It was now time to pay a debt to Gorbachev. The Soviet leader had been promised a role in the search for an overarching peace in the Middle East and a renewed effort to resolve the Israeli-Palestinian conflict in return for his support of American action against Iraq. Perhaps working together, the Soviet Union and the United States could put an end to hatreds they had exacerbated by their Cold War struggle for dominance in the region. Without Soviet support for their confrontation with Israel, radical Arab states such as Syria and Yemen might be ready for peace. The Palestinian leader Yasser Arafat, who had supported Saddam Hussein against the American-led coalition, was assumed to be suitably chastened and amenable to reason. Israel, however, was certain to be difficult. Its leaders mistrusted the Soviets, and had no use for a United Nations that had voted to equate Zionism with fascism. The country was governed by a right-wing coalition committed to a vision of Greater Israel, adamantly opposed to surrendering any of the territory it had occupied in the Six Day War of 1967.

Secretary of State Baker had begun his tenure determined to stay away from the Arab-Israeli conflict. There was no evidence of willingness to compromise on either side and there was the potential for serious domestic political trouble if Israel's many supporters in the United States, Jews and non-Jews alike, thought the administration's commitment to Israel was faltering. Former president Richard Nixon warned against any effort to promote peace in the region, reinforcing Baker's predisposition.

Beginning with Lyndon Johnson, every American president had endorsed UN Resolution 242 that called upon Israel to surrender the occupied land in exchange for peace treaties that would constitute Arab recognition of the right of the state of Israel to exist, the "land for peace" formula. The Bush administration seemed a little less tolerant of Israel's rejection of the formula and a little less accepting of its persistent building of settlements in Arab East Jerusalem and amidst the Arab populations of the West Bank and Gaza. At one point Bush infuriated the Israelis by insisting that Israel stop building new settlements and conditioning loan guarantees on their response. They ignored him. But Arafat's support for terrorism made him an unlikely beneficiary of American diplomacy. Prior to Gorbachev's proposal, the Bush team chose to stand clear of the Arab-Israeli issue.

In March 1991, Baker determined to honor his commitment to Gorbachev, despite reservations elsewhere in the administration. He talked to Israeli leaders and to leaders of most of the Arab states. He was particularly encouraged by discussions with the Saudis and Jordanians who had been astonished by Israel's restraint during the Gulf War. It was clear King Hussein of Jordan was ready for peace with Israel. The Saudis indicated that they would participate in the proposed conference and were willing to establish diplomatic and economic relations with Israel if the Palestinians gained a homeland. The Egyptians had already recognized Israel and were quick to agree to attend. The Arab states of the Persian Gulf, having witnessed the exercise of American power, assuming the Americans were in the region to stay, were eager to line up behind Washington. But Syria, Israel, and the Palestinians tried Baker's patience.

One incentive Baker was able to deliver to Israel was the reestablishment of diplomatic relations offered by Gorbachev – essential for winning agreement to Soviet cosponsorship of the conference. Back and forth he flew, winning agreements after tedious negotiations, only to have them unravel within days. But Baker stayed with it and somehow won the approval of all the players to a conference scheduled for Madrid at the end of October 1991. It was an extraordinary display of diplomatic skill. On the day the conference opened, the ceremonies were hosted personally by Bush and Gorbachev and there was, however briefly, renewed hope for peace between Israel and the Arab states.

By the time the conference met, however, Gorbachev's days of power were running out. In August, a coup against him by Communist Party stalwarts, long anticipated by American intelligence, was launched. Gorbachev refused to comply with the orders of the coup leaders and was placed under house arrest. But in Moscow, more than a hundred thousand Russians took to the streets to protest against the coup. Boris Yeltsin, the president of the Russian Federation, assumed leadership of the demonstrators who blocked the movement of tanks through the streets. When the tanks commanders refused to open fire on the demonstrators, the coup failed. In marked contrast to the events at Tiananmen in 1989, a peaceful demonstration in favor of democracy succeeded in Moscow.

Although Gorbachev returned to the Kremlin after the collapse of the coup, his control of the country slipped away. In the days that followed, Yeltsin, riding a wave of enormous popularity because of his resistance to the coup, engineered the break-up of the Soviet Union. On December 31, 1991, the Soviet Union, the land of Lenin and Stalin, the great communist superpower of the post-World War II era, ceased to exist. And then Yeltsin had the Communist Party banned within Russia.

The Americans could do no more than watch from the sidelines as these incredible events occurred. The Bush administration had to decide how to deal with a host of new issues, not least of which was Yeltsin's drinking problem which caused the Americans and his own entourage considerable anxiety. Of greater concern was the need to determine responsibility for the Soviet era nuclear weapons that remained scattered among the now independent former Soviet republics. Specialists on issues of nuclear weapons proliferation considered this new situation incredibly dangerous. Nor could Yeltsin's Russia be written off as a possible rival to the United States. It was no longer a communist state, but it still had a powerful military, including an enormous nuclear force. Yeltsin's Russia had no intention of dropping out of the ranks of great powers.

Of course, the rest of the world did not stand still while Baker focused on Soviet affairs or the Middle East. Satellite photos in the mid-1980s had indicated that North Korea was building a nuclear reactor at Yongbyun. By June 1988, American intelligence analysts suspected North Korea was attempting to develop nuclear weapons. In February 1989, they briefed the Chinese and the Soviets and Baker personally took up the issue with Shevardnadze and the Chinese foreign minister. Before the Tiananmen massacres damaged Chinese-American relations, Washington was working with Beijing in the hope that the Chinese would use their presumed influence with Kim Il Sung to persuade him not to build a bomb. But the lines of communication broke down after Tiananmen. Any hope that the Soviets could help evaporated when Gorbachev chose to establish diplomatic relations with South Korea in September 1990 – although Baker expressed pleasure at Soviet assistance in isolating North Korea.

One important goal was to get Pyongyang, which had signed the Nuclear Nonproliferation Treaty in 1985 as the price for a Soviet commitment to provide light-water reactors for civilian power use, to sign an overdue safeguard agreement with the International Atomic Energy Agency (IAEA). The North Korean position was that they would allow no inspections as long as they were threatened by American nuclear weapons, especially those positioned in South Korea. The commander of U.S. forces in Korea indicated that he had no need for nuclear weapons and the Defense Department concurred. In October, 1990, the American ambassador in Seoul recommended removal of the weapons to facilitate negotiations with the North, but removal was opposed by Scowcroft. He persuaded the president that removal would be perceived as giving something for nothing: the North Koreans had not earned a reward. Despite intelligence estimates that Pyongyang might have nuclear weapons as early as mid-1990, the Bush administration was too divided on the issue to take action and was preoccupied with Chinese, Soviet, and Iraqi affairs.

The attempted coup against Gorbachev triggered an announcement by Bush that the United States would remove all of its overseas-based land and sea tactical nuclear weapons. Washington assumed Gorbachev would reciprocate and wanted to lock in an agreement while the Soviet leader retained some vestige of authority. Secretly, Bush went a step further and approved the removal of all nuclear weapons from South Korea. In December 1991, the president of South Korea declared his country nuclear free.

Kim Il Sung, his economy in serious trouble, unable to obtain any support from the Soviets, came under pressure from the Chinese to do something to ease American concerns over his nuclear program. The Chinese were eager to expand their relations with Seoul and wanted the issue out of the way. Kim could not have been pleased by the direction of Chinese diplomacy. He may, however, have seen appeasing the Americans on inspections as a means not only of retaining Chinese aid but also of obtaining economic assistance from South Korea and conceivably the United States.

In December 1991, the Bush administration communicated its willingness to have the high-level meeting the North Koreans had long demanded. Kim's representatives met quickly with their South Korean counterparts and before the month was out had reached agreement on a nonaggression pact with the South and a ban on the reprocessing of uranium. Perhaps most importantly, in exchange for a South Korean agreement to cancel the intimidating US-ROK Team Spirit military exercise, the North Koreans agreed to sign the safeguards agreement with IAEA and to allow inspections of its Yongbyon facilities.

Later that month, a senior State Department official met with a representative of Kim Il Sung's in New York, at the U.S. Mission to the UN. Reflecting the divisions in the administration over the decision to allow the meeting and about what might be said, the American was severely restrained. He was to insist that North Korea drop its nuclear weapons program and permit IAEA inspections. He had nothing to offer in return. Nonetheless, Pyongyang seemed satisfied and signed the safeguards agreement shortly afterward.

Unfortunately, the hopes and promise of the winter of 1991-2 were vanquished as soon as the IAEA began its inspections. A series of discrepancies between what Pyongyang declared and what the inspectors found quickly emerged and the political situation on the Korean peninsula turned sour. In South Korea, as well as the United States, 1992 was a presidential election year and in neither country was appearing soft in dealing with Kim Il Song considered a political asset. South Korean military and intelligence leaders expressed renewed suspicion of the North. The presidential candidate of the ruling party feared that continued improvement of relations with the North would benefit the opposition. Relations cooled again and Seoul asked the Americans to back away from Pyongyang. In particular, the South Korean military wanted to resume the Team Spirit exercise, as did U.S. Secretary of Defense Cheney. The decision to run the operation in 1993 was made without consulting the State Department – and Kim Il Sung was outraged.

Unquestionably the saga of the North Korean nuclear program was an ugly story. The North Koreans, unwilling to rely on their allies or the international community for their security, had decided that possession of nuclear weapons was their best protection. They tried to hide their efforts to develop these weapons from their friends as well as their enemies. They knowingly violated their commitments under the NPT. When suspicions were voiced they lied about their activities. Their agreement to allow IAEA inspections of the Yongbyon facilities was predicated on the assumption that there were political gains to be made with China, South Korea, and the United States – and on the additional assumption that they could hide the truth about their activities.

Before the end of 1992, Kim Il Sung must have concluded he had made a bad bargain. The South Koreans were being difficult again. The Americans were unresponsive. Resumption of the Team Spirit exercises had been announced. And the inspections were far more intrusive – and successful at uncovering deception – than he had anticipated. As Lyndon Johnson might have said, it was time to "hunker down." North-South talks on all issues were cancelled and the North Koreans threatened to bar the access of IAEA inspectors to Yongbyon.

The Bush administration, badly divided as to how to approach North Korea, would not touch the issue during the election campaign. When tensions between the IAEA and Pyongyang mounted in November 1992, a defeated President Bush and his team refused to act. Bill Clinton was president-elect: let him cope with the problem.

Although Bush and his advisers went out with a whimper, they had initially responded extraordinarily well to the evidence of North Korea's nuclear program. Amidst the tensions with China after the Tiananmen massacres, the unraveling of the Soviet empire, the reunification of Germany, and the war with Iraq, their ability to address the concerns of North and South Korea was remarkable. They developed a package of incentives – removal of American nuclear weapons from the peninsula, cancellation of Team Spirit 1992, and a direct meeting between senior officials – to indicate to Kim Il Sung that there might be more to be gained by dropping the program. Had they been able to focus on the problems that emerged in mid-1992, perhaps they could have provided Kim with sufficient assurance for North Korea actually to put aside its effort to build nuclear weapons. They couldn't – and he didn't. Perhaps nothing the Americans could have done would have persuaded Pyongyang to settle for anything less than its own nuclear deterrent.

Other signs that the peaceful world many Americans expected after the Cold War was a fantasy were apparent across the globe. To be sure, there were many positive signs, especially the emergence of stable, democratic regimes in Eastern Europe and the possibility of a democratic Russia. Analysts persuaded that democracies were always peace-loving were heartened by new regimes in places as diverse as South Korea and South Africa, Mongolia, and Chile. But they might best have recalled the words of Sir Thomas More, the sixteenth-century English statesman who wrote "it is not possible for all things to be well, unless all men were good. Which I think will not be yet this good many years."

Most troubling was the disintegration of Yugoslavia and the outbreak of wars between some of its constituent parts. Croatia and Slovenia, two of the six republics in the federation, had been pulling away from the rest of the country since the death in 1980 of Tito, the independent communist leader who had founded modern Yugoslavia after World War II. By the spring of 1991, it was evident that they would not wait much longer. At the same time, the Serbian leader, Slobodan Milosevic, was fanning Serbian nationalism. A Serbian attack was likely if Slovenia and Croatia declared independence – which the German government, with longstanding ties to the nationalist movements in both republics, was encouraging them to do.

The future of Yugoslavia was not a question to which the Bush administration wished to address itself. Secretary of State Baker's plate was full and events in the Balkans did not impress him or his colleagues as being of great importance to the United States. Nonetheless, in June 1991, Baker stopped off in Belgrade and met with the various Yugoslav leaders. He advised the Croat and Slovene leaders against independence. He chastised Milosevic for human rights violations against Kosovars of Albanian ethnicity. To all he stressed American opposition to the use of force to resolve their differences. The United States would accept any peaceful outcome. Baker had no illusions about the impact of his words and his skepticism was justified four days after his visit when Croatia and Slovenia declared independence and Serbia attacked a day later.

All of this seemed minor when compared with events in the Soviet Union and the Bush administration concluded that what was to become of Yugoslavia was a question best left to the Europeans. Washington was delighted when the European Community stepped in and tried to mediate, and it welcomed the willingness of the UN Security Council to send former American secretary of state Cyrus Vance to Belgrade to assist in the mediation efforts. The United States would recognize the independence of the various republics as they demonstrated their adherence of the norms of the international community.

Germany decided not to wait for the outcome of mediation efforts and unilaterally recognized Croatia and Slovenia in December and the European Community followed suit in January 1992. Vance and his associates won a cease-fire in January, but it left Serbia in control of a substantial chunk of Croat territory. Serb behavior – early indications of ethnic cleansing and the unnecessary shelling of Dubrovnik – began to trouble neutral observers, but there was no will in any capital to use force to stop it. The U.S. government, eager to avoid involvement, remained distant through March 1992.

The decision of another Yugoslav republic, Bosnia-Herzegovina, to request recognition of its independence from Belgrade, eventually drew the reluctant Americans into the morass. Bosnia was the most ethnically diverse of the republics, made up of Croat Catholics, Serb Orthodox Christians, and a plurality of Bosnian Muslims. The Serbs and Croats did not let their hostility toward each other prevent them from colluding to divide Bosnia between them. Hoping to preserve the territorial integrity of Bosnia, Washington, in concert with the European Community, recognized it as an independent state in April 1992. The UN Security Council sent a peacekeeping force, but the situation quickly spun out of control.

The obvious point was that Milosevic was determined to seize control of Bosnia and was using Bosnian Serb fighters as his surrogates. The UN peacekeepers had no peace to keep and they lacked the strength to deter Serb onslaughts against majority Muslim towns. Bosnia quickly became a humanitarian nightmare with innocent civilians driven from their homes, raped, and murdered. The cosmopolitan city of Sarajevo, capital of Bosnia, came under siege. In May, the Security Council imposed an economic embargo on Serbia, but the Serbs were undaunted. Milosevic sent in irregulars, including many notoriously brutal thugs, and reports of atrocities mounted.

In Washington, there was a growing sense that the United States, the world's greatest power, the only remaining superpower, had a responsibility to stop the Serbs. Scowcroft was deeply troubled by the horror stories. The Air Force chief of staff agreed that America's great power obligated it to act, whether or not it had strategic interests at stake – and he was convinced he could do the job with air power alone. Paul Wolfowitz, Cheney's subordinate at Defense, argued for action. But Cheney and Powell were opposed and more importantly, so were Baker and Bush. As Baker famously phrased the argument, the United States "had no dog in this fight."

There might be a political price to pay for inaction, however, and Bush decided to approve the use of force to deliver humanitarian relief to Sarajevo, over the objections of Powell and Cheney. He insisted that American action be part of a multilateral operation under the UN and he requested and obtained Congressional support. In face of this display of determination, the Serbs backed off and allowed the relief supplies to be delivered.

Elsewhere in what was once Yugoslavia, conditions grew worse and evidence of concentration camps in which Muslims were held, tortured, raped, and massacred appeared in the international press. Within the administration, as fear of genocide in Bosnia grew, support for action against Serbia intensified, the most popular known as "lift and strike" – shorthand for lifting the arms embargo that prevented the Bosnians from defending themselves and striking Serb positions from the air to improve Bosnian prospects. But it was too close to the election and Bush was under fire for paying too much attention to foreign affairs. He was not about to order American forces into an action in which no vital national interest was apparent. This too, became an issue to be passed on to the next administration.

Another problem that the Bush administration attempted to dodge had emerged in September 1991 when the democratically elected president of Haiti, the mercurial Jean- Bertrand Aristide, was overthrown by a coup and fled to the United States. The United States quickly suspended all aid to Haiti and persuaded the OAS (Organization of American States) to apply a trade embargo. But Aristide was perceived as an irrational radical and despised by American conservatives. The administration would do nothing to restore him to power. Powell noted that the job probably could be done by a handful of marines, but that once U.S. forces went in, it would be difficult to take them out – that an occupation of indeterminate length would be necessary before democracy could take hold in Haiti. Baker later defended inaction by arguing that although the administration perceived a national interest in restoring democracy to Haiti, it was not a vital interest and did not justify the use of force.

The terrible conditions in Haiti after the coup had other ramifications less easily escaped. Thousands of Haitians attempted to flee the country and seek refuge in the United States. Poor and black, they found no welcome on Florida shores. Unlike Cuban refugees, presumably escaping communist oppression – and encouraged by the politically powerful Cuban-American community – Haitians were sent back or interned at Guantanamo Bay. Something had to be done to staunch the flow, but the administration found the issue both trivial and nettlesome and left it for its successor.

Bush had two major concerns in 1992: working out a healthy relationship with Boris Yeltsin and getting himself re-elected. He did as well as could be hoped with the first – and failed miserably with the second. Yeltsin's reputation as a reformer and critic of Gorbachev had long interested Bush and his advisers, most of whom were eager to reach out to him even before his heroic stand during the coup attempt against Gorbachev in August 1991. The Soviet specialists at the NSC (National Security Council), Robert Gates and Condoleezza Rice, saw him as an important player with whom the United States needed contact. Cheney, the secretary of defense, was uninterested in supporting Gorbachev, and saw Yeltsin as a man who might hasten the collapse of the Soviet Union. Bush believed American interests were served best by supporting Gorbachev and the continued existence of a reforming central government for the erstwhile Cold War adversary of the United States. Nonetheless, when Yeltsin came to Washington in September 1989, Bush agreed to see him. A "drop-in" visit to Scowcroft's office was arranged as the way for the president to meet Yeltsin without giving offense to Gorbachev.

In May 1990, Yeltsin became chairman of the Supreme Soviet of the Russian Federation, the newly elected Russian Legislature. In that capacity – and a month after he had publicly demanded Gorbachev's resignation – he returned to Washington and met again with Bush in March 1991. In that meeting he assured the president of his support for Gorbachev and dismissed reports of a planned coup. In June 1991, Yeltsin became the first democratically elected president of the Russian Federation. In August came the actual coup attempt by Communist Party conservatives opposed to the Gorbachev reforms and profoundly troubled by the declining power of both the Party and the Soviet Union. This, of course, was Yeltsin's proudest moment. With Gorbachev a prisoner in his dacha in the Crimea, Yeltsin risked his life leading the successful opposition to the coup. Bush publicly supported Yeltsin, giving CNN an interview to be sure the message reached Moscow.

In the months that followed, Yeltsin left Gorbachev with no doubt that the power relationship between them had shifted and that he, Yeltsin, was the winner. And he took a series of steps that endeared him to many of Bush's aides. He immediately banned the Communist Party in Russia and then recognized the independence of the Baltic states, Estonia, Latvia, and Lithuania – the treatment of which was a potentially divisive issue in Russian-American relations. The United States had never recognized the reabsorption of those three states into the Soviet Union during World War II and Americans of Baltic ancestry had become a potent political force in domestic politics. Bush had worried about Gorbachev's management of the demand of the Baltic states for independence and the issue had come close to disrupting his admiration for Gorbachev. Yeltsin resolved the issue in precisely the way the Bush administration had hoped.

In December 1991, Yeltsin met secretly with the leaders of Belarus and Ukraine and they signed an agreement announcing the dissolution of the Soviet Union and the creation of the Commonwealth of Independent States (CIS), which Yeltsin intended to lead. No more Soviet Union – and no place for Mikhail Gorbachev in the Kremlin. There was no grieving in Washington, although Bush unquestionably regretted the humiliation of Gorbachev. Yeltsin as top man in Moscow soon abandoned his populist democratic supporters, surrounded himself with cronies, most of them former high-ranking communist officials. As he consolidated his power, the Americans continued to hope he would bring democracy and free markets to Russia, but they were no doubt satisfied that the threat from the Soviet Union had been greatly depreciated. His welcome to Washington in February 1992 could not have been warmer – although Yeltsin surely would have preferred a more positive response to his request for aid. Bush, unfortunately, was still handicapped by an empty treasury and a public ill-informed about the difficulties and dangers involved in the dissolution of the Soviet Union.

Overall, the Bush administration had performed ably in the international arena. In the great events of the era – the end of the Cold War, the collapse of the Soviet empire, the reunification of Germany – it had played a secondary role, but played it well. Certainly there were questions about its actions in Panama and the Persian Gulf, serious reservations about its response to the Tiananmen massacres, but the American people graded their president highly for his efforts and his leadership. Nonetheless, by mid-1992, it was clear that his campaign for re-election was in trouble. His support from the right wing of his own party had never been more than lukewarm and his inability to drag the country out of economic recession left him an easy target for the opposition Democrats. He was hurt also by the third party candidacy of Ross Perot, a wealthy Texas businessman with a knack for memorable sound-bites. His best one was probably his reference to a "giant sucking sound" caused by Bush's negotiations to bring Mexico into the North American Free Trade Association (NAFTA) – which Perot alleged was the sound of American jobs being sucked into the cheap labor market south of the border.

One major Bush effort to provide jobs and to carry the states of Texas and California had major foreign policy implications. For ten years the Taiwan government had been begging the United States to sell it F-16 fighter planes. Fearful of antagonizing Beijing and unconvinced that Taiwan needed the planes, the Americans had refused. But in 1992, several members of Bush's national security team argued that the time had come to make the sale. The law – specifically the Taiwan Relations Act of 1980 – required the United States to provide the weapons Taiwan needed to defend itself. China had just purchased all-weather jet fighters from Russia and was threatening Taiwan's long-standing air superiority. If the Americans held back it was deemed likely that Taiwan would buy planes from France.

Bush wavered, fearful that the fragile relationship he was trying to preserve with Beijing would be destroyed if he allowed the sale. But he was being pilloried for "coddling dictators," for his efforts to explain the importance he attached to cooperative Chinese-American relations. Finally, trailing Clinton in the polls, in August 1992, he announced the sale of 150 F-16s to Taiwan. Domestic political considerations overcame his doubts as to the wisdom of the action. As he anticipated, the Chinese were furious – and he lost the election anyway. (Taiwan, not expecting Bush to approve the sale of F-16s, had committed itself to buying the French Mirages, and ended up with both the French and American planes.)

There was, however, one further foreign policy issue from which Bush could not escape. Civil strife in Somalia was costing hundreds of thousands of lives, many through starvation. The country, strategically located on the Horn of Africa, had been of interest to both the United States and the Soviet Union, but had dropped off the screen with the end of the Cold War. American aid ended in 1991: the country and its people were no longer of any importance. No one in the U.S. government called for military intervention, but Africanists in the State Department urged humanitarian support in cooperation with UN efforts and American television began to show images of starving Somalis. Criticized by Democrats for doing nothing, in August 1992 a distracted and disinterested president authorized Operation Provide Relief, an airlift of food under UN auspices. The administration was responding to the relatively new phenomenon labeled the "CNN effect," the ability of television reporters to force the American government to attend to political or humanitarian crises it preferred to ignore. The president's advisers also suggested that aid to Somalia might deflect attention from the administration's unwillingness to aid Bosnia.

After the elections in the United States, the television cameras returned to Somalia and despite the opposition of the CIA, the Pentagon, and the Africanists at the State Department, Bush decided to send a major American force, 25,000 troops, to lead Operation Restore Hope, a multilateral military intervention designed to stop food theft and oversee the equitable distribution of famine aid. The United States no longer had a strategic interest in Somalia that would justify the expedition, but Bush was being pushed by Congress and public opinion. Clearly his reputation in the history books was on the table. And the intervention saved lives, tens of thousands of lives, but it did nothing to resolve the underlying problem of clan warfare in Somalia. What would happen when the troops came home – as Bush intended them to do in a matter of weeks, not months? The answer would be of great interest to Bill Clinton.

2

In Search of a Compass

There is general agreement that the George H. W. Bush administration did a credible job managing the end of the Cold War. There is also a consensus on Bush's lack of what he called "the vision thing." With the disappearance of the Soviet Union, the defining element of American foreign policy since George Kennan, which was articulated in the concept of containment in the mid-1940s, was lost. Bush and Baker, Scowcroft and Cheney had neither the time nor the inclination to ponder grand theory. But that does not mean that no one in the administration was thinking about what the post-Cold War world would be like and what the role of the United States should be. In Kennan's day, the Policy Planning Staff at the State Department would have been the most likely source of such reflections. Certainly that was what George Marshall had in mind when he created that group and brought Kennan in to head it in 1947. By the 1990s, however, the Department of Defense was playing a much larger role in American foreign policy generally and had its own group of policy planners. Every two years that group provided the secretary of defense and the president with a Defense Planning Guidance (DPG) document. The DPG for 1992, the first provided after the Soviet collapse, produced a sensation when an early draft was leaked in March 1992.

The DPG was, perhaps primarily, a rationalization for the Defense Department's budget request. Given that purpose, its drafters inevitably scanned the horizon for potential threats to the United States and its interests abroad. There was no virtue in underestimating these. The greater the danger, the more money the organization might be expected to obtain. In 1992, the Defense Department's budget hopes for the future were grim. The Cold War was over and Americans were expecting a "peace dividend" – a major reduction in defense spending and the taxes required to support it. Somehow the DPG had to provide an argument that would persuade the president and the Congress to provide funding that would allow the Defense Department to remain the enormous organization it had grown into in the course of the worldwide confrontation with the Soviets – in the absence of a comparable adversary.

The leaked draft document noted that the United States was the sole surviving superpower. Its task for the foreseeable future – perhaps for all eternity – was to prevent the rise of rivals. Scan the globe for potential rising powers – China, perhaps, or Japan and Germany, perceived by some to be the principal beneficiaries of the Cold War that had bankrupted the Soviet Union and left the United States deeply in debt – and act as necessary to prevent them from becoming threats to America's national interests. To be able to do so would require a military at least as powerful as that of the Cold War years – and a Defense Department organization large enough to support it. In short, it would be unwise to cut the department's budget.

The public outcry after the draft DPG was leaked necessitated a rephrasing that softened the language without surrendering the argument for protecting the budget. Rather than imply the need for the United States to take preventive action to bat down rising powers, the revised document indicated the desirability of an American military so strong that no country would be tempted to compete. The document also made clear that if international support for the world order envisaged by Americans was not forthcoming, the United States would act alone to create and preserve it.

In addition to government planners, there were dozens of men and women, national security or international relations specialists and public intellectuals in the universities and research institutions ("think tanks") across the country, who were mulling over some of the same issues. These were people for whom foreign affairs was the ultimate concern. Usually teaching and writing about policy issues provided their livelihood. Their reputations depended on their ability to publish "op-ed" essays in the major newspapers and articles in the most important journals. Some were frequent public speakers at fora around the country and appeared on television talk shows. The writings of the most prominent among them were read by policymakers. They served as advisers and consultants at the Departments of State and Defense, the CIA, and the National Security Council. Frequently they held government positions, as did some of their students. The most famous of them was, of course, Henry Kissinger, the Harvard political scientist who became national security adviser and secretary of state under Richard Nixon and Gerald Ford. Harvard's McGeorge Bundy was Kennedy's national security adviser – the man who brought in other intellectuals whom the writer David Halberstam labeled "the best and the brightest." MIT's Walt Rostow headed the Policy Planning Staff under

Kennedy and was elevated to national security adviser by Lyndon Johnson. These men and women, the foreign policy elite, provided the ideas and rationales for foreign policy.

As the Cold War ground to a halt and in the years immediately afterward, they, too, were asking: What would the world be like now that the Cold War was over? What should the role of the United States be? In the absence of superpower rivalry, could the United Nations serve as the world's policeman? Some shared the perspective of the defense planners and may in fact have influenced them.

As evidenced in the principal American journals of world affairs, such as *Foreign Affairs, Foreign Policy, International Security*, and *The National Interest*, the foreign policy elite was divided on all questions. The sharpest divisions on some issues seemed to be between traditional conservatives and libertarians on the one hand, and neoconservatives on the other. Traditional conservatives and libertarians, as always, sought to restrict the role of the government – and favored restraint for the United States in the absence of any deadly threat. Neoconservatives, once allied with conservatives in their shared hostility to Soviet communism, demanded a much more active role for the country and were eager to extend the blessings of democracy to benighted peoples everywhere – and especially in the Middle East. Traditional conservatives tended to favor *Realpolitik*: use American power only when vital interests were threatened. Neoconservatives were generally more ideological, almost Wilsonian in their crusading zeal – but for the overwhelming exception of their unilateralism. Both, however, had little use for the United Nations.

Centrists – or liberals as they were labeled in the American political context – were most likely to argue for internationalism or multilateralism. They continued to be supportive of the United Nations, eager to see it assume the role envisioned for it at its creation: an organization that would have the power and the will to preserve peace and justice across the globe. In particular, they argued in favor of humanitarian interventions, such as Bush had undertaken in Somalia and they contended he should have taken in Bosnia. In their view the national interest encompassed more than the nation's strategic interests. Much like the neoconservatives, the centrists wanted to see a world in which American values thrived, but they hoped to see such a world emerge as a result of a more effective United Nations. Should the UN be unable to prevent genocide, protect the weak against the transgressions of the strong, or come to the aid of the world's needy, they accepted an obligation to use the might of the United States, but only as the leader in multilateral efforts such as the coalition Bush had mustered for the rescue of Kuwait.

The Left in American politics hardly existed. The views of leftist intellectuals were most readily found in the venerable journal *The Nation*. They were predictably antimilitary, fearful of American imperialism, and suspicious of the role of business interests in defining the national interest. They, too, were supportive of the United Nations and multilateralism. Most favored humanitarian interventions, but challenged the tendency of the U.S. government to come to the aid of people who had oil and to ignore the suffering of those who did not. They differed from liberals specifically on the matter of free trade and opposed NAFTA, recognizing that although free trade might be advantageous for the nation as a whole, there would be losers as well as winners – and their government was unlikely to do much for workers who lost their jobs, for families that lost their source of income. They were also receptive to the concerns of Latin Americans who feared NAFTA would destroy their way of life.

As always, definitions of the national interest were disputed, but most of the foreign policy elite seemed to be pessimistic about the shape of the post-Cold War world. Utopian visions vanished quickly and were replaced by gloomy assessments of the likelihood of ancient quarrels resumed, of new nationalist and ethnic problems, of failed states, international terrorism, and, worst of all, the proliferation of weapons of mass destruction. The best known optimist – perhaps the only optimist – was Francis Fukuyama, sometime member of the State Department's Policy Planning Staff who wrote a widely publicized essay in *The National Interest* (1989) and subsequent book titled *The End of History* (1992) in which he argued that humankind was now progressing inexorably toward democratic societies organized around free markets. An analyst who offered both good news and bad was Richard Rosecrance who contended that with the end of the Cold War, the world was entering an era of trading states in which military power could be discounted. The economic power of Germany and Japan would make those countries the dominant powers of the twenty-first century – unless, of course, the United States stopped worrying about maintaining military superiority and shifted its resources to become more competitive economically.

There was consensus, also, on the world's hot spots. Control of Persian Gulf oil was considered a vital national interest – and threatened by both Iraq and Iran, countries hostile to the United States. Although some writers, especially those who had served in the Bush administration, defended Bush's decision not to extend the war to Baghdad and the removal of Saddam Hussein, no one doubted that Saddam was a significant menace. His quest for weapons of mass destruction would continue and knowledge that he had used chemical weapons against Iran and his own people left no illusions as to the danger he posed. Somehow the threat from Iraq would have to be contained at minimum and eliminated if at all possible. Iran, too, appeared to be seeking nuclear weapons and its leaders continued to spew hate against the United States and to support terrorism.

Equally threatening to the American conception of world order was Kim Il Sung's North Korea. The Bush administration had responded quickly and sensibly to evidence that the North Koreans had a nuclear weapons program, but lost momentum, largely because of divisions within its foreign policy team. Those favoring a carrot and stick approach to Kim lost out to those who insisted the North Koreans deserved no concessions and would respond only to force.

On other potential dangers to the republic, the men and woman who surveyed the horizon were divided. China worried many of them. Its economy was strengthening rapidly as it edged away from socialism toward a market economy. Some predicted that it would have the largest economy in the world by the middle of the twenty-first century. Its armed forces were huge and, although poorly equipped, were modernizing rapidly – in part with purchases from Russia. It was already a nuclear power. The regime in Beijing had demonstrated its capacity for brutality in 1989 and it was clear that the Communist Party leadership did not share American values. There was also the powder keg of Taiwan, the island enjoying de facto independence with American support but, according to the men in Beijing, a wayward province of China, to be returned to the fold by force if necessary. Other analysts dismissed the alleged threat. Some argued the Chinese economy was a house of cards that would collapse before long because of a failing banking system and corruption. Others imagined south China and Hong Kong breaking away to unite with Singapore and Taiwan. Some insisted that China had never been an aggressive power and that its current leaders, concerned primarily with modernizing their country, had no interest in foreign adventure. Chinese actions and American domestic politics seemed to be equally influential in shaping the course of the debate.

And then there was the threat of Japan as "number 1." For years a relatively small group of writers, perceived by the Japanese and their American defenders as "Japan bashers," had been arguing that Tokyo was engaged in economic warfare with the United States. They pointed to the enormous imbalance in bilateral trade relations and to Japan's mercantilist restrictive trade practices that they held responsible. The United States was certain to lose the war to what the renowned political scientist Chalmers Johnson called the "developmental state" unless it recognized that it was at war and fought back. This was a battle the incoming Clinton administration was virtually sure to join, given its commitment to revitalizing the American economy and provide jobs for American workers.

The debate on the likely nature of the post-Cold War world began even before the fall of the Berlin Wall. In 1989 and 1990, most writers did not anticipate the complete collapse of the Soviet Union and Moscow's future standing seemed to be the principal question mark. Some, much like Secretary of Defense Cheney, underestimated the significance of the changes Gorbachev had instituted and refused to recognize that the Soviets had surrendered on the ideological front – that the competition was over. For them, the future would differ little from the past.

One of the most interesting analysts was Charles Krauthammer, generally associated with the neoconservatives. Writing late in 1989, he was not quite ready to relax the anti-Soviet vigil, but he foresaw a world that would resemble the nineteenth century: a multipolar system with five probable major actors. He expected the Soviet Union to continue to play a superior role, along with the United States, and pointed to China, Japan, and either a united Germany or confederated Europe rounding out the field. Eventually a balance of power likely would emerge, with the United States playing the traditional British role of balancer. But Krauthammer was not satisfied with that outcome. He wanted a "unipolar" world dominated by some sort of Western confederation including democratic Europe, North America, and Asia. This community of democratic states would have unrivaled power and its continued success would lead inexorably to the spread of democracy. He anticipated nothing less than "universal domination" in the unlikely event this Western confederation came into being.

Much of the debate was waged by political scientists, often at an incomprehensible theoretical level. The tocsin was sounded early by John Mearsheimer, a well-regarded scholar who never hesitated to go where no one had dared go before. Writing early in 1990, he contended that the Cold War and the "long peace" that it had brought to Europe would be missed and that an end to the Cold War would create more problems than it would solve. Peace had depended on the bipolar distribution of power, the rough military parity between the two superpowers, and the fact that each had a sufficient number of nuclear weapons to deter the other. He was willing to accept a reduction of tensions between the United States and the Soviet Union, but insisted that the retention of the Cold War international system was the world's best hope for the avoidance of conflict in the years ahead. Certainly, he maintained, there had been less suffering in Europe during the Cold War than in the first 45 years of the century. If the superpowers withdrew from Europe, a multipolar system would arise and it would be more prone to instability, more likely to be undermined by hypernationalism, especially in Eastern Europe. Perhaps intending to shock, Mearsheimer argued that if the Soviet and American arsenals were removed from Europe, Germany – and Germany alone – should be allowed nuclear weapons, ostensibly to deter war in Europe.

Another prominent scholar, Stanley Hoffmann, also warned that the post-Cold War world would be a mess. Although relatively sanguine about Europe, he foresaw the re-emergence of traditional quarrels that the super-powers had repressed, each reining in potential troublemakers in its own orbit. In the absence of competition between them, neither the United States nor the Soviet Union would be willing to expend much effort in moderating these disagreeable tendencies among their erstwhile allies. Hoffmann also raised the specter of Islamic fundamentalism, a concern that had penetrated American consciousness with the rise of Khomeini in Iran, but had remained subordinate to Cold War issues.

Perhaps the most prominent resister of the multipolar image of the world to come was Joseph Nye, Hoffmann's colleague at Harvard. Nye rejected the idea of the decline of the United States – popularized by the Yale historian Paul Kennedy – and insisted that all potential challengers were deficient either economically or militarily. No state had a range of power resources comparable to that enjoyed by America. He did concede that there would be a general diffusion of power, but the challenge to America would come not from competitors for hegemony but from transnational interdependence. He stressed the importance of technology and its empowerment of nonstate actors, like terrorists. Nye saw a unipolar but fragmented world – with the United States, in his words, "bound to lead."

Another concern that cropped up frequently in the debate was of the proliferation of weapons of mass destruction (WMD) – biological, chemical, and especially nuclear. The American intelligence community was surprised at how advanced Iraqi's nuclear program had been and that discovery intensified anxieties about North Korea and Iran. The always thoughtful journalist William Pfaff warned that Third World countries were seeking and obtaining WMD as equalizers, giving small and relatively weak countries protection against bullying by more powerful neighbors – or by the United States. Nye worried about regional bullies, Iraq for example, using such weapons. And there was also the possibility of such weapons falling into the hands of terrorist organizations.

One important turning point in the debate came after the Persian Gulf War. The focus on America's imminent decline vanished. Anticipation of a multipolar world in which economic power replaced military power also found fewer voices. Owen Harries, then editor of *The National Interest*, noted the widespread emergence of "unipolarists." The United States, alone of all the world's nations, had been able to mount a response to Iraq's invasion of Kuwait. The acclaimed economic power of Germany and Japan had proven irrelevant in the crisis. But Harries was not rejoicing over the future he now perceived. Summing up much of the debate as it had evolved as of the winter of 1990–91, he predicted more regional imperialism as middle powers gained more freedom of action, more opportunities for the explosion of ethnic, national, and religious passions – and not least the greater availability of sophisticated weapons for which the Cold Warriors on both side no longer had any use. Perhaps his most striking point was the belittling of the demonstration of American power against Iraq – a smaller middle power. The lesson he drew was that Desert Storm had proven to be enormously expensive and established that the United States could not handle two such encounters at once.

Probably the most provocative argument about the shape of the post-Cold War world came from Samuel Huntington in his notorious article, "The Clash of Civilizations," published in *Foreign Affairs* in 1993. Huntington, yet another prominent Harvard political scientist, had trained many members of the foreign policy elite and his pronouncements always galvanized the debate. Earlier, in 1991, writing in the British journal *Survival*, he had echoed ideas spreading among analysts: military power was declining in importance while economic power was becoming more important; the post-Cold War world would be a jungle full of danger, traps, and unpleasant surprises. He thought the end of the Napoleonic wars the best analogy and recommended that President Bush read Castlereagh, the great British statesman of that era. It was a world in which the United States had best remain top dog – as it would, he contended, be best for all. A year or so later, he focused on Japanese economic power and called for economic renewal in the United States to preserve American dominance in the world.

In 1993, however, his focus shifted to cultural divisions. These, he argued, rather than ideological or economic divisions, would define the post-Cold War era. Conflicts would occur along cultural fault lines separating civilizations – ultimately between the West and the rest. Notably, he contended that interaction between Islam and the West was perceived by both sides as a "clash of civilizations." He advised the West to develop a better understanding of other civilizations, but warned that it would have to maintain the military and economic power necessary to protect its interests.

Critics challenged Huntington's definition of civilization or argued that states not civilizations determined the course of international affairs. He was accused of feeding Western paranoia about Islam or of ethnocentrism for his conviction that the Western model was best for the world. Nonetheless, to the men and women trying to prepare the United States for the new world order, Huntington's analysis, although readily challenged at the margins, seemed plausible at the core. Russia was struggling with Muslims. Iran had been a problem since Khomeini seized power. Most Muslim states were hostile to Israel's existence as a Western cancer in their midst. And there had been the attempt by Muslim radicals to blow up the World Trade Center in New York in 1993.

Of course, mulling over the probable nature of the post-Cold War era was merely the prelude to deciding America's place in it. What role would or should or could the United States play in the years to come? Perhaps the first call for a debate came from Charles William Maynes, then editor of *Foreign Policy*. Writing early in 1990, he recognized that the Malta meeting between Bush and Gorbachev meant that the Cold War was virtually over and that it was time to discuss future policy options. He was dismissive of the contentions that terrorism and Japanese economic power were the next generation of security threats and could find no challenge to American pre-eminence on the horizon. Nonetheless, the country needed a foreign policy. He saw the problem clearly and phrased it beautifully: the United States was losing not only an enemy, but also the "sextant by which the ship of state has been guided since 1945" (Maynes, 1990).

Maynes perceived three different foundations for future policy: national interest, democratic values, and global partnership. He argued that a national-interest based policy would allow a drastic drawback of U.S. forces overseas as the Third World faded into insignificance in the absence of a Soviet-American confrontation. He doubted that a narrow definition of national interest would survive the scrutiny of a Congress pressed by ethnic and other interest groups and, in any event, he was opposed to extensive retrenchment. Prudence was the word of the day. The neo-Wilsonian quest for spreading democracy, readily apparent in neoconservative circles, troubled him. Maynes was afflicted with the liberal's discomfort at imposing values on others – although he would have welcomed a universal endorsement of Franklin's Roosevelt's Four Freedoms (of speech and religion, from fear and from want) as central to a definition of democracy. His enthusiasm seemed to grow with the prospect of the United States and the Soviet Union joining in strengthening the United Nations, using their forces for peacemaking as well as peacekeeping. But he knew his people and feared that they would demand freedom of action, that they would be uneasy allowing any international organization a voice in their country's future.

Robert Tucker, a prominent scholar at the Washington-based Johns Hopkins School for Advanced International Studies, was also reflecting on the apparent end of the Cold War. He was a little more concerned than Maynes about how the end game would be played, but he, too, looked ahead and came to compatible conclusions. He was more troubled by the prospect of Germany and Japan emerging as major powers as military capability declined in importance, but saw neither as a threat to the United States. Indeed he saw little likelihood of any major power using force in Europe or Asia. American security was assured because the values and institutions for which it had intervened in World War II and contained the Soviets in the Cold War, presumably democracy and free markets – perhaps Roosevelt's Four Freedoms – were triumphing.

For the future, Tucker saw less need for the United States to play the world's policeman, but feared that it would because Americans liked being "number 1." He doubted that its allies would be as deferential in the absence of the Soviet threat and was skeptical about public support for policies designed to maintain world peace and stability – and the interventions that would likely be required. He hoped the U.S. government would be moderate in its future use of force, citing as positive examples Reagan's minor forays against Libya and Grenada and Bush's easy rout of the Panamanian Defense Force. But he knew that historically great powers did not go gently into the night – that the Pentagon and others in the foreign policy elite would seek and probably find new demons to combat.

Indeed, there were respected analysts who seemed to fear the Cold War would end or had ended before Americans achieved as much as they might. Some, such as Selig Harrison and Clyde Prestowitz (1990), complained that the Bush administration was ignoring an opportunity to restructure what they labeled the obsolete postwar order in East Asia. Their principal concern seemed to be Bush's continued emphasis on security issues when, they contended, he should have been seizing the opportunity Gorbachev had presented to focus on economic priorities. Martin Indyk (1990), a leading specialist on Middle Eastern affairs, was eager for the Bush administration to restructure the Middle East. Indyk was particularly disappointed when, after Desert Storm, Bush did not eliminate the baleful influence of Saddam Hussein or use the opportunity to gain control of weapons of mass destruction or press for democracy in Arab states. Indyk's agenda would not disappear.

Mayne's call for a debate was answered immediately by *The National Interest* which ran several articles, including a symposium in the fall issue (1990), on the question of America's purpose. Quickly most of the approaches that would be proposed and contested in the next decade were tabled. Isolationism – an abstention from world affairs that the United States had never actually practiced – was dismissed by all but the extreme Right, personified by the boisterous Pat Buchanan, sometime Republican speechwriter and presidential candidate. Virtually all other participants assumed that at least a modicum of international involvement was unavoidable, like it or not.

Irving Kristol (1990), perhaps the first of the old left intellectuals to emerge as a neoconservative, seemed annoyed with the debate. He was displeased especially with liberals and conservatives whom he perceived as expanding the idea of human rights to include the rights and liberties of modern liberal democracy and he was dismissive of the idea of a foreign policy designed to enhance democracy abroad. To him, America's national interest was clear: to prevent the emergence of another superpower with hostile political and social values – and he saw none on the horizon. He argued that the United States should protect nations that shared its values from those that did not. In addition, it should support those that are friendly and with whom good relations were important, such as Saudi Arabia, even if the Saudis did not share the American view of civil liberties and civil rights.

Ted Galen Carpenter (1990) of the libertarian Cato Institute was probably least supportive of the idea of a Pax Americana, of the need for the United States to continue to play the dominant role on the planet. Separating himself from Buchanan, he declared opposition to economic autarky or intolerant nationalism. He was bemused, however, by what he perceived as a frantic search for new missions by American foreign policy experts who assumed that the United States had to continue to lead to stave off global catastrophe. Carpenter wanted a narrower definition of the nation's vital interests and insisted there was no need to risk war to suppress ethnic conflicts in the Balkans or take the chance of being dragged into conflicts by irresponsible client states such as Israel, South Korea, or Pakistan. He insisted that the United States could be actively involved without being the world's policeman. He hoped for a two-third's cut in the defense budget and a strategy that somehow promoted American values without constant military interventions.

Others, such as Joseph Nye (1990) and the German journalist Josef Joffe (1990), argued that the United States could not escape its pre-eminent role. It alone had the power to dominate in every arena of world affairs – military, economic, and cultural. Joffe could not imagine any international crisis being managed without American participation. Nye, writing in *Foreign Policy* (1990), warned that the problem for the United States would not be the challenge of a new rising power, but of the diffusion of power. Nonstate actors – multinational corporations and terrorists, for example – were becoming increasingly important. As always he urged the use of "soft power," the attractiveness of American culture, ideology, and institutions to get others to want what Americans wanted. He also left no doubt that he believed that increasing transnational interdependence required international cooperation and collective action.

It was in the midst of the debate, in August 1990, that Saddam Hussein sent his forces into Kuwait and that George Bush, in due course, sent hundreds of thousands of American troops to the Persian Gulf to throw the Iraqis out of Kuwait, a task accomplished with relative ease early in 1991. It was then, too, that Charles Krauthammer revisited assumptions about the nature of the post-Cold War world and the role of the United States in it. There would not be, after all, a multipolar world. In fact, he contended, this was the "unipolar moment." It was the United States, acting unilaterally, that had prevented Iraq from gaining control of the Arabian Peninsula. Forget about German and Japanese economic power: it was clearly not enough to award them great power status. The Germans and Japanese had disappeared as soon as the first shots were fired. He labeled American action "pseudo-multilateralism," a recruiting of token support to pacify those Americans uncomfortable with unilateral action.

Krauthammer had three fears. The first, widely shared across the political spectrum, was of an underlying American weakness apparent in the state of the nation's economy. He was profoundly troubled by the national debt, which he attributed to the low tax ideology of the Reagan years and the usual desire of the American people for a free lunch – a higher standard of living without paying for it. Writing at the same time, William Pfaff (1991) took Krauthammer's concern a step further, arguing that superpowers pay their own way and that Bush's appeal for other nation's to pay for the Gulf War was a renunciation of superpower status. Robert Hormats, a well-regarded international banker with ties to leading Democrats, expressed similar thoughts (1991). Hormats insisted that the Reagan and Bush administrations had neglected the roots of American economic power and contended that the coming danger was not of imperial overstretch but of underperformance of the domestic economy.

Krauthammer and Pfaff shared a second concern: the proliferation of weapons of mass destruction among small aggressive states such as Iraq and North Korea. Krauthammer insisted they had to be disarmed – and by the United States. For him there was no alternative to unilateral preemptive action.

Krauthammer's third fear was of resurgent isolationism in America, a fear derived from the widespread opposition to the Gulf War among some conservatives and many liberals. He never doubted that the Gulf was an area of vital interest to the United States and was troubled by what he viewed as a narrow conception of the national interest held by analysts who imagined themselves to be "realists." Krauthammer foresaw the curious alignment that defined the debate in the years ahead. Traditional conservatives and liberals, for differing reasons, would call for limiting the use of American power abroad while neoconservatives would insist there was an opportunity to use that power to spread American values across the world.

Cato's Ted Galen Carpenter (1991), not surprisingly, was profoundly troubled by Krauthammer and the overall neoconservative expansiveness. Like Owen Harries and many other specialists in international relations, Carpenter disparaged the idea of a unipolar moment, insisting that if the United States attempted to reorder the world as it pleased, if it acted as though no effective opposition could arise, it would surely prompt creation of an opposing coalition of second tier nations. Writing in 1991, after the Gulf War, he was utterly contemptuous of the claim that the United States could create democracy in Iraq – pointing to earlier failures in Chile, Guatemala, Iran, Korea, Nicaragua, and the Philippines. Instead of looking for new rationales to intervene abroad, American officials should adopt a less interventionist role, acting against lethal danger – but not for what he considered unattainable, utopian objectives.

And then, of course, the Soviet Union disappeared at the end of 1991. There is no doubt that all of the American foreign policy elite liked the idea of the United States as the world's only remaining superpower and hoped the nation would enjoy that status for a very long time. Maintaining American global primacy was a consensus goal and most analysts agreed with Samuel Huntington's contention that the world was best off with the United States as "number 1." But primacy was not the same as dominance. Leading the world was not the same as forcing it to accept American values. The debate over how and when American power would be used continued, erupting anew with every perceived international crisis.

In late 1991 and 1992, foreign policy issues were considered against the backdrop of the presidential election campaign – a campaign in which Bush, initially conceived of as the invulnerable leader of a nation victorious in the Cold War and the Persian Gulf War, found himself in trouble. Not unlike Winston Churchill in 1945, Bush faced a nation that thanked him for winning the wars, but judged him insensitive to their postwar economic needs. World dominance was fine, but the demand for more jobs and higher family income came first.

One idea, of which Larry Diamond, a senior fellow at the Hoover Institution was probably the most persistent spokesman, was that the United States should work assiduously to promote the spread of democracy in the post-Cold War world. The underlying assumption was that democracies don't go to war against each other, ergo the promotion of democracy had security ramifications. It would make the world safer for America. Richard Nixon – of all people – had complained that the response of the United States to the needs of the Soviet Union as it tried to move toward democracy and a market economy was "pathetically inadequate." Diamond proclaimed that Bush's policy toward the postcommunist states was timid and called upon the United States to rally Europe and Japan to provide far greater aid, insisting democratization of Russia was the highest strategic interest of the West. He also argued that success depended on collaboration with the other industrial democracies – that the United States could not succeed unilaterally.

David Hendrikson, writing in *Foreign Affairs* (1992), was intensely critical of the Bush administration's efforts to maintain military power and build alliances in the absence of a Soviet threat. He accused it of equating aggression in remote areas of the world with threats to world order and American security. The idea of costly military interventions at a time when the nation faced an enormous budget deficit troubled him greatly. He insisted that with the collapse of the Soviet Union, disorder in the Third World no longer posed a danger for the United States – and that Americans should avoid an imperial role. Unimpressed by the performance of the United States in the Third World during the Cold War, he suggested it was likely to get worse without Soviet restraints. Paraphrasing Lord Acton, he warned that unrestrained power would be corrupting. Hendrickson was also uncomfortable with the way the United States had fought in Iraq. He saw a new approach in which casualties were minimized, engagement avoided, and massive use of firepower followed by rapid withdrawal: "While assuming an imperial role, there is no intention of assuming the responsibilities of imperial power."

In the same issue of *Foreign Affairs*, Joseph Nye – who had Democratic Party candidate Bill Clinton's ear – took the opposite tack, insisting that world order was exceptionally important to the United States. He described a world of transnational interdependence in which international disorder could have a negative impact on most Americans. He pointed to the usual culprits – proliferation of weapons of mass destruction, terrorism, and drug trafficking – but warned that the United States could not manage such problems alone. Aware of the widespread desire to reduce the country's military and economic commitments abroad, he argued for renewed allegiance to multilateral institutions, the middle path between doing too much and doing too little. Increasingly, the call for multilateralism became the liberal's mantra.

Any discussion of multilateralism inevitably demanded arguments about the future role of the United Nations. American support for the organization, once the nation's hope for a peaceful, orderly, and just postwar world, had declined over the years. In the late 1940s and 1950s, the United States had usually been able to dominate the organization, rallying its allies and client states. As membership increased in the 1960s with decolonization and many of the new African and Asian states proved less pliable than hoped, the UN ceased to be an instrument of American policy. Too often, UN fora became sounding boards for Third World grievances against the United States and its allies. Too often, the Soviets and their allies were able to block actions Washington would have liked the organization to take. Perhaps the decisive blow came in 1975 when the UN General Assembly voted to equate Zionism with racism, outraging a significant segment of American opinion previously among the UN's strongest supporters.

With the end of the Cold War, the original vision of an organization to which the United States might turn over many of the responsibilities for keeping the peace and providing justice for peoples in areas remote from American vital interests resurfaced. Maynes, as early as the spring of 1990, envisioned the United States and the Soviet Union cooperating to strengthen the UN. He imagined that no longer competitors, they might use their military forces for peacekeeping, peacemaking, and arms control verification under the UN flag.

Some analysts were heartened by the role the Security Council had played during the Gulf War. It passed the necessary resolutions to facilitate action against the Iraqi aggressors. None of the permanent members threatened a veto – although the Chinese abstained rather than support the use of force. It was Joseph Nye who made the critical point on the UN's role: its resolutions provided the cover the Saudis needed to participate in the American-led coalition against Saddam Hussein and enabled the United States to persuade other states, must notably Germany and Japan, to pay the bill for Desert Storm.

There was little evidence, however, of optimism about the UN enabling the United States to reduce its responsibilities – and little sense that Washington would be willing to step down from its position of dominance on any issue of interest to it. Owen Harries (1990–1) was quick to discount the UN role in Kuwait, arguing that the UN still could function only when the villain was not one of the veto-possessing permanent members of the Security Council. Krauthammer (1991) dismissed the UN resolutions as a fig leaf for American unilateralism, an argument not very different from that of Nye. He accepted the idea that it made intervention more palatable to the American people, but his contempt for the UN was underscored when he expressed dismay at the idea that the United States needed the support of the "butchers of Beijing" represented in the Security Council. Pfaff (1991) warned that those who imagined a future in which the United States led UN actions around the world were assuming, falsely, that UN members would have opinions on events consistent with those of Americans. That had not been true since the Korean War and was not likely to get any better. He saw unilateralism as deeply rooted in American society: Americans were certainly not going to accept UN influence and any expectation they had that the UN would follow them was unrealistic.

The most thoughtful exposition about the place of the UN in the post-Cold War world came from Yale scholars Bruce Russett and James Sutterlein in the spring of 1991. They thought that in the Gulf War the UN had shown itself able to act decisively and that this might serve as a deterrent to potential aggressors. But they contended that the organization needed its own standing multilateral force, an argument long identified with Brian Urquhart who had served as UN under secretary general in the 1960s. In the absence of such a force, the country providing most of the troops would control the action and pursue its interests – which might not be congruent with those of other member states. Russett and Sutterlein warned that the essentially unilateral way in which the United States and its followers acted in the Gulf was likely to preclude Security Council approval of a similar process in the future. Other council members would want more control over military operations, especially the decision as to when to end them. In Korea, in 1950, the United States pushed beyond the initial intention of the UN in a classic case of "mission creep," deciding not merely to repel aggression but to unite the Korean Peninsula under noncommunist control. Security Council members were not unaware that some American leaders would have liked to go on to Baghdad and eliminate Saddam Hussein's regime, an aim with which other states were not in sympathy.

And then, in November 1992, the American people abandoned George Bush and elected Bill Clinton to be their next president. In the campaign, Clinton had been critical of Bush for failing to come to the aid of the Bosnians in the face of Serb aggression. In the interim between the election and Clinton's inauguration, the issue of humanitarian intervention took a central place in the debate over America's role and that of the UN.

The question of whether the United States should intervene in the wars over the breakup of Yugoslavia was joined by the question of what to do in the face of famine resulting from civil strife in Somalia. Bush had chosen to stay out of the struggle among the Yugoslav succession states, but chose to act in Somalia, sending American troops in under UN auspices to distribute food to starving Somalis. What should Clinton do?

Few analysts perceived the UN as the solution to the problem of humanitarian interventions and most were sharply divided as to how the United States should respond to such crises. It seemed clear to all that without American leadership, the UN could and would do little. Stephen John Stedman, writing in *Foreign Affairs* (1993), expressed fear that the demand for humanitarian interventions would involve the United States in domestic conflicts around the world. He saw support for such missionary action coming from across the political spectrum, culminating in the UN effort to feed Somalis – and he thought Clinton was sympathetic to such actions. Stedman argued that there was no moral obligation to ride to the rescue of the people of failed states and that the UN lacked the resources to do the job. Paralleling Stedman's contentions, Doug Bandow insisted in *Foreign Policy* (1992–3) that with the end of the Cold War, global disorder posed no threat to the United States and that the country should stop acting like an empire. He worried about the collecting of client states and the establishment of military installations all over the globe. He even argued that the Gulf War had been unnecessary. He dismissed the UN as good merely for providing cover for American actions in Korea and the Gulf, but unable to resolve issues itself. Echoing hostility to China that had been part of Clinton's campaign, Bandow found the Security Council to be at the mercy of Beijing and suggested that the United States had paid too much to gain China's abstention in the UN vote to authorize force in the Gulf.

Writing in the same issue of *Foreign Policy*, Edward Luck clearly favored intervention in Bosnia and Somali and implicitly criticized the Bush administration for failing to explain adequately the post-Cold War strategic underpinning for American policy. He seemed to want a clear moral basis for policy, rejecting claims that democratization was an important administration goal: how could it be when the absence of it was ignored in China? He had even less use for the contention that the Gulf War had been fought for democratic principles when it restored the hereditary emir of Kuwait and left Saddam Hussein in power in Baghdad. How could Bush have looked away while Somalis starved? How could he refuse to act to stop ethnic cleansing in Bosnia?

Luck wanted Clinton to stress human rights and humanitarian concerns, norms he contended served American economic and strategic interests. But like Stedman and Bandow, he had little expectation of the UN playing a major role. He saw it as useful, however, for determining the global division of labor. Multilateralism was good – except, he conceded, when American national interests were not congruent with that of others on the Security Council. Then the United States might have to act alone. The critical point was that responsibility for humanitarian interventions could not be dumped on the UN: it could not do the job.

Enter Bill Clinton – with American troops on the ground in Somalia and pressure mounting for action in Bosnia to protect Muslims there and for action against the perpetrators of the Tiananmen atrocities. Clinton had promised to do better on all three counts and had promised also to promote democracy and respect for human rights everywhere – and strengthen the UN. But at the heart of his campaign was the determination to revive the American economy. Many analysts, on the right and on the left, insisted that reducing the budget deficit was essential for the restoration of American power – and that American economic power was essential to the preservation of the nation's survival as the sole superpower.

3

CLINTON AND HUMANITARIAN
INTERVENTIONS

George H. W. Bush had amassed an enviable record in his management of
foreign affairs. There was, to be sure, a bit of carping from the human rights
community about his alleged coddling of the Chinese Communist government after the brutal Tiananmen massacres, and Richard Nixon had been
critical of his parsimonious aid to the former Soviet Union and the aspir-
ing democracies of Eastern Europe. But Bush had presided over the victorious end of the Cold War and jailed the thuggish Panamanian dictator
Manuel Noriega. He had assembled and led the coalition that threw the
Iraqi aggressors out of Kuwait. Having eliminated all imminent threats to
the security of the American people and proclaimed a "new world order"
in which American values would thrive, he had, unfortunately for his political future, made it possible for his people to view foreign affairs as no
longer important – and allowed them the luxury of electing as their next
president a small state governor who promised to focus his attention on the
domestic economy.

Bill ("it's the economy, stupid") Clinton was a so-called New Democrat
who emphasized fiscal conservatism. The labor-based New Deal coalition
that had once led the Democrat Party to victory after victory beginning with
Franklin Roosevelt in 1932 had faltered after the election of Lyndon
Johnson in 1964. New Democrats believed it was essential to move
the Party to the center if it was to regain the support of middle-class
Americans. Moreover the accelerating costliness of election campaigns
made it essential, in their minds, to attract campaign funds from bankers
and corporate leaders, if the Party was to remain competitive.

Clinton was determined to balance the federal budget and reduce the
deficit without damaging programs that benefited his party's core working-
and middle-class constituents. He knew he would have to take the unpopular step of raising taxes to compensate for the profligacy of the Reagan

years, but he and his supporters also saw substantial savings coming from the "peace dividend" – the monies that could be cut from defense spending in the absence of a threat to the country. Before taking office, he told Lee Hamilton, chairman of the House Foreign Affairs Committee, that no one in America cared about foreign policy but a handful of journalists. As he entered the White House in January 1993, the only foreign policy issues that seemed to hold his attention were trade-related. More than most Democrats, he was a fervent believer in free trade, eager to gain Senate approval for NAFTA, and convinced that for the remainder of the century, international economic issues would take precedence over security concerns. Support for Clinton from American firms engaged in international business strengthened his convictions.

Clinton's foreign policy team was more representative of the foreign policy establishment, but proved to be uninspired – and uninspiring. His secretary of state, Warren Christopher, had served as deputy secretary in the Carter administration, believed in service to his president and country, multilateralism and international cooperation generally, and, if given the opportunity, would have placed the protection of human rights high on his agenda. He was a highly intelligent and decent man, but he was never as close to Clinton as Baker had been to Bush and could rarely count on strong support from his president. Les Aspin, Clinton's first secretary of defense, was a very knowledgeable congressman who proved to be an abominable administrator, and quickly lost the confidence of the uniformed military. The highly respected Colin Powell, inherited as chairman of the Joint Chiefs, opposed the president's policy on gays in the military and openly undermined the president. Tony Lake, appointed the president's national security adviser, had served briefly on Henry Kissinger's staff in the Nixon administration, but had learned little about deviousness or salesmanship from Kissinger. In the Carter years he had directed the State Department's Policy Planning Staff and had strengthened his reputation for thoughtfulness and sober judgment. He imagined himself an idealist, committed to expanding democracy throughout the world and protecting human rights.

The most charismatic figures on the team were a step removed from the White House, most notably Madeline Albright, ambassador to the United Nations, Richard Holbrooke, briefly ambassador to Germany and then assistant secretary of state for European and Canadian Affairs, and Winston Lord, an apostate Republican who served as assistant secretary for East Asia and the Pacific. All three were successful at attracting press attention and easily overshadowed the colorless Christopher and Lake. Albright was determined to reinvigorate the UN and to strengthen U.S. ties to it. She promised a policy of "assertive multilateralism." Holbrooke, Carter's assistant secretary for East Asia and the Pacific, was notoriously aggressive and proved to be the right man to take on Slobodan Milosevic when the administration eventually confronted the Serbian leader. Lord had served as ambassador to China in the Bush administration, and perceived Bush's management of Chinese-American relations as weak, especially on human rights issues. During the 1992 election campaign, he became Clinton's point man on policy toward China, urging less accommodation and more pressure. His role in the administration generated anxiety in Beijing.

But there were four others who had greater access to the president and whose activities reflected Clinton's priorities. First was his long-time friend, Strobe Talbott, whom he named special ambassador. Talbott, a prominent journalist, had exceptional knowledge of Russian affairs and focused almost exclusively on efforts to reform Russia – to assist the Russians in developing a democratic government and a market economy. The other three were Samuel ("Sandy") Berger, Lake's deputy on the National Security Council, Ron Brown, secretary of commerce, and Mickey Kantor, who served as United States Trade Representative (USTR). All three were intensely concerned with trade issues, especially opening foreign markets to American exports and gaining American corporations greater access to the cheap labor and natural resources of less-developed countries.

One transcendent issue that had emerged clearly in the Bush administration and concerned the Clintonites no less was how to maintain the preeminence of the United States in world affairs. The controversial Defense Planning Guide attributed to Paul Wolfowitz had emphasized challenges to American military power – as one might expect from Department of Defense planners. Initially, at least, the Clinton team seemed to see the threat primarily in economic terms, perhaps perceiving the future as had Roger Rosecrance in his contention that trading states, specifically Germany and Japan, would dominate the post-Cold War world and that military power would become less relevant.

By 1993, concern about the rise of German power was fading. Reunification, the absorption of East Germany, had proven enormously costly for the Federal Republic. But the threat of Japan as number one continued to be of grave concern to analysts in and out of government. Samuel Huntington (1993) the influential Harvard political scientist, argued that the Japanese were practicing economic warfare against the United States, attempting to use their economic power to replace U.S. influence in the world. He insisted that the continued primacy of the United States was essential for the entire world, as well as for Americans. He worried about

American dependence on imports and capital from Japan and perceived Japanese lobbyists buying elections and scholars. If the Japanese succeeded in wresting primacy from the United States, we would have a world "with more violence and disorder and less democracy and economic growth".

Clinton's response was to minimize the importance of the Japanese-American security relationship and take the offensive in trade relations with Japan. Mickey Kantor was his chosen instrument. For roughly three years, Kantor badgered and threatened the Japanese in a modestly successful effort to get them to liberalize their trade practices. The American struggle to open up Japanese markets had begun in the 1960s, but more often than not during the Cold War, trade had been subordinated to security. The Clinton administration did not hesitate to put economic concerns first, to the chagrin of analysts and officials preoccupied with maintaining the Japanese-American alliance as the lynchpin of American strategy in East Asia.

Further indication of Clinton's priorities appeared in his struggle to win ratification for NAFTA. The president's enthusiasm for globalization, for what he called the spread of "market democracy," troubled important interests within the Democratic Party, most notably labor and the environmentalists. In the election campaign, he had supported Bush on the issue of NAFTA in the face of third party candidate Ross Perot's warning of a "giant sucking sound" of jobs being lost to Mexico if NAFTA were ratified.

To mollify the AFL-CIO (American Federation of Labor and Congress of Industrial Organizations) and the environmentalists, he had promised side agreements with Mexico to meet their concerns. In the summer of 1993, despite the opposition of the majority of Congressional Democrats, he pushed hard for ratification. It was clearly an issue he deemed important and upon which he was prepared to expend considerable political capital – and he won, thanks to strong support from Congressional Republicans. On few other foreign policy issues was Clinton comparably engaged in the early years of his presidency.

NAFTA was probably of minimal value to the United States. Economists thought it would bring a small net gain to the country, although obviously there would be jobs lost as well as gained. Henry Kissinger and the prominent liberal economist Paul Krugman argued for ratification on political rather than economic grounds. Ratification would help a friendly Mexican government succeed in moving from import-substitution protectionism to free trade. Failure to ratify the agreement would have been devastating to Mexican reformers. Ultimately, the Mexican financial crisis of 1994–5 – the collapse of the Mexican peso – and the need for an American bail out overshadowed the NAFTA issue.

In the election campaign of 1992, the Democrats had sought to make political capital out of Bush's handling of relations with China after the Tiananmen massacres of 1989, his inaction in the face of the fragmentation of Yugoslavia, and his administration's treatment of Haitian refugees in the aftermath of a military junta deposing Jean-Bertrand Aristide, the democratically elected president of that hapless country. But a different and seemingly more remote problem the incoming administration faced in January 1993 was Somalia, where the lame-duck Bush administration, with the unanimous support of the UN Security Council, had intervened in a chaotic civil war for strictly humanitarian reasons. Thirty-thousand American troops were on the ground when Bill Clinton was inaugurated. Events there had an enormous impact on the evolution of Clinton's foreign policy.

Bush's decision to send marines to Somalia was criticized at home on the grounds that the United States had no strategic or economic interest in Somalia, a sometime Cold War ally. President-elect Clinton, however, supported Bush: hundreds of thousands of Somali lives would be saved if order sufficient to allow the distribution of food relief could be maintained. And this phase of the operation was successful. But once in office, Clinton's attention was directed in a myriad of different directions. Somalia was not one of them. Many months passed before the president was forced to focus on events there. In the absence of presidential leadership, his foreign policy apparatus functioned poorly and did not serve him well.

By March 1993, the apparent success of the intervention had led to the reduction of American forces in Somalia – and mission creep. The UN resolved to create a secure environment throughout the country and intensified efforts begun by the Bush administration to pacify the warlords whose rivalries had brought such misery to the local people. Albright perceived an opportunity for the United States to do good through multilateral action: it would lead the UN in the reconstruction of a failed-state. American forces continued to be withdrawn and command of the UN forces, including the remaining 4,000 Americans passed to the UN in May – although the UN commander was a retired American naval officer.

The turning point came early in June, when the forces of Mohammed Farah Aidid, probably the most powerful Somali warlord, ambushed a UN patrol and killed 24 Pakistani peacekeepers. Aidid was angered by UN restraints on his operations and had concluded that UN forces were a threat to his power. Outraged by the attack, the Security Council authorized the arrest of Aidid. Albright, in an extraordinary flight of rhetoric, pronounced him an obstacle to the emergence of democracy.

When it became clear that UN forces in Somalia were not sufficient to do the job, the United States sent in Rangers and Delta Force commandos. A humanitarian mission designed to save Somali lives was now causing Somali casualties as air attacks and raids intensified. Robert Oakley, a former ambassador to Somalia, originally appointed special ambassador by Bush, had attempted to reach a diplomatic solution with Aidid. But Boutros Boutros-Ghali, the UN secretary general, and the UN command in Somalia were determined to overpower the Somali warlord.

No directions came from the White House. The president and his national security adviser were content to leave control of Somali affairs to the men in the field – until disaster struck on October 3. On that day, after helicopter gunships attacked Aidid's headquarters in Mogadishu, two American Black Hawks were downed by Aidid's forces. Eighteen U.S. soldiers were killed, the body of one dragged in front of television cameras and a captured pilot mistreated by the Somalis, to the horror of millions of Americans. It was a wake-up call at the White House where an angry president demanded to have the mess cleaned up. Aspin became the scapegoat of choice, but Clinton was also intensely dissatisfied with the performances of Powell and Lake. And he wanted out of Somalia as quickly as possible short of further humiliation of the United States.

The congressional and media reaction to the tragedy in Mogadishu was to question the American presence in Somalia. What interest did the United States have there that was worth American lives? Intervening for humanitarian purposes was an attractive idea, but as with most overseas adventures, Americans were reluctant to pay the price. If there was no apparent benefit for the United States, American troops should not be put in harm's way. If the people the United States and the UN were trying to help were shooting at their would-be saviors, something was wrong and it was time to get out.

Pulling itself together, the Clinton's foreign policy team agreed on the necessity of a rapid exit from Somalia. First, American troops there would be reinforced in the vain hope the world would perceive that the United States could not be intimidated by some tin-pot warlord. At the same time, Oakley was authorized to negotiate with Aidid for the release of the captured pilot – which he did successfully. Then Clinton ordered the phased withdrawal of American forces. Wisely, Aidid held back until the Americans were gone and events in Somalia ceased to be of interest to the public or politicians in the United States.

Different folks learned different lessons from the American intervention in Somalia. The prevailing view in the United States was that nothing like it could be allowed to happen again. The United States would not support any future UN actions unless all parties to a conflict consented to the deployment. Peacemaking operations, where UN forces intervened to stop the fighting, were precluded. Risking American lives for strictly humanitarian purposes would not be acceptable. Hereafter it would have to be evident that the national interest was involved. As Clinton expressed it, rebuilding Somalia was "not our job." Presumably rebuilding failed states elsewhere would not be part of America's mission. After several months of discussions within the administration, in May, 1994, the president signed a directive "reforming" multilateral peace operations–a document that greatly reduced the likelihood of American troops providing the muscle for the UN.

Elsewhere in the world, a perception grew that the sole surviving superpower, despite enjoying its unipolar moment, could be outmaneuvered simply by killing a few American soldiers – or merely threatening to do so. Evidence of this "lesson" of the American withdrawal from Somalia came quickly and close to home, in Haiti. Again, the president was only minimally engaged by the issue, despite his criticism of Bush's policy of forced repatriation of Haitian refugees. His promise to reverse Bush's practice was dropped quickly when the CIA informed him that in celebration of his election, 200,000 jubilant Haitians were building rafts and preparing a mass exodus for the United States. The Haitians were black, they were poor (perhaps worst of all they spoke French) and, unlike the Cuban refugees from Castro, they were not welcome in politically important Florida.

Since Aristide's overthrow by a military junta in 1991, the official position of the United States was to demand that he be restored to office. In fact, powerful forces within the U.S. government, especially the CIA, the Department of Defense, and Senator Jesse Helms (R-NC), chairman of the Senate Foreign Relations Committee, were opposed to Aristide's return. He was, after, all a priest who had been defrocked for his adherence to liberation theology – preaching the need to free the masses from the oppression of the ruling class – and a demagogue who angered American investors by promising to double the minimum wage in Haiti. Bush, Baker, and Cheney had agreed that the effort to regain Aristide's presidency for him was not worth one American life.

Lake, Talbott, and Albright, however, focused on the fact that Aristide had received 67% of the vote in a fair election. The junta could not be allowed to thwart democracy, the will of the Haitian people. They intensified diplomatic efforts to arrange for Aristide's return and reached an agreement with the junta in July 1993 to terms that satisfied Haitian elites and that Aristide reluctantly accepted. Unfortunately, the junta reneged on the agreement.

The clearest sign that the Haitian military had no intention of relinquishing power came in October – and indicated what the Haitian generals had learned from the events in Somalia. The junta had agreed to allow a small force of 200 American and Canadian troops to land in Haiti to train local security forces. When the *U.S.S. Harlan County*, carrying the troops, attempted to dock, it was met by a mob brandishing pistols and chanting "Somalia." Unprepared to land under fire, the ship left. Faced with the likelihood of losing lives, the United States retreated – and no military action to relieve the humiliation followed.

The Clinton administration's next step was to tighten economic sanctions in hope of bringing the junta to heel. But by the spring 1994, it was obvious that the sanctions were not working. Equally obvious was the increased flow of refugees, the bulk of whom were caught and sent back to Haiti. Human rights groups were increasingly active on behalf of the Haitians. In Washington the Congressional Black Caucus was growing restive and angry. Randall Robinson, director of TransAfrica (an NGO that had played a prominent role fighting apartheid in South Africa), began a hunger strike to force Clinton to act. To the dismay of the Pentagon, Lake and Talbott pushed plans for an invasion.

The OAS (Organization of American States) had indicated grave concern when Aristide was overthrown in 1991. In July, 1994, the OAS approved the use of force to drive out the junta and restore Aristide to his presidency. Albright then succeeded in getting the UN Security Council to authorize "a coalition of the willing" to invade Haiti. Despite congressional opposition and polls that showed the American public opposed, Clinton insisted he had the constitutional authority to send in the troops. In September the operation was ready when the Haitian junta blinked.

The junta invited former president Jimmy Carter to Haiti to help find a peaceful resolution. The administration agreed to Carter's mission, but insisted he be accompanied by former Georgia senator Sam Nunn and Colin Powell. Clinton gave them one day, until noon September 18, to reach an agreement. He accepted several hour delays as the junta stalled and bargained and then told the mission the attack would commence in 30 minutes. With that the junta folded. Led by the United States, coalition forces landed unopposed in Haiti the next day, September 19.

Clinton justified the intervention by arguing that brutality close to America's shores threatened the national interest. His critics were unpersuaded, but because the landing of American troops was not resisted, because there were no casualties, debate about his policy evaporated quickly. Distaste for Aristide among American conservatives did not disappear and they were delighted to call Clinton's attention to evidence of corruption, incompetence, and undemocratic practices by Aristide's government in the years that followed.

Clinton's advisers on domestic affairs left the president with no doubt that humanitarian interventions would be a political liability, reinforcing his disinclination to use force and his general disinterest in noneconomic foreign policy issues. His vacillating response to the crisis in Bosnia reflected his unwillingness to provide strong leadership. His refusal to intervene when confronted with genocide in Rwanda – indeed his administration's obstruction of UN efforts to save the lives of hundreds of thousands of Tutsis in Rwanda – was probably the most reprehensible moment of his presidency. The experience in Somalia could not have been far from his thoughts in both crises.

The breakup of Yugoslavia that led to the atrocities against civilians in Bosnia had been abetted by Europe, most obviously by German support for the independence of Croatia and Slovenia. As the war to create a "Greater Serbia" produced inescapable evidence of "ethnic cleansing," European governments appeared to prefer to end the bloodshed without any help from the United States. The Cold War was over and Europe's leaders were eager to demonstrate that they were no longer dependent on the Americans – an idea which suited both Bush and Clinton administrations just fine. But neither the Europeans nor the UN was prepared to intervene forcibly to stop the fighting and certainly not to roll back Serb aggression.

Mediation efforts by the European Union (EU) and the UN Security Council had failed to stop the fighting between Serbs and Croats. In 1992 in an attempt to preserve some semblance of Bosnian independence, Cyrus Vance, former American secretary of state, acting for the UN, and David Lord Owen, former British foreign secretary, acting for the EU, had devised a peace plan that left the Serbs in de facto control of roughly two-thirds of Bosnia. It was a highly repugnant arrangement on moral grounds, but unquestionably the best the Bosnian Muslims could hope for in the absence of a foreign military intervention to do to the Serbs what the Muslims were unable to do for themselves.

The incoming Clinton administration was not prepared to send troops to throw the Serb army out of Bosnia, but it was unwilling to endorse the Vance-Owen plan that patently rewarded the aggressors. Clinton was troubled by the suffering in Bosnia, by the evidence of atrocities and spoke out against ethnic cleansing, but no action followed. Lake was eager to intervene, also on humanitarian grounds, but the Pentagon was adamantly opposed. Military leaders were convinced that air power would not suffice to stop the Serbs and they were unwilling to send in ground troops, foreseeing a Vietnam-like quagmire. It was in this context that Albright outraged Colin Powell by asking what the point was of having a superb military if we were unwilling to use it. Powell and his supporters in and out of the Pentagon were clearly averse to risking casualties.

Under pressure from Lake, Albright, and Vice President Al Gore, by April 1993 Clinton was leaning toward the strategy known popularly as "lift and strike." Men and women eager to come to the rescue of the beleaguered Bosnian Muslims called on the president to lift the embargo on the sale of arms to the Muslims and to hit the Serbs with air strikes. Clinton sent Christopher to Europe to sound out NATO allies, but gave up the idea when he found all opposed. Unquestionably, staying on the same page as his allies was more important to him than undertaking a dangerous intervention on behalf of Bosnian Muslims. He allowed himself to be persuaded that the strife in the Balkans was rooted in centuries' old disputes, that atrocities were a natural part of Balkan culture – and unstoppable.

Clinton doubtless would have been happiest if the war in Bosnia had disappeared from the media and was forgotten by the public. That did not happen, not least because of the extraordinary efforts of one television journalist, Christiane Amanpour of CNN. Amanpour was appalled by the atrocities and convinced that stopping the Serbs was a moral duty. She was not alone, but CNN had great credibility in the United States and abroad, and many other reporters picked up on her stories. The Bosnian cause was also kept alive by a number of foreign service officers who shared her view and pressed from within the Department of State. Throughout the country, the desire to do something – short of sending in American troops – intensified. But the administration dithered.

Meanwhile, in distant Africa, in Rwanda where the United States had no interest whatever, a peace accord was reached in August 1993, which promised to end the civil war between the Hutus and Tutsis. In this post-Cold War world, Africa received little attention from the American government and initially none from the president. Any earlier inclination to do good in that part of the world had gone down the drain with the debacle in Somalia. Peace accords, however, were always welcome.

The handful of Americans who followed the affairs of Rwanda noted in the months that followed that militant Hutus were preventing the implementation of the accord. A tiny UN multinational force was sent to help, but it was not adequate to the task. Assembling a larger force was impossible, largely because the United States had reduced its contribution to peacekeeping operations and was uninterested in participating in a region in which it perceived no national interest. Indeed, after the experience of Somalia, the United States did everything it could to prevent the UN from intervening in areas where it had little or no interest.

On April 6, 1994, the president of Rwanda was killed when his plane was shot down. Concerned midlevel officials in the State Department immediately recognized the possibility of mass killings and alerted Secretary Christopher. But the massacres had already begun. Hutu soldiers rounded up and murdered one after another of Rwanda's moderate politicians, including the prime minister. They seized the fifteen peacekeepers at her home, released the five Ghanaians, and butchered the ten Belgians – apparently assuming, correctly, that Belgium would then withdraw its men, as the Americans had done in Somalia.

Almost immediately it became clear that the Hutu militants were intent on killing every last Tutsi in the country. In the first days Tutsis were murdered by the thousands, then the tens of thousands, then hundreds of thousands. Over a period of roughly one hundred days, 800,000 Tutsis and moderate Hutus were massacred – an unquestionable case of genocide. And the United States did nothing to stop it.

According to the Genocide Convention which the UN had adopted in 1948 and the United States belatedly ratified in 1988, the nations of the world were obligated to intervene to stop genocide. But the Clinton administration did not want to intervene and refused to acknowledge that genocide was occurring. The "G-word" was deliberately omitted from all discussion of events in Rwanda. Washington rejected all requests to reinforce the peacekeepers, demanded their withdrawal from Rwanda, and blocked UN efforts to reinforce them. The most powerful country in the world, an administration that prided itself on its commitment to the protection of human rights, to a higher morality in foreign policy, made no effort to stop the slaughter. The journalist Samantha Power noted that Clinton did not call a single meeting of his senior advisers to consider an American response to events in a country in which the United States had no strategic or economic interest. They knew what was happening, but were unwilling to accept the responsibility that accompanies great power. Least of all were they willing to risk the lives of American soldiers in a country few Americans could find on a map. And the results were catastrophic – for the Tutsis of Rwanda.

The inability of the UN to act and the unwillingness of the United States to act in Rwanda did nothing, of course, to discourage the Serbs in their determination to eliminate the Muslim population of Bosnia. Talbott, at the State Department, was increasingly discouraged by the passivity of his own department (from which several foreign service officers had resigned in protest), by the unwillingness of the Defense Department to act, and the failure of Lake to engage the president. It was time for strong medicine. He maneuvered to bring Holbrooke back to Washington in September 1994, to manage European and especially Balkan affairs – much to the distaste of Christopher and Lake. Widely perceived as abrasive and overbearing, Holbrooke was a man who could make things happen, get things done – and he did, but it took another year and the loss of many thousand more lives in Bosnia.

When the Americans, the Europeans, and the UN failed to aid the Bosnian Muslims or punish the Serbs in the spring of 1993, the UN announced that it would set up "safe areas" where civilian refugees would be shielded from the fighting. Six such areas were named, including the capital of Sarajevo and the city of Srebrenica. UN peacekeepers were deployed to protect the safe areas, but, because the United States refused to send troops, the numbers available were not adequate for the assignment. Serb forces constantly harassed the peacekeepers, cutting off their supplies and occasionally taking them hostage. In February 1994, the Serbs launched a mortar attack on a crowded market in Sarajevo, killing 67 shoppers. Clinton denounced the attack, threatened the Serbs with retaliation by NATO if they persisted – and may have intimidated them for the moment. In April, pushed by Washington, NATO actually began "pinprick" strikes against Serb artillery positions, but it was soon apparent no ground troops would be used and that neither NATO nor the UN was prepared to take serious military action.

Holbrooke came back to Washington demanding that NATO bomb the Serb "fuckers" (Power, 2002). Albright was ready, as were Gore, and Lake, but Clinton was not; nor was the will to act apparent among European leaders. And the Serbs murdered and raped thousands more.

The cat and mouse game between the Bosnian Serb army and NATO and the UN continued well into 1995 with Serbs growing bolder and the would-be protectors of the Muslims increasingly helpless. The point of no return was reached in July 1995, when the Serbs pushed aside a handful of Dutch peacekeepers at Srebrenica and ignoring international protests, systematically and brutally murdered 7,000 Muslims who had taken refuge there. At last the arrogance and monstrous behavior of the Bosnian Serb army forced NATO to respond. Jacque Chirac, who had become president of France in May, pressed for action. This time France would not obstruct. Clinton remained unwilling to send American troops, but on August 30, NATO commenced a massive three-week bombing campaign that for the first time gave Serb leaders pause. At almost the same time, urged on by

American officials including Holbrooke and the American ambassador, Croatia began a ground offensive driving the Bosnian Serbs out of territory they had taken from Croats and Muslims. The Serbs stopped their attacks on civilians.

In August, just before the Serbs began to pay a price for their aggression and atrocities, Holbrooke went to Yugoslavia and took charge of the Bosnian issue. With the tide turning against him, Slobodan Milosevic, the Serb leader, who always alleged he had no control over the Bosnian Serbs, proved amenable to negotiations. Holbrooke was able to win a cease-fire in September and he arranged a meeting in Dayton, Ohio in which he bullied Milosevic and the Croat and Bosnian Muslim leaders into accepting a settlement he designed. The Bosnian Serbs were represented by Milosevic who quickly abandoned them. The settlement called for the de facto division of Bosnia on ethnic and religious lines, a solution the United States had criticized when a comparable solution had been presented in the Vance-Owen Plan. But the Serb share of Bosnia was reduced significantly and the semblance of a unified Bosnian state retained. It would be led ostensibly by a three-person presidency, representative of its three major religious groups.

For Clinton, perhaps the hardest part was the necessity to agree to deploy 20,000 American peacekeepers to Bosnia. The polls left no doubt that such a deployment was unpopular and there was much unhappiness in Congress, but the president promised to bring the troops home after one year and assured the country that there would be no mission creep: there would be no repeat of Somalia. It was a difficult decision for Clinton to make less than year away from an election, but his likely Republican opponent, Kansas Senator Robert Dole, was a leading advocate of a tougher policy to stop Serb aggression and helped win Senate approval. Success at Dayton seemed to defuse the issue and presented the Clinton administration with what it could claim as a major foreign policy success.

After his successful re-election campaign, Clinton was forced to admit American troops would have to remain in Bosnia for an extended period. The Bosnian Serbs were determined to destroy the single state agreement reached at Dayton, to turn the line separating the Muslim/Croat and Serb "entities" into an actual border. Without NATO troops in Bosnia, peace would not have lasted very long. Perhaps worst of all, the NATO commanders failed to arrest those Bosnian Serb leaders who had been indicted as war criminals for the atrocities they ordered or carried out. Evidence eventually emerged that a mole (a French officer) within NATO headquarters tipped off the Serbs whenever an effort, however half-hearted, was made to round up suspects. It was not until General Wesley Clark, who had been with Holbrooke in Bosnia in 1995, took over the command of NATO in 1997, that a vigorous effort to enforce the Dayton accords began.

Of course, the United States was not quite free of Milosevic and Yugoslav problems. Milosevic had ridden to power after the death of Tito by appealing to Serb nationalism. One step exceptionally popular with his Serb constituents had been the revocation of the autonomy of Kosovo, a Yugoslav republic inhabited primarily by Albanian Muslims – a territory of great historic significance to Orthodox Christian Serbs, even if relatively few still lived there. There were indications in the early 1990s that Milosevic was considering further repressive measures in Kosovo, perhaps even an effort to drive out the Muslims. President Bush had warned him not to attack Kosovo and Clinton also sent several warnings – and the situation remained stable through the mid-1990s. Kosovo was not discussed at Dayton because Holbrooke suspected correctly that Milosevic would sell out the Bosnian Serbs, but would not, perhaps could not, give assurances on Kosovo.

In the late 1990s, moderate Kosovar leaders were quickly overshadowed by the emergence of the Kosovo Liberation Army (KLA). KLA guerrilla units ran raids against Serb police and vandalized Orthodox churches and cemeteries, deliberately provoking Milosevic with the expectation of winning NATO support when the Serbs attacked. The American government considered the KLA to be a terrorist organization and neither Washington nor any of its allies favored the KLA's goal of an independent Kosovo. But as the Serbs retaliated, Albright, now secretary of state, feared the destabilization of the region with the possibility of Albanian, Macedonian, Greek, or Turkish involvement. She warned Milosevic that ethnic cleansing would not be tolerated.

In early 1998, Clinton, preoccupied with the surfacing of his affair with a White House intern, was even further removed from foreign policy concerns than usual. He and those in his administration determined to protect him did not want a major overseas distraction before the mid-term election. It was a job for Holbrooke who went over to Belgrade and in October succeeded in cajoling Milosevic into an agreement to halt the repression in Kosovo – but the deal collapsed quickly as it served the purpose of neither the KLA nor Milosevic. In January 1999, Serb irregulars and police massacred dozens of Kosovar civilians in the village of Racak.

Visions of Sebrenica and Rwanda filled Washington. The United States could not stand aside again and allow such atrocities. But what to do? Berger, who had replaced Lake as national security adviser and William Cohen, who had become secretary of defense, were not eager to act. Indeed, the Pentagon still had no taste for battle. Albright led the demand for action and on this occasion she had strong support from NATO allies, especially the British. In February a conference was held at Rambouillet, in France, in which the KLA was forced to agree to disarm if the Serbs would agree to remove most of their forces from Kosovo, restore a high degree of autonomy, and accept the deployment of armed NATO peacekeepers. The Serbs were warned that they would confront NATO airpower if they refused. They refused nonetheless and in March NATO began to bomb Serbia.

At the same time Clinton authorized General Clark to order the bombing, he declared that he would send no ground troops. Neither he nor Cohen were willing to risk American lives. Even Albright apparently thought three or four days of bombing would be enough to bring Milosevic back to the table, but she and those who shared her expectation clearly underestimated the importance of Kosovo to the Serb leader and his appeal to his people. Undeterred by the bombing, buoyed by indications no NATO troops were on the way, hopeful of Russian support, the Serbs began a massive offensive in Kosovo that resulted in more than a million Kosovar Muslims fleeing their homes, hundreds of thousands seeking refuge in Albania and Macedonia.

The humanitarian disaster the administration had hoped to avoid had begun. The Serbs had not been deterred by threats or the commencement of a bombing campaign. The credibility of the United States – and of NATO – was in question. Clark wanted to take whatever action would prove necessary to stop the Serbs, including the use of attack helicopters, even ground troops, but the Pentagon resisted: casualty avoidance was still a top priority. Clark never received authorization to use either the helicopters or ground troops. He was, however, able to use his planes for increasingly more intense bombing of Serbia, bringing misery and death to Serbian civilians. After 11 weeks of devastating attacks by NATO that included the accidental bombing of the Chinese embassy in Belgrade, and after a clear signal the Russians would not help him, Milosevic finally capitulated. He agreed to withdraw his forces from Kosovo and allowed 50,000 NATO peacekeepers to enter the province. Perhaps equally important to Clinton, Clark had prevailed without a single American death – although his aggressiveness alienated the Pentagon, cost him his job, and forced his retirement.

The administration's record on humanitarian interventions left much to be desired. It was reasonably clear in Somalia, Haiti, Rwanda, Bosnia, and Kosovo that if the United States would not act forcefully, no other state would provide the leadership or the troops. Certainly the UN lacked the means. Even in Bosnia, where the European Union might have been expected to lead, to demonstrate that Europe could manage its affairs without the United States, all the European states abdicated responsibility, stood by and docilely tolerated atrocity after atrocity. But the Americans, with all their power, acted reluctantly, belatedly, if at all.

Albright had a point when she asked why American military leaders were so unwilling to send their forces into harm's way, why Powell and others stipulated conditions that all but precluded interventions. The answer is doubtless mistrust of civilian leadership, based on the lessons senior officers drew from their memories of Vietnam. Jeffrey Record, a historian at the Air Force War College, has called this attitude "force protection fetishism" (2002) wherein the military's mission is subordinated to the goal of avoiding casualties, resulting in military timidity. Similarly Clinton, having avoided military service during the Vietnam War, was hesitant to send others into battle. After losing 18 lives in Somalia, the United States withdrew from that benighted county with indecent haste and then allowed hundreds of thousands of innocent civilians to be murdered in Rwanda. Scared off once, it finally took action in Haiti, but then allowed thousands more to die in Bosnia and Kosovo before it took even limited risks.

Ultimately, responsibility for these policies rested with Clinton. He rarely provided his foreign policy team with guidance; he rarely led. His interests and concerns were elsewhere and when events forced him to engage, his first inclination seemed to be to test the domestic political winds. On the one hand, one can argue that in a democracy, a president must be responsive to public opinion. On the other hand, an American president has enormous power to mold that opinion, using the "bully pulpit" to lead. The great presidents of the United States were men who led. If judged by his responses to humanitarian disasters, Clinton will never make the first rank.

MANAGING THE GREAT POWERS

It was readily apparent that Bill Clinton's principal foreign policy interest was in expanding markets for trade and investment, but his stated priority was Russian-American relations. Although greatly weakened, Russia retained an enormous nuclear arsenal and posed the greatest potential threat to the security of the United States. Few disputed the president's contention that it was in the interest of the United States to assist in the transformation of its erstwhile adversary into a democratic, market-oriented, and friendly state. Indeed, Richard Nixon had criticized Bush for not doing enough and urged Clinton to provide more aid to Moscow. And Strobe Talbott, who assumed responsibility for Russian-American relations, was Clinton's closest friend in the foreign policy apparatus and had excellent access to the president. As a result, Clinton's level of involvement was generally high.

Efforts to carry out the political and economic reforms Gorbachev had begun in the last years of the Soviet Union had accelerated under the leadership of Boris Yeltsin. Opposition to change was very strong, however, certainly among many who had not surrendered the Marxist-Leninist vision, but also among those angered by Russia's declining status in the world – and others who were being hurt by reforms that cost them benefits they had enjoyed in the old regime and offered little in return. Clinton and Talbott unhesitatingly sided with Yeltsin in his struggle to maintain control of his government and the direction it would take. To underline that support, Clinton met with Yeltsin in Vancouver in April 1993 and the two men seemed to get on well.

In the months that followed, the challenges to Yeltsin's policies intensified. His health was questionable and his drinking bouts notorious. By September 1993, he and the Russian parliament, the Duma, constantly at odds, had reached the point of no return. Yeltsin, like many an American president, disliked legislative restrictions on his power. Unlike any American president, however, when he tired of parliamentary recalcitrance, he sent in the tanks. There is no doubt that Yeltsin had been provoked by his enemies, who had called their supporters into the streets and began the violence, but the order to fire on the White House, the parliamentary building which the offending legislators – led by the vice president – were using as their head-quarters, might have been considered excessive and undemocratic, to say the least.

Nonetheless, the Clinton administration was unwavering in its support of Yeltsin, apparently convinced that he alone of potential Russian leaders was committed to the reforms Talbott and his colleagues considered essential to Russia's liberalization and integration into Europe. Moreover, his rule promised a Russia that would be friendly to the United States and supportive of American foreign policy more generally. Certainly his erratic behavior and occasional disappearances were troubling, certainly shelling the parliament was undesirable, but the Clinton team concluded that we live in an imperfect world and Washington would have to tolerate Yeltsin's foibles.

The first major test of the Russian-American relationship during the Clinton years came over the American decision to push for the expansion of NATO – to invite former Soviet satellites, the Czech Republic, Hungary, Poland, and Slovakia to join the Western alliance. Perhaps not coincidentally, Clinton announced this controversial plan only days after the United States had indicated its continued support for Yeltsin.

American public intellectuals and government officials were still fretting about the role of NATO in the post-Cold War world and uneasy about European affairs generally. Some advocated the expansion of NATO to protect the new democracies of Central and Eastern Europe from a resurgent Russia. Certainly many leaders of countries in what had long been a Soviet, and was still considered a Russian, sphere of influence were eager to embrace the protective custody of the West. Others in the United States and Europe were apprehensive about the role a united Germany would play, mindful that Germany was once again in a position to dominate Europe. NATO had been viewed in Washington, London, and Paris, as a means of containing German as well as Soviet power throughout the Cold War. If the organization could be revitalized with new members beholden to the United States, it would perform its Cold War roles and dampen growing resistance to American leadership among Europeans. And, as always for Bill Clinton, there were compelling domestic political reasons for sponsoring the rapid integration of the new democracies into Europe: bipartisan support for the idea in Congress and the votes of Americans of Czech, Hungarian, Polish, and Slovak ancestry.

The principal argument against NATO expansion was the strong probability that it would anger Russians and serve to undermine those Russians most willing to cooperate with the United States in world affairs. Countless analysts warned against humiliating the Russians by extending the Western alliance to Russia's borders. Talbott, wanting to build a strong relationship between NATO and Russia first, was opposed, as was the legendary foreign policy guru, George Kennan. The Pentagon resisted, fearful of being called upon to defend a region to which American power had never before been extended – and without additional resources. The principal proponent in the administration was Albright, her position perhaps reflecting her Czech roots. In Congress she had the strong support of the ordinarily obstructionist chairman of the Senate Foreign Relations Committee, Jesse Helms.

Clinton's decision to move toward NATO expansion was facilitated by a gambit proposed by the Chairman of the Joint Chiefs, General John Shalikashvili. He recommended that every nation in Central and Eastern Europe, including Russia, be invited to join a Partnership for Peace, a relationship with NATO that was short of membership and involving no commitment on the part of the members to defend such "partners" – the primary fear of the Pentagon. In October 1993, Christopher, apparently the designated flak-catcher of the administration, was sent to Moscow to sell the idea to Yeltsin.

To Christopher's astonishment, Yeltsin, possibly inebriated, expressed great pleasure with his friend Bill's proposed Partnership for Peace. Perhaps Yeltsin was still celebrating his victory over parliament and grateful for the support he had received from Washington. Perhaps he misperceived the Partnership as a substitute for NATO expansion. In the months that followed, apprehension that the Russians had misunderstood was allayed as Talbott kept them informed of the intent to expand NATO and the Russians did not protest.

There was further cause to hesitate with NATO expansion when Russian reformers were defeated badly in the parliamentary elections of December 1993, largely because of the suffering of the Russian people during the bumpy transition from communism to a market economy. Jobs in state-owned industries and the social safety net were being eliminated, bringing misery to millions. But there was also resentment against the United States, in large part because of the American consultants pressing the economic reforms, insisting on the need for "shock therapy." In addition, many ordinary Russians were unhappy with the country's declining status in the world, preferring to be citizens of a feared superpower than of an international basket case. When the votes were tallied it was evident that the

Russian people had turned to extremist nationalists and the remnants of the Communist Party – although in a possibly fraudulent process, a referendum on a constitution strengthening the power of the president did pass.

Nonetheless, in November 1994, the Russian foreign minister asked to meet with NATO foreign ministers to join the Partnership. A few days later, however, at the meeting, the Russians suddenly refused to sign. With the foreign minister out of town, a skeptical minister of defense prevailed. And a few days after that, Yeltsin denounced the Partnership for Peace and NATO expansion as a threat to Russia: a "cold peace" was descending upon Europe, he declared. Most likely, Yeltsin's domestic policy advisers had warned him that NATO expansion was not playing well at home, that even the warmest supporters of the new Russian-American relationship perceived the United States as taking advantage of Russia's weakness.

Most Russian analysts and the politically aware Russian public saw American power being extended to Russia's borders and were angered by American arrogance. Defense specialists in the Duma were warning that relations would deteriorate unless Washington compromised on NATO expansion, gave assurances it would not create a national missile defense system, and revised the START II arms limitation agreement. Stalin could have ignored their opinion; Yeltsin could not. He was being outmaneuvered by extremists appealing to nationalist themes. It was time to play to his domestic audience and perhaps give pause to the Americans, force them to treat Russia with a little more respect.

The reality, of course, was that Americans no longer feared Russia and few saw any need to defer to Russian sensibilities. As demonstrated in Bosnia and Kosovo, the United States was prepared to bypass the UN where the Russians had veto power and act through NATO or unilaterally as its own interests dictated. The Russians might be consulted, they were welcome to come along or not, as they pleased, but they no longer had the ability to deter American action. In calling for Russian cooperation – which the U.S. government unquestionably wanted – it was looking for a compliant junior partner. If it ever did – which is doubtful – Washington no longer viewed Moscow as an equal.

The influence of the minister of defense and the perceived need to play to greater Russian chauvinism led Yeltsin to the disastrous decision to use force in December 1994 to crush a separatist movement that emerged in Chechnya, a Russian republic in the Caucasus. Stalin had deported the Muslim Chechens during World War II, but Khrushchev had allowed them to return in the late 1950s. For years, the Chechens nursed their hostility toward Russians and a few of their leaders saw an opportunity for independence – or at least greater autonomy – after the collapse of the Soviet Union. Led by a former Soviet general, they became increasingly provocative in 1994.

The bombing and invasion of Chechnya did not arouse the international community at first. In many nations there was a strong tendency to consider unrest within national borders a domestic affair, outside the realm of world affairs and the jurisdiction of the United Nations. In this specific case, none of the great powers wanted to see the disintegration of Russia and there was an assumption that the Chechen rebellion would be suppressed quickly, with a minimum of bloodshed. When warning signals went up in late fall 1994, the Clinton administration took little notice. When the invasion began, Clinton called it an internal Russian affair and Christopher argued for allowing Yeltsin to do what he deemed necessary. The administration was determined to support Yeltsin and persisted in the belief that he was Russia's best hope for democratic and economic reform. Certainly no word that came out of Washington gave Yeltsin reason to pause.

For about a month, criticism of the Russian use of force in Chechnya was muted. Quite likely, the world's leaders hoped the issue would disappear and they would not have to act. But it soon became apparent that the Chechens were not going to collapse in the face of the onslaught by the Russian army. It was equally clear that Russian troops were incompetent and behaving brutally toward people who were still Russian citizens. Atrocities against civilians multiplied, as did the casualty rate among the invading forces.

Helmut Kohl, in January 1995, was the first prominent statesman to speak out against Russian actions in Chechnya. By then there was considerable anxiety in Washington and arguments for distancing the administration from Yeltsin increased. There was also a growing fear that Yeltsin was losing control of his government to the military, that Russia might end up with a military dictatorship or at best a government strongly influenced by the military. In fact, the Russian general staff had opposed the invasion, for which Yeltsin and his defense minister were responsible.

Anxiety also grew in the capitals of the former Warsaw Pact nations of Central and Eastern Europe. If the Russian army was on the move, might they be next? They lobbied even harder for admission to NATO, for the protection membership in the Western alliance would presumably provide. And Clinton was responsive, arguing that the expansion of NATO was urgent – even if the American military was still less eager to accept additional responsibilities.

In May 1995, Clinton flew to Moscow for a celebration of the 50th anniversary of VE-Day, of the surrender of the German government to end

World War II in Europe. Meeting with Yeltsin, he raised the issue of the war in Chechnya and referred to the human rights violations of which the Russian army was accused. American complaints were dismissed, but apparently they had been raised in so inoffensive a manner that Yeltsin agreed to sign the Partners for Peace Agreement – which Moscow did later that month. The war in Chechnya went on, with mounting casualties and cruelty on both sides and growing opposition from the Russian people until a peace agreement was reached in August 1996 and Russian troops withdrew in mid-1997.

Yeltsin needed American support, political and economic, but he obviously needed support from Russians even more. His mercurial behavior was partly due to his health and drinking problems, but to a much greater extent by the necessity of playing to multiple audiences at home and abroad. With his political fortunes looking poor in 1995, he fought his war in Chechnya and made anti-Western speeches at home. He continued to rail against the expansion of NATO. He decried the bombing of Serbia and the increasing role of the Americans in the Balkans. But privately, to Clinton and to Kohl, he indicated his unchanged desire to cooperate with the West, to integrate Russia into Europe. When NATO troops went to Bosnia as peacekeepers after the Dayton accords – and after the Duma elections in December – Russian troops accompanied them.

Pandering to the electorate did not help Yeltsin's followers in the election. They were routed by the communists and extreme nationalists. Yeltsin's future looked grim and in the course of 1996 he seemed less inclined to cooperate with his friend Bill Clinton. The men and women responsible for shaping American policy toward Russia gradually became responsive to charges that they had focused too narrowly on Yeltsin and that their expectations of a democratic and friendly Russia were unrealistic. They began looking around for other partners in the region among other former Soviet republics. As for alternatives to Yeltsin within Russia, they knew they did not want to see the communists return to power and they had no use for the extreme nationalists, but were otherwise clueless. So they stayed with Yeltsin who was polling in the single digits in the Russian electorate.

The Russian presidential election was scheduled for June 1996, and the polls consistently showed the Communist Party candidate in the lead. Nothing could have scared Western leaders more. Nor could the new "oligarchs," the robber barons who had made great fortunes in the privatization of Soviet state-owned assets, risk the return of the communists. As Yeltsin struggled to hold on to his presidency, support came from the West and from the oligarchs. Gradually, Yeltsin closed the gap and in the first round of voting he had a slight lead over the communist candidate, but fell far short of the majority needed for election. But once it seemed clear that the choice was between Yeltsin and the communists, support for Yeltsin grew. In the second round Yeltsin won a majority handily – so handily as to raise suspicion that the election had been rigged.

Less than a year later, while Russian forces still struggled haplessly against Chechen guerrillas, Russia signed an agreement with NATO that all but made it an honorary member of the Western alliance. Two months later, the Czech Republic, Hungary, and Poland were invited to join NATO. Expansion would proceed whether the Russians liked the idea or not. Clinton and Yeltsin united to sugarcoat what must have been a very bitter pill for the once-feared Russian military to swallow.

Difficulties in Russian-American relations persisted. Various actions of each country irritated the other. By 1998, American intelligence had confirmed the earlier discovery that the Russians were selling nuclear reactors to Iran and training Iranian scientists, facilitating that nation's efforts to develop nuclear weapons. The Russians were also selling weapons to Iraq, in violation of UN sanctions. In both instances, the sales probably were made primarily for economic reasons rather than as part of a quest for geopolitical gain. The Russian defense industry, no longer benefiting from Cold War policies, was in trouble, cash starved – and so was the nuclear industry. The country was in desperate straits, aid from the West was inadequate, and sales abroad the only available answer: the Americans be damned.

There could be little doubt that Russian officials were not willing to accept a unipolar world in which Russia – and the rest of the world – were expected to play by rules laid out by Washington while the Americans did as they pleased. American efforts to intrude in areas perceived as within Russia' s historic sphere of influence, not least American determination to exploit the oil and gas of the Caspian Sea, angered them. They wanted to work with the West. Yeltsin still favored integration and perceived a need for aid from the West. But they insisted on a multipolar world in which Russia remained a great power. To this end they worked assiduously to improve relations with China and India as well as seeking to exploit differences within NATO as a means of checking American power.

The critical test of whether Russia would stay on the path to democracy, a market economy, and cooperation with the West came in August 1998 when the Russian economy collapsed, the ruble was devalued and Moscow defaulted on loan repayments to the IMF. The possibility of a financial crisis had been anticipated by some American analysts and they feared that if it occurred, it would lead to a reversal of policy in Russia. And there were

major changes. The last of the liberal reformers widely considered responsible for the troubles were fired and Yeltsin appointed, and conceded significant powers to, Yevgeny Primakov, a new prime minister favored by the
parliament and mistrusted by Washington.

The Russians rejected the so-called Washington Consensus calling for
rapid privatization of state-owned property, abolition of price controls,
lowering trade barriers, opening the door to foreign investment, and count-
ing on the market to solve all problems and provide economic growth. It
was not working and the results had been chaotic, bringing misery to millions through the undermining of the existing system of social welfare while
jobs were lost and real wages declined. Efforts to repair the social safety
net were inevitable, but economic liberalization did not end entirely; nor
did Russia's halting movement toward strengthening democratic institutions; nor did Yeltsin's determination to integrate Russia with the West
disappear.

In the months that followed, the Clinton administration had to reassess
its posture toward Russia and more specifically Yeltsin. Although the
Americans had surely been mistaken to support Yeltsin when he ordered
the attack on parliament in October 1993, and when he sent troops into
Chechnya in December 1994, the Clinton-Yeltsin relationship had proved
useful. Despite frequent grumbling, a scream of outrage or two, Yeltsin had
accepted NATO expansion, tolerated NATO intervention in the Balkans,
and sent peacekeepers to Bosnia and Kosovo to serve alongside NATO
forces. Despite frequent backsliding, he had set Russia firmly on a course
toward democracy and a market economy. But he was clearly weakening,
physically as well as politically. Clinton might reasonably claim success for
his policy toward Russia, but he and his advisers had to prepare for a post-
Yeltsin era in which none of the potential successors looked attractive from
Washington's perspective. It was also obvious that the United States could
do little more to shape the course of events inside Russia.

In August 1999, Yeltsin surprised virtually everyone in Russia and abroad
by firing Primakov, who had been accruing power steadily, and replacing
him as prime minister with Vladamir Putin, an unknown former KGB agent.
Yeltsin was attempting to sideline the man best able to challenge his authority within the government and the country. Primakov and his supporters
were perceived as likely to gain strength in the parliamentary elections
scheduled for December and Primakov was himself a likely candidate for
the presidency in the election scheduled for March 2000. Yeltsin's maneuver fueled apprehension that he would never relinquish power voluntarily.

Putin asserted himself quickly and seemed driven primarily by a determination to assure the primacy of the central government against challenges

from regional governors and separatists. Political democracy did not appear to be a high priority for him and he was clearly unhappy with a free press and the carping of opposition politicians. Confronting a situation in which Russians were shaken by Chechen military actions and terrorist acts in Russia attributed to Chechen operatives, he resumed forceful, brutal, military action against Chechnya. One can argue about who ignited it, but a second phase of the war had begun.

Although polls had shown popular displeasure with Primakov's dismissal, the Russian public seemed accepting of Putin's approach. He was less mercurial than Yeltsin; his was a steadier hand on the tiller. He appealed to Russian nationalism and pride. He promised law and order. As is so often the case, the people tolerated inroads on their new found freedoms in exchange for an increase in their sense of security.

When the parliamentary elections were held in December, a political party hastily formed by the Kremlin attracted more votes than that of Primakov, dashing his hopes. And then, on December 31, 1999 came perhaps the biggest surprise of all. Yeltsin announced that he was stepping down from the presidency and anointing Putin as his successor. Suddenly Putin emerged as the favorite in the forthcoming presidential election.

The Clinton administration had no idea of what to expect next and how to respond. The president was weakened by a sex scandal and Republican attempts to impeach him. Talbott, National Security Adviser Sandy Berger, and Secretary of State Madeline Albright were accustomed to functioning without him, but the level and tone of partisan attacks on the administration had grown increasingly vicious and accusations that the administration had "lost" Russia had them on the defensive. And, of course, 2000 was a presidential election year in the United States as well.

Putin won easily in March, gaining a majority on the first round. Subsequently, analysts of the first year of his presidency described a man confident of his own powers – confident enough to turn on the oligarchs who had supported Yeltsin and to dismantle the bases of Yeltsin's support. The security services from which he had emerged gained new influence as did the bureaucracy. Nonetheless he professed to be determined to continue Yeltsin's policies of economic reforms and cooperation with the West. But there was little doubt that he governed even more autocratically than Yeltsin, that the progress Russia had made toward democracy was in danger, and that Putin was obsessed with the restoration of state power.

To those Americans less concerned with events inside Russia, anxious about Putin's foreign policy choices, 2000 offered no reassurance. Putin was unquestionably setting a course designed to counter Washington's influence everywhere in the world. He was determined to revive Russian influence in the former states of the Soviet Union, in many of which the United States had made significant inroads. As Yeltsin had, he worked assiduously at developing closer ties with China, India, and Iran. He also reached out to nations intensely hostile to the United States – Cuba, Iraq, North Korea – nations abandoned by Gorbachev and Yeltsin. No wonder critics feared the United States had "lost" Russia.

And then there was China, ruled by the "butchers of Beijing," ostensibly the responsibility of Winston Lord. Americans appalled by the brutality of the Chinese government in its massacre of its own people in the 1989 Tiananmen "incident" anticipated a stiffening of sanctions against China, as promised by Clinton and Lord in the 1992 election campaign. An unusual coalition of anticommunist conservatives and liberal human rights advocates were eager to punish the Chinese government, specifically by withdrawing most-favored-nation or MFN status, granted in 1979, from its exports to the United States. Without MFN status, Chinese goods entering the United States would be subject to tariff rates higher than those imposed on the goods of other nations, placing China at a competitive disadvantage. Bush had blocked such sanctions. Clinton was expected to approve them. Policy decisions would now be made by men and women determined to hold Beijing accountable for its transgressions, at home and abroad.

Clinton's ultimate concern, however, was reviving the American economy. Stimulating economic growth, putting Americans back to work, were also campaign promises. A trade war with China would almost certainly have the opposite effect. His economic advisers warned such a confrontation could cost tens of thousands of jobs – and he heard them. His dilemma was to find a way to honor – at very least appear to honor – promises likely to have conflicting results.

Clinton's decision was to temporize. He persuaded his supporters in Congress to delay legislation to eliminate MFN for China and to give him a year to gain the actions desired from the Chinese government: the release of political prisoners, the protection of Tibet's cultural heritage, an end to the jamming of Voice of America broadcasts, and an end to missile sales to Pakistan and Iran. In May 1993, he issued an executive order renewing MFN for China for another year, but setting conditions for the next renewal scheduled for the spring 1994. The sighs of relief in Beijing were palpable. Nonetheless, China presumably would be required to improve its human rights record and respond adequately to other American demands or lose MFN in 1994.

American corporations with interests in trading with China were intensely apprehensive about the policies advocated by the Clinton administration. They undertook a major lobbying campaign designed to head off the potential conflict. In addition to the economic arguments they raised, Henry Kissinger and Cyrus Vance, former secretaries of state, argued publicly that the strategic relationship with China was too important to jeopardize by pressing what they considered less significant human rights issues.

In August 1993, the administration denied licenses for the sale of satellites to China in retaliation for Chinese missile sales to Pakistan. The Chinese turned to European suppliers, only too happy to oblige them. Representatives of the affected American companies, including major donors to Clinton's election campaign, rushed to the White House to persuade the president to grant them a waiver. Clinton then made an extraordinary decision. At the request of Ron Brown, his secretary of commerce, he agreed to take the decision on the licensing of technology sales to China away from the Departments of State and Defense and to give it to the Department of Commerce. In other words, commercial rather than political or military considerations would be privileged.

It became increasingly evident that the State Department, the Defense Department, and the National Security Council would have less influence on American policy toward China than Clinton's economic team. The administration's interest in threatening to take away China's MFN status evaporated. Not only Brown at Commerce, but the key players at the Department of the Treasury, Department of Agriculture, and U.S. Trade Representative's office were opposed. And even at the Defense Department, arguments emerged in opposition to further sanctions against China. The American military favored resuming meetings with its Chinese counterparts, contacts terminated after Tiananmen. Military officers argued that the Chinese might be helpful with the burgeoning crisis over North Korea's nuclear weapons program. And most incredibly, lobbyists for the business community and other opponents of sanctions brought forth the idea that the results China's critics desired – democracy in China and respect for human rights by Beijing – would be brought about by increased trade. Presumably trade would strengthen the private sector and the nascent middle class in China who would then demand a share in governing the country – and one day China would be a middle-class democracy, just like America.

That MFN would lead to democracy was a contention that won few converts among human rights advocates or on the anticommunist right. But other arguments for avoiding confrontation with China, for continued "engagement," obviously had merit. Economic warfare between the United States and China would be harmful to the American economy and have repercussions throughout East Asia – and perhaps further abroad. Americans concerned about the prospects for democratic reform in Hong Kong heard cries from admired reformers that elimination of MFN for China would hurt Hong Kong. And the strategic reasons for restoring a working relationship with the Chinese government could not be ignored. China had a veto in the UN and could obstruct American efforts to work with that organization. It probably had more influence with North Korea than did any other state. Perhaps China's proclivity for proliferating missile and nuclear technology could be constrained.

What the administration needed as it backed away from confrontation over MFN were some indications that China was responding to American concerns. It got none. Deng Xiaoping and his colleagues concluded that Washington was bluffing. They were confident that American businessmen, desperately eager for a larger share of the market in China, would force the Clinton administration to grant renewal of MFN.

Without support from the president, the Department of State was left with the thankless task of trying to persuade the Chinese to meet the conditions Clinton had set forth in 1993. In March 1994, Christopher flew to Beijing to see what concessions he might extract from China's leaders. He was preceded by his assistant secretary for human rights, who met with Wei Jingsheng, China's most vociferous and best known dissident, only recently released from prison. Shortly after the meeting, Wei was picked up by China's public security service and returned to prison. By the time Christopher arrived, other dissidents had been rounded up – a demonstration of intention to defy American wishes. A meeting scheduled between Christopher and Chinese president Jiang Zemin was canceled and he was sent to meet instead with Premier Li Peng, widely despised even in China as one of the leaders responsible for the Tiananmen massacres. Li proved worthy of his reputation, treating Christopher with contempt. He informed the American diplomat that the Chinese embassy in Washington had reported that Clinton would renew MFN no matter what China did – and that he knew that Christopher did not speak for Clinton. In the days that followed, Clinton did nothing to change Li's mind. He said nothing in support of Christopher, nothing about the importance of the human rights issue. When Christopher returned to Washington, Clinton did not bother to attend the meeting at which his secretary of state reported on his mission.

Although many were disappointed, few were surprised when, in the spring of 1994, Clinton abandoned his expressed concern for human rights and renewed MFN for China without any conditions. Clinton appeared to have resurrected Calvin Coolidge's best remembered adage, "the business of America is business" as the guideline for his administration. He threatened sanctions only once, when he responded to the complaints of the American entertainment industry and demanded an agreement on intellectual property rights to stop China from pirating movies, CDs, and computer software.

Gradually the memory of Tiananmen faded in the American imagination. The Chinese government continued to deny its people political, intellectual, and religious freedom. It continued to suppress minority cultures, exploit prison labor, market organs harvested from those executed by the state, and force women to have abortions, but human rights issues had little impact on American policy. On the contrary, American officials pointed to the increasing openness of Chinese society, the improvement of the quality of life of ordinary Chinese citizens as a result of Deng's reforms. But the most compelling point they made was that whatever China's failings, decent working relations with Beijing were essential to American economic interests and to stability in East Asia.

Trade between the United States and the People's Republic of China (PRC) grew rapidly in the mid-1990s as the PRC became an increasingly important American trading partner. Even this presumably mutually beneficial relationship caused friction as the Chinese exported far more than they imported, creating a serious balance of trade problem for the United States. China's restrictive business practices limiting the import of foreign goods cost it the support of some American businessmen, but tensions over trade relations were trivial compared to those that exploded over Taiwan in 1995 and 1996.

By the mid-1990s, Taiwan was evolving into a fully fledged democracy. In March 1996, it was scheduled to hold the first direct election for president that the Chinese people had ever known. But the ruling Kuomintang, party of Chiang Kai-shek and his son Ching-kuo, no longer exercised the overwhelming power it had known when the Chiangs, father and son, were alive. The younger Chiang had allowed an opposition party, the Democratic Progressive Party, to emerge. Its popularity, stemming largely from its appeal to the Taiwanese majority native to the island and its call for independence from China, threatened the Kuomintang – and specifically its presidential candidate, Lee Teng-hui, Ching-kuo's designated successor as president. Lee was himself a native Taiwanese and his candidacy assured the Kuomintang a substantial share of the Taiwanese vote, but his advisers were uneasy. They urged him to play a more assertive role internationally, to hint, at least, that he, too, favored independence. It was a role that suited him perfectly.

American specialists on Taiwan affairs recognized the changes that had occurred on the island. They understood the broad desire among the island's political elite for an international role commensurate with Taiwan's de facto independence. In Washington, a desire to adjust to these changes without provoking Beijing prompted an ineffectual reassessment of Taiwan policy in 1993. The United States could not easily treat Taiwan authorities as leaders of a sovereign state without appearing to violate the commitment to the principle of one China, accepted by every administration beginning with that of Richard Nixon. Only a few senior officials from Taiwan had been allowed to visit the United States after derecognition in 1979 – and those visits had attracted little media attention.

In 1994, President Lee Teng-hui decided to force the issue by requesting a visa to stop over in Hawaii enroute to Central America. His request was denied, but as a sop, the Department of State offered him a reception in a transit lounge at an air force base. Lee brushed aside the gesture and began a strikingly successful lobbying effort with the American congress. Since the end of World War II, only Israel had been more successful than Taiwan at manipulating the American government. The Senate passed a resolution calling upon the State Department to issue visas to Taiwan officials. Lee's lobbyists then generated enormous pressure on the administration to grant him a visa to attend a reunion at Cornell University, where he had earned his doctorate. The administration refused and assured Beijing that Lee would not be allowed to enter the country.

In May 1995, Lee saw a return on his investment. The U.S. House of Representatives demanded that he be granted a visa by a vote of 396-0. The vote in the Senate was 97-1. Taiwan's well-paid lobbyists had performed ably, but the key to their success was the democratization of Taiwan, assuring it support across the political spectrum rather than merely from the aging cadre of right-wing supporters of Chiang who had served the island so well in the 1950s and 1960s. Delight in the political evolution of Taiwan combined with anger at Beijing's human rights transgressions prompted American political leaders to support Taiwan. They did so with full knowledge that their actions would give offense to China, but without anticipating the forcefulness of Beijing's response. It was the political equivalent of an obscene gesture. Given the vote in Congress, the Clinton administration surrendered and allowed Lee to visit Cornell in June 1995.

Chinese leaders were outraged. The Americans were giving a platform to a man Beijing saw as an obstacle to reunification – after providing assurances they would not. They directed their anger toward both the United States and Taiwan. They recalled their ambassador to the United States and refused to accept the credentials of the newly appointed American ambassador to China. They broke off the "cross-strait" dialogue they had been having with Taipei – a positive effort toward peaceful reconciliation. A few weeks later, the PLA (People's Liberation Army) conducted military exercises in the Taiwan Strait, including the firing of nuclear-capable missiles into the sea north of Taiwan. Beijing's intimidation of the people of Taiwan was successful. Support for independence declined on the island, its stock market fell sharply, as did the value of its currency in international markets.

As tensions rose, Clinton's advisers succeeded in gaining his attention. He wrote to Jiang Zemin, president of China, inviting him to Washington and assuring him that that the United States would oppose Taiwan's independence and its admission to the UN. The letter brought the Chinese ambassador back to Washington and the American ambassador was received in Beijing. The crisis of the moment passed.

To remind the Chinese of the American insistence on a peaceful resolution of the issues between Taiwan and China, the Clinton administration also protested against the PLA exercises. Beijing was disdainful, reminding the Americans that unlike the 1950s when the United States could with impunity threaten to use nuclear weapons to protect Taiwan, China now had the capability to strike American cities with nuclear weapons. Relieving American concerns was not high on China's list of priorities. The United States responded by sending a carrier and support ships through the Taiwan Strait, joining in a dangerous test of wills.

Disregarding American protests, in February 1996 the PLA began massing troops across the Strait from Taiwan. In March, just before the presidential election in Taiwan, the PLA bracketed the island with missiles, demonstrating its ability to devastate Taiwan without an invasion. Again, Taiwan's stock market fell and fear wracked the island's people.

Few in Washington doubted that the United States had to respond to the challenge. Lake warned a senior Chinese diplomat that military action against Taiwan would have "grave consequences." To give weight to the words, Clinton ordered two carrier battle groups to the vicinity of the island. It was the first significant military confrontation between China and the United States since rapprochement in the 1970s.

Despite the threat from China, Taiwan held its presidential election on schedule and Lee Teng-hui won an impressive victory. His defiance of Beijing had not hurt his political career. He was now the first popularly elected president in Chinese history. The PLA troops concluded their exercises and returned to the barracks. The American warships sailed away without firing a shot. Another phase of an apparently unending crisis was over.

Clinton's advisers understood that the Chinese-American partnership of the 1970s and 80s had ended with the Tiananmen massacre in 1989. They realized that the efforts by both Bush and Clinton to accommodate China's rising power had not been reciprocated by the Chinese. It was time for a new approach. Friendly relations were not likely in the absence of a shared enemy, such as the Soviet Union had been in the last two decades of the Cold War. The events at Tiananmen had demonstrated the enormous gap between the values of the American people and those which motivated the Chinese government. However, given China's great capacity for jeopardizing American interests around the world, it was essential to develop a good working relationship. The two governments had to accept their differences, cooperate when possible, and avoid confrontation when cooperation was not possible. To this end, the Clinton administration proclaimed a policy of "comprehensive engagement," remarkably similar to the Bush administration policies of which Clinton had been so contemptuous.

Although anti-American feeling ran high in the PLA as a result of the March confrontation, Chinese leaders concluded that a working relationship between the two countries was in China's interest as well. Washington and Beijing agreed to exchange presidential visits. Jiang prepared to visit the United States in 1997.

It was thus incumbent upon the aides of the two presidents to come up with an agreement that would demonstrate the substantive importance of their discussions. For months Chinese and American diplomatists labored in vain. The Americans wanted the Chinese to stop helping Iran with its nuclear program, stop selling missiles to Pakistan and various Middle Eastern states, and to release some well-known dissidents. The Chinese wanted the remaining Tiananmen-inspired sanctions lifted. But most of all, they wanted a public statement from Clinton repeating his private assurances that the United States would not support Taiwan's independence and adhered to the "one China" policy.

The American negotiators refused the Chinese demands and the Chinese refused to discontinue missile sales. They did offer, however, to release the most prominent dissident, Wei Jingsheng, and to stop aiding Iran's nuclear program – if they were granted access to American nuclear power equipment and technology. In Washington, Jiang and Clinton agreed on the last point: Jiang would end China's role in Iran's program and Clinton would allow sales of restricted nuclear technology to China. As Jiang left Washington, a State Department spokesman offered the public assurances regarding Taiwan that Jiang had hoped to get from Clinton, but it was enough to win Wei Jingsheng's release and exile to the United States where, as the Chinese government anticipated, he was soon forgotten.

China and the United States had agreed to disagree on human rights and missile sales and to resume a working relationship. For Beijing that meant the United States would restrain Taiwan's urge to independence and that China would have access to the American market and American technology. In return, the Chinese offered limited access to their market, assistance in coping with the dangerous North Korean regime, and the occasional release of a political prisoner. The administration may have been satisfied, but many interested Americans were not, including many Republican members of Congress. Criticism of Clinton's approach increased in 1998.

The focus of anger at Clinton was on his intervention to permit the sale of a satellite to China at a time when the corporation making the sale was under investigation on charges that it had enabled the Chinese to improve their ballistic missile guidance systems. The corporation in question had been an important contributor to Clinton political campaigns and it appeared that the president was focused less on national security concerns than on repaying major donors. At best, he was putting corporate interests – and the jobs allegedly at risk – ahead of what many analysts believed to be the national interest in minimizing assistance to the PLA.

Despite the partisan attacks on the administration's policy toward China, Clinton was committed to go there in 1998. Once again, he needed gestures from the Chinese government that would justify the trip and his efforts to improve Chinese-American relations. He wanted the Chinese to release more dissidents, including Wang Dan, the most appealing of the student leaders of the 1989 Tiananmen demonstrations. He wanted them to sign the United Nations Covenant on Civil and Political Rights committing the Chinese to international norms on human rights. Neither step would necessarily signify change in China's actual human rights practices, but they would play well in the American media. In return, Clinton was prepared to drop the annual American effort to have China condemned by the UN Commission on Human Rights. A deal was struck and Wang Dan was shipped off to the United States in April 1998 – where, like Wei Jingsheng, he became another story with a short shelf life. In June, Clinton went to China.

On the eve of Clinton's flight, the Chinese detained more dissidents. They denied visas to journalists from Radio Free Asia, a U.S. government-funded network devoted to promoting democracy in Asia. And they insisted that the welcoming ceremony for the president's party be held in Tiananmen Square, symbol of the atrocities the Chinese government committed against its own people on June 4, 1989. Human rights advocates in America were outraged. But Clinton delighted them with a forceful condemnation of the Tiananmen massacre in his televised joint press conference with Jiang and his criticism of China's human rights record in a second public address televised across China. He called upon China's leaders to undertake political reforms, to allow free speech and to move toward political democracy.

Clinton's forthright censure of China's human rights record and his affirmation of values shared by most Americans assured him of a public relations success at home. Less attention was given to remarks he made in Shanghai a few days later. There, in return for the opportunity to speak to the Chinese people directly, he gave the Chinese leaders what they wanted regarding Taiwan. In a staged forum, he declared that the United States remained committed to the "one China" principle and it would not support Taiwan's independence or admission to any international organization, such as the UN, that required statehood for membership. Across the Strait in Taipei, Lee Teng-hui and his colleagues were not pleased. But there was never any doubt that American leaders wanted the issue to go away and hoped, however unrealistically, Beijing and Taipei would find a peaceful solution to the issues that separated them.

For the remaining months of 1998 and the early months of 1999, Clinton was preoccupied by the scandal involving his sexual improprieties and Republican efforts to remove him from office. If that wasn't enough to distract him from Chinese affairs, there was also the American-led NATO attack on Yugoslavia. In those rare moments when he was forced to focus on China, he had to cope with charges that his administration had jeopardized national security by failing to respond adequately to evidence of Chinese espionage. Not surprisingly under the circumstances, he stumbled badly during the April 1999 visit of Chinese premier Zhu Rongji. Fearful of seeming too friendly toward China, he dismissed as inadequate concessions offered by Zhu in exchange for American acceptance of China's entry into the World Trade Organization (WTO). Pressed by outraged corporate lobbyists delighted by the concessions, Clinton reversed field and promised Zhu a deal before the end of the year. It was an embarrassing performance, largely unnoticed by the media preoccupied with the plight of the Kosovo refugees.

As the Kosovars fled the murders and rapes inflicted on them by Serb forces, NATO intervened by bombing Serbia – with a disastrous impact on Chinese-American relations. The Chinese, sensitive about their own transgressions in Tibet, opposed NATO's operations as interference in the internal affairs of Yugoslavia and an illegal sidestepping of the UN Security Council – where they had veto power. And then, in May 1999, NATO accidentally bombed the Chinese embassy in Belgrade, killing three Chinese. The Chinese government rejected American explanations and encouraged its people to believe the attack had been deliberate. Outraged demonstrators besieged the American embassy in Beijing and set fire to the home of the American consul general in Chengdu. Washington seemed surprised at the intensity of anti-American sentiment among ordinary Chinese. It was apparent that Chinese leaders unfriendly to the United States had been strengthened by the incident – and it might be a very long time before the level of civility Jiang and Clinton had attained through summitry could be retrieved.

As the Clinton administration ground through its last months, the American foreign policy elite, especially its Republican component, was divided. On the one side stood those who perceived China as the next great threat to the nation's security, supported by men and women troubled by human rights abuses in China. They groped unsuccessfully for a policy that would force Chinese leaders to be more responsive to their concerns. On the other side could be found those whose eagerness to trade with China transcended any anxieties they might have had about security or human rights issues. They perceived no alternative to continued engagement with a government that frequently behaved reprehensibly.

"Engagement," the pursuit of a working relationship with a disagreeable regime, has rarely been attractive to Americans of any political persuasion. When a government's leaders are openly unsympathetic to American values and frequently pursue policies contrary to the interests of the United States, Americans are not easily persuaded of the value of befriending it. During World War II, most understood that the United States allied with Stalin's Soviet Union out of a desperate need to keep it in the war against Nazi Germany. Similarly, during the Cold War, they grudgingly accepted the fact that the American government developed strategic partnerships with reprehensible regimes including that of Mao Zedong's China, as it struggled to contain the Soviet empire. In the 1990s, with no apparent threat to the security of the United States, it was much more difficult to provide a compelling case for paying court to the "butchers of Beijing." But thoughtful men and women understood there was no alternative.

Neither Germany nor Japan, the two countries some theorists predicted would dominate the post-Cold War world, ever came close to emerging as "number 1" in the 1990s. No one had suggested either would rival American military power, but military power was presumably going to count for less in the future. Japan and Germany appeared to have the strongest economies as the world entered an era in which economic power would prevail. But Germany was quickly preoccupied with assimilation of the East Germans and their ruined society, at great cost to the West German state of the Cold War era. And Japan, attacked fiercely by the U.S. Trade Representative (USTR) in the early years of the Clinton administration, faded quickly in the mid-1990s, its sagging economy a threat primarily to itself.

In general, the Clinton administration handled affairs with Japan badly, in large part because of Clinton's disinterest. The Commerce Department and the USTR office pushed the Departments of State and Defense aside, demanding that Japan accept "results-oriented" trade agreements – agreements that would reduce Japanese exports to the United States and increase Japanese imports of American products. Ignoring security issues, the Americans continued to press very hard even after the real estate and stock market bubbles burst in Japan and its economy went into free fall. Christopher justified the American approach by contending that a continued trade imbalance between the two countries would erode domestic support for the Japanese-American relationship, including the security relationship. Lord, as assistant secretary for East Asian and Pacific Affairs, was deeply troubled by the nearly exclusive focus on economic affairs – and by his inability to gain the president's attention.

It was 1995, with the American economy booming, and the Japanese economy obviously weakening, before the Clinton administration eased its trade pressures. The United States still had legitimate grievances against Japanese commercial practices, but Japan-bashing had gone out of style. American economic primacy as well as military primacy seemed assured for at least the remainder of the century. William Perry, successor to Les Aspin as secretary of defense, and Joseph Nye, the Harvard political scientist serving as assistant secretary for international security, were able to make the case for more attention to security affairs. Facts on the ground – specifically a crisis that evolved in 1994 when it became evident that North Korea was developing nuclear weapons and had the missiles to deliver them (see below, chapter five) – helped Washington to shift its focus. The Japanese, too, demonstrated their renewed concerns by revising their National Defense Program Outline to increase their defense capabilities.

The so-called Nye Initiative resurrected the Cold War mantra that the Japanese-American alliance was the linchpin of American security policy in East Asia. The initial purpose of the alliance, defense of Japan and the containment of the Soviet Union, was redirected toward maintaining peace and stability in the Asia-Pacific region. American troops and bases would still be needed, although the U.S. base area on Okinawa, a constant irritation, exacerbated when three U.S. Marines raped a young Japanese girl there in 1995, would be reduced. The key American concerns were clearly North Korea's nuclear program and tensions in the Taiwan Strait. In 1996, Clinton and the Japanese prime minister issued a Joint Declaration reaffirming the security relationship between their nations and promised a revision of the Cold War era Guidelines for U.S.-Japan Defense Cooperation. Missile defense was mentioned specifically. In 1997, the new Guidelines were issued and extended the range of bilateral cooperation from the defense of Japan to undefined "surrounding areas," a deliberately oblique and ambiguous reference to North Korea and Taiwan that succeeded in arousing anxiety in Beijing and Pyongyang – although there was no assurance the Japanese Diet would pass the necessary enabling legislation.

Japanese relief at the indications of renewed American determination to keep U.S. forces in East Asia and the reiteration of the central place reserved for Japan in American policy toward the region was short-lived. Ever since the rapprochement between the United States and China in the 1970s, Japanese leaders and foreign affairs analysts have feared that they would be abandoned by the Americans – who would resume their pre-Cold War romance with China. The Madam Butterfly syndrome is still very much alive in Tokyo. When Clinton paid his long visit to China in 1998, he did not bother to stop in Tokyo to brief his ally on the way over or on the way back. To the Japanese, Clinton's action symbolized not merely a welcome reduction in Chinese-American tensions, but also contempt for the alleged "lynchpin" of American security in East Asia. The Americans appeared to have eased up on Japan bashing; now the Japanese became anxious about "Japan-passing."

Another unsettling moment for the Japanese in 1998 came when North Korea fired an intermediate range ballistic missile that crossed over Japan. The Japanese had understood for some long time that much of their country was within range of Pyongyang's short range missiles, but this further evidence of North Korean prowess left Tokyo yet more eager for the security provided by the alliance with the United States – and more responsive to the persistent American efforts to get the Japanese to agree to participate more fully with the United States in military operations. Once again the Japanese were forced to contemplate revision or reinterpretation of Article 9 of their constitution in which they renounced any right to go to war.

In the absence of presidential leadership, other American officials worked assiduously to strengthen the Japanese-American alliance and to give the Japanese the assurances they craved. But those most concerned, such as Nye and Perry, left the government and their successors never provided their subordinates with the support needed to maintain momentum. The Japanese government, however, demonstrated its good faith in 1999 when the Diet authorized logistical support for the United States in the event that the Americans became involved in a military confrontation in East Asia outside of Japan. With strong backing from the Japanese Defense Agency – Japan's equivalent of the U.S. Department of Defense – conservative newspapers, and key players in the Ministry of Foreign Affairs, the alliance remained central to Japan's security outlook and adjusted glacially to the demands of the post-Cold War era.

There were in the world other nations that imagined themselves to be great powers – Great Britain and France perhaps – but they posed no threat to the United States or its interests and received minimal attention from the Clinton White House. Clinton's good friend Tony Blair, the British prime minister, could usually be counted on to support American policy around the world or to be polite when demurring. French pretentions to great power status were a constant source of irritation. More troubling was their delight in undermining sanctions regimes, such as those the United States eagerly sought to maintain against Iraq and Iran. But occasionally they, too, could be helpful. Futurologists postulated a time when the European Union might challenge the United States, economically if not militarily. In the 1990s that day seemed very far off.

★ 5 ★

THE CLINTON YEARS ASSESSED

Any effort to assess the Clinton administration's management of the nation's foreign affairs must include its responses to situations that involved other great powers only indirectly – or not at all – and did not constitute humanitarian interventions – or what Michael Mandelbaum (1996) called "foreign policy as social work." There were, of course, a host of these, most handled reasonably well. If not terribly much was accomplished, disasters were averted, few lives were lost, and the problems passed on to Clinton's successor were troubling but did not seem to constitute an immediate threat to the United States or any of its major interests abroad.

Iraq was one of the most irritating problems. The G. H. W. Bush administration had driven Saddam Hussein's forces out of Kuwait but left him in power in Baghdad. Hopes that he might be overthrown came to naught. Those members of the Bush administration, such as Paul Wolfowitz, who had argued unsuccessfully for marching into Iraq, continued to demand action against Saddam in response to his never-ending pinprick challenges to the United States, its friends, and the UN. For the most part, the Iraqi taunts were limited to firing ineffectively at American and British planes policing the no-fly zones imposed on Iraqi fixed-wing aircraft in 1991. The Gulf War and the UN economic sanctions that followed meant that Iraq, never more than a third-rate power, was significantly weaker than it had been in 1990, but Saddam seemed irrepressible.

In June 1993, the Iraqis appear to have raised the stakes with a plan to assassinate former president Bush, who was visiting Kuwait. There was some doubt as to the reliability of the reported Iraqi plot, but Christopher persuaded Clinton to respond aggressively. The weapon of choice was the Tomahawk cruise missile, several of which were directed against the headquarters of the Iraqi intelligence agency in Baghdad. Cruise missiles had the virtue of avoiding the risk of American casualties for a president who was unquestionably risk averse – at least in military matters. Saddam-haters and Bush loyalists were contemptuous of what they perceived as a mere slap on the wrist, an inadequate response to the alleged assassination attempt.

The policy of the Clinton team toward the region was one they called "dual containment," an effort to contain Iran as well as Iraq. The Republicans, who gained control of the American Congress in the 1994 elections, demanded tougher measures against Iran. The United States tried to isolate both countries, but with increasing difficulty as France and Russia, eager to resume trade and investment ties, did what they could to subvert American efforts. Moreover, neighboring Turkey and Jordan were being hurt by economic sanctions targeting Iraq. Saddam played the fracture lines between the United States and the others with considerable virtuosity.

In 1996, there was another escalation of the problems in Iraq. Saddam, in violation of the 1991 settlement, sent troops into Kurdish-held territory in the north – at the invitation of one Kurdish faction that was fighting another. Clinton wanted no part of the issue. It arose in the midst of a presidential election campaign he was likely to win easily, but he was not eager to take any chances. There were problems enough in the Balkans and in East Asia. But an unsuccessful appeal to the UN to take action emboldened Saddam: it was evident that the United States was reluctant to use force. Ultimately Clinton's advisers agreed to settle for throwing a few more cruise missiles at Iraqi targets in the south – with no apparent impact.

Saddam launched a more serious challenge in 1997, obstructing the efforts of UN inspectors to carry out their assigned duty to assure the UN Security Council that Iraq had complied with the requirement that it destroy all of its weapons of mass destruction (WMD). The Baghdad regime denied the inspectors access to some sites and then declared it would allow no American members of the inspection teams – charging, with some basis in fact, that they served as intelligence agents for the U.S. government. Rejecting the Iraqi maneuvers, the UN pulled out all of the inspectors. The conviction grew in Washington that Saddam was hiding WMD and resuming efforts to build nuclear weapons and Clinton ordered an aircraft carrier to the Persian Gulf and strengthened American ground forces in the region.

The United States sought new sanctions against Iraq, but its efforts were blocked by France and Russia in the UN Security Council. China, too, worked to thwart the Americans. Only Great Britain continued to support the American position. Frustrated, Clinton agreed to allow the Russians to negotiate with Saddam for the return of the inspectors. Widely perceived as a victory for Baghdad, a deal was struck which permitted Iraq to sell oil in exchange for purchases of food and medicine.

Within the Clinton administration, Secretary of State Albright and Lake's successor as national security adviser, Samuel ("Sandy") Berger, argued that the time had come to get rid of Saddam. The Pentagon, however, insisted that ground forces would be necessary – that air strikes and cruise missiles would not bring down Saddam's government. The Saudis would not cooperate: they would not allow the United States to use bases in Saudi Arabia for an invasion of Iraq. Nearly isolated, the Clinton administration backed off. It would not act unilaterally. Arab leaders, fearing a reprise of 1991 in which Saddam would be hurt but remain in power, were relieved. There was doubtless some Arab proverb warning against poking tigers with sticks. Moreover, Arab governments were reluctant to oppose a fellow Arab amidst rising tensions between the Palestinians and Israelis.

Continued Iraqi obstruction of the inspection regime convinced Clinton's advisers that the time had come to act unilaterally, if necessary. Albright, Berger, and Secretary of Defense William Cohen set out to prepare the country for a major air campaign against Iraq, but failed. The nadir of their effort was a televised town hall style meeting at Ohio State University in February 1998. Their discussion failed to persuade either the university community or the television audience. Even the sanctions were losing support among the American people, some of whom were shaken by statistics that indicated that Iraqi civilians, especially children, were bearing the brunt of the punishment inflicted on Iraq. More such suffering rather than regime change was perceived as the likely outcome of bombs and missiles launched at Baghdad. Even some Americans eager to go after Saddam did not seem to think an aerial attack would be effective – and the administration had no intention whatever of sending in hundreds of thousands of troops to do the job.

Clinton's advisers concluded they could not gain sufficient support at home or abroad for the kind of military campaign they contemplated. They would do the best they could to isolate Iraq and to prevent it from attacking any of its neighbors. However desirable regime change might be, their assessment of the political realities convinced them that they would have to settle for containment.

The Republican-controlled Congress had a different idea. It was politically useful to attack the administration for its failure either to improve Saddam's behavior or get rid of him. But the Congress had a new plan for which Paul Wolfowitz was the intellectual driving force. Wolfowitz was still demanding the overthrow of Saddam as the only way to protect America's vital interest in the Persian Gulf region. If the public would not accept a major U.S. invasion, there was another way. Congress passed the Iraqi Liberation Act to funnel $97 million to the Iraqi opposition. The obvious point was that the Iraqi opposition, presumably with American air support, would be able to topple Saddam. Clinton's foreign policy team ridiculed the concept, arguing that the opposition Iraqi National Congress had more support in Washington than in Iraq, but his political advisers persuaded him to sign the bill into law. Some analysts compared the idea to the disastrous Bay of Pigs operation when U.S.-backed Cuban exiles tried to overthrow Castro in 1961.

In December 1998, as Saddam continued to obstruct UN inspection teams and Clinton was facing impeachment for lying about a sexual liasion in the White House, the administration executed Operation Desert Fox, a new and sustained air and missile attack on Iraq. American and British pilots patrolling the no-fly zones were granted greater leeway to engage Iraqi air defenses. Critics accused Clinton of attempting to divert attention from his peccadilloes, to rally support behind a president struggling to protect the nation's interests abroad. The critics may indeed have had a point, but Saddam, perceiving a wounded president, unquestionably had been provocative. Ultimately, Desert Fox had little impact on either the impeachment debate or Saddam.

Iraq posed an excruciatingly difficult problem for the United States. Saddam's ability to frustrate UN inspectors and capitalize on the fault lines among the members of the Security Council meant the UN would not be able to prevent him from maintaining programs for the development of weapons of mass destruction – or indeed from hiding stockpiles that had existed in 1991. Iraq was certainly a threat to its neighbors, to American interests in the Persian Gulf, and to the international system many people throughout the world had imagined would emerge with the end of the Cold War. But the United States could not muster significant support at home or abroad to end that threat. The greatest power the world had ever known seemed helpless to cope with a tin-pot dictator ruling over a Third World country with a decrepit military force that had deteriorated since being thrashed in 1991. And Saddam missed no opportunity to taunt Washington.

All that was left for the Clinton administration was to continue the unrewarding policy of containing Iraq and hoping that at some point Saddam's actions would be sufficiently provocative to persuade the French and the Russians of the need for stiff reprisals – or perhaps his own people, tormented beyond tolerance, would rise against him. Unhappily, both scenarios seemed highly unlikely. As the presidential election campaign began in 2000, Wolfowitz was prominent among the advisers to the Republican candidate and criticism of the Clinton administration's failure to rein in Saddam sounded loudly in discussions of foreign policy. Condoleezza Rice, another such adviser accused Clinton of having been weak in handling rogue regimes: Saddam must go, she insisted.

The Clinton team's approach to Iran also proved problematic. Congress and the American public remained intensely hostile to the Islamic Republic that in the late 1970s had held the American Embassy staff hostage for a year and mistreated its captives. Diplomatic relations had been severed in 1980. There was little indication that Iran had modified its view of the United States as the Great Satan or eased its threat to American interests in the Persian Gulf region. It continued to support Islamic fundamentalists in the Middle East and South Asia, including some terrorist organizations. The Reagan administration's search for Iranian moderates had ended in disaster and few in Washington were disposed to risk new overtures, least of all Christopher who had negotiated unsuccessfully for the release of the hostages in 1980. Moreover, there was increasing evidence that Iran, too, was developing weapons of mass destruction, specifically seeking a nuclear weapons capability, with the assistance of Russia and China. Apprehension about Iranian intentions and capabilities was growing and some analysts argued it was more dangerous than Iraq. Unable to attempt the Bush administration strategy of supporting Iraq against Iran, the Clinton administration announced its policy of "dual containment."

As the new administration conducted an extensive review of policy toward Iran, Christopher foreshadowed the outcome by labeling Iran an "international outlaw." His language was harsher than that used by his predecessor and the press anticipated a stiffening of American policy. When the review was completed, the administration began a major effort to isolate Iran. Referring to Iranian support for Hamas and Hezbollah, both frequently involved in terrorist acts, to its support for terrorist training camps, and its quest for WMD, Washington asked its allies and friends to cut loans, investments, and arms sales to Iran.

The prospects for success with this approach were poor. The World Bank approved a major loan to Iran over U.S. objections. The Chinese and Russians may have been eager to win American favor, but not at the expense of lucrative deals with Iran. American influence at the World Bank was strong enough to get the Bank to put loans to Iran on hold temporarily, but the Clinton administration ran into a stone wall with its allies. As was so often the case, only Great Britain endorsed the American effort. The Germans angered Christopher in their determination to maintain their trading relationship with Iran. France, Italy, and Japan rejected Washington's proposed tactics. At a meeting with European Community foreign ministers, Christopher was told they believed *increased* trade with

Iran was the best way to moderate its behavior and reintegrate it in the world community.

As the months passed fruitlessly, divisions within the administration on policy toward Iran began to emerge. Lake lumped Iran with what he called "backlash" states such as Iraq, Libya, China, and North Korea. Over at the CIA, the overall assessment suggested Iran should not be a comparable concern. It certainly remained hostile to the United States, but it had reduced its arms purchases sharply. It no longer seemed to be a threat to its neighbors. At the Pentagon there was apprehension that increased pressure would further radicalize Iran. Analysts in and out of the government pointed to its economic difficulties, largely the result of declining world oil prices and Iran's declining production capability. By mid-1994, some senior officials in the administration appeared to distance themselves from Lake's position, arguing that Iran was not as troublesome as Iraq. Clinton personally had concluded that sanctions were not working, but Christopher and Albright persisted in advocating more far-reaching sanctions.

Any plan to ease pressures on Iran that might have evolved among Clinton's advisers was forgotten when the Republicans won control of the Congress in the mid-term elections of 1994. Republican congressional leaders, especially Newt Gingrich (R-GA), demanded tougher policies toward "rogue" states, including Iran. The American Israel Public Affairs Committee (AIPAC), the powerful pro-Israel lobby, pressed for legislation to ban all commercial contact. Running before the tide, Clinton endorsed a complete economic boycott, much to the consternation of American oil companies who were buying Iranian oil legally for sale to third countries. But Gingrich wanted much more: he called for covert operations to overthrow the Iranian government (and several others he opposed). In 1996, the Congress passed legislation mandating sanctions against foreign companies that contributed to the development of Iran or Libya – infuriating allies of the United States who preferred not to be coerced into supporting an American policy they considered counterproductive.

Zbigniew Brzezinski and Brent Scowcroft, national security advisers under Democratic and Republican presidents respectively, publicly criticized the harsher approach toward Iran that had emerged. They conceded that Iran's support of terrorists and its nuclear program threatened the United States, but argued that there were better ways to address these concerns than by crude – and improbable – efforts to isolate the country. Carrots, as well as sticks, would be more likely to persuade the Iranian government to stop supporting terrorism and to halt its nuclear weapons program. They belittled Iran's buildup of conventional forces, insisting it was no threat to American supremacy in the region. Demonizing Iran was not a useful tactic, nor was coercing allies into enforcing American sanctions. In fact, they favored the revival of commercial relations.

Other prominent analysts joined in the criticism of sanctions, but to no avail. Gingrich was unmoved by their arguments and Clinton, who would have preferred to resume trade and investment with Iran, was not willing to do battle on the issue. The critics gained a powerful new argument in May 1997, however, when the Iranian people elected Mohammad Khatami, a prominent reformist cleric, as their new president. There could be no doubt that the Iranian people wanted to change course – and with Christopher gone, there was a greater willingness among Clinton's advisers to explore the possibility of some level of rapprochement. The fact that the Israelis appeared less hostile to Khatami's Iran removed another obstacle.

By 1998 it was evident that Khatami was trying to end Iran's pariah status in the international community. Although the Ayotollah Ali Khameni, Iran's supreme religious leader, was the ultimate power, Khatami had considerable success in reducing Iran's deviant behavior. Support for terrorist attacks and assassination of exiled dissidents declined. Iran ratified the Chemical Weapons Convention, presumably surrendering one WMD option. Perhaps of greatest impact on the American public was an interview Khatami gave to CNN. Exuding moderation from every pore, he expressed regret for the embassy hostage transgression and called for increased cultural and educational exchanges with the United States.

Khatami's performance as Iran's president gave Clinton sufficient cover to waive the congressionally mandated sanctions of foreign companies that invested in Iran. The United States would not obstruct Iran's efforts to obtain development capital. Secretary Albright publicly expressed interest in improving relations and the administration signaled in several ways its interest in rapprochement. It renounced its earlier policy of dual containment, arguing that Iraq was far more dangerous than Iran and that the United States, while seeking regime change in Baghdad, recognized the legitimacy of the Tehran government. It stopped referring to Iran as the most active state supporter of terrorism. As a result, tensions between Iran and the United States eased markedly, but Khatami, very likely restrained by Khameni, seemed unable to move any closer to the Americans during Clinton's remaining years in office.

State-supported terrorism, however, was not the only – or even the most threatening – form of terrorism the United States faced. There was always the danger posed by the home-grown lunatic fringe capable of atrocities such as the bombing of a federal building in Oklahoma City in 1995. But increasingly, the threat came from nonstate actors with grievances rooted in the Middle East. American support for Israel was one source of hostility to the United States. Support for conservative Arab leaders such as the Saudi royal family was another. Most Arabs assumed the American-led war against Iraq in 1991 was designed to preserve American oil interests and the security of Israel rather than to liberate Kuwait. And not least was the perception in the Muslim world of a western assault on Islamic values – an assault presumably led by the United States, the most powerful state in the West.

As evidence of American military power, U.S. forces were frequently sent abroad to protect American interests or what were perceived as the interests of the international community – peace, stability, the free flow of commerce, including oil. Overseas, in foreign cities and ports, they became targets. Reagan had sent U.S. marines to Lebanon to stabilize the situation in that benighted country and 241 of them were killed when a suicide bomber drove a truck into their barracks in Beirut in 1983. In 1996, using a gasoline truck as a bomb, attackers killed 19 and wounded 240 American troops sleeping in Khobar Towers in Dharan, Saudi Arabia, where their mission was to deter Iraqi aggression. In 2000, the *U.S.S. Cole* was attacked in port in Yemen resulting in the deaths of 17 sailors.

American diplomats abroad also lived with danger. The American embassy in Beirut was hit by a car bomb in 1983. The worst episode came in August 1998, when the American embassies in Nairobi, Kenya, and Dar es Salaam, Tanzania were struck with car bombs almost simultaneously, injuring a total of 5,500 people, over 200 of whom died in Nairobi as did eleven others in Dar es Salaam.

In 1993, terrorists struck in New York City, setting off a car bomb in a parking facility under the World Trade Center, killing five and injuring hundreds of others. Suddenly it was apparent that simply staying home was not adequate protection, that terrorists could strike Americans anywhere in the United States. The World Trade Center survived the attack and the terrorists responsible were captured before their planned attacks on the Lincoln Tunnel and the United Nations building, but the vulnerability of ordinary Americans was apparent. Military bases might be shielded by increasing security, but it was extraordinarily difficult to guard against attacks in civilian settings. Perhaps most appalling was the revelation of the ease with which terrorist groups could move in and out of the United States.

All of the men involved in the 1993 attack on the World Trade Center were Muslims from the Middle East, led by an Egyptian cleric, Sheik Omar Abdul Rahman. In the course of the investigation, American officials learned that the group's activities had been financed by a Saudi business-man, Osama bin Laden, a multimillionaire whose whereabouts were unknown. Later in the year, a lone gunman stood at the entrance to CIA headquarters in Langley, Virginia, and began picking off employees as they arrived for work, killing two and wounding three others. He escaped, but was identified as a Pakistani, possibly one of the 20,000 "Afghans," Muslims from all over South Asia and the Middle East, including bin Laden, who went to Afghanistan to fight the Soviets in the 1980s, often with American assistance.

The Reagan administration had provided weaponry for the *mujahadin* in Afghanistan, especially Stingers (shoulder-fired antiaircraft missiles) that proved highly successful against Soviet helicopters. Having developed a taste for killing infidels in Afghanistan, in the post-Cold War world they turned their attention to Americans, whom they now perceived as the gravest threat to Islam. Some analysts called this pattern "blowback," retribution for what they considered ill-conceived, imprudent American actions abroad.

It is likely that bin Laden was also behind the attack on U.S. forces in Saudi Arabia in 1996. In many of his pronouncements of the 1990s he raged against the presence of non-Muslims on holy Saudi soil, insisting it was a sacrilege, an offense against Allah. But Saudi officials obstructed the investigation and later executed several Saudis they held responsible, without allowing them to be interrogated by Americans.

In 1998, bin Laden issued a declaration of *jihad* against the Jews and the "crusaders" – his label, intended pejoratively, for Westerners present in the Middle East. He called American actions in the region, including the 1991 liberation of Kuwait, a declaration of war against Islam. *Jihad* was thus the duty of every Muslim. Killing Americans and their allies was the duty of every Muslim until their armies were driven out of the lands of Islam. Americans were to be killed wherever they could be found and their possessions plundered. Relatively few Muslims accepted an interpretation of the Koran that called for terrorism, for the murder of innocent bystanders, but implementation of bin Laden's vision required only a few.

Stopping bin Laden and those throughout the Muslim world who might respond to his call posed a much more difficult assignment than deterring state-sponsored terrorism. The United States could issue credible threats to countries such as Iran, Libya, or Syria, as Christopher did in 1996, but deterring generally anonymous nonstate actors may well have been impossible. Even the world's most powerful military had few options. The Department of Defense developed plans for pre-emption: whenever a terrorist group targeting Americans was discovered, the U.S. would strike first, crush it before it could act. But bin Laden's organization, al Qaeda, proved to be exceptionally diffuse, with cells operating all over the world, held together primarily by hostility to the West, especially Israel, perceived as a crusader outpost on Arab land, and the United States, the leading power in the West and the principal supporter of Israel.

The emergence of bin Laden as the apparent instigator and financier of attacks on Americans led inevitably to efforts to capture or kill him. On one occasion, when U.S. intelligence determined he was living in Sudan, the administration failed to reach agreement with a Sudanese government that seemed willing to turn him over. In 1996, under threat of UN sanctions for harboring terrorists, Sudan forced him to leave. He moved back to Afghanistan. After the attacks on the American embassies in Kenya and Tanzania in 1998, the hunt intensified. By this time bin Laden was in Afghanistan, collaborating with the Taliban rulers of the country and running training camps for terrorists. Clinton authorized the launching of cruise missiles against a bin Laden camp in Afghanistan and a chemical factory in Sudan suspected – probably wrongly – of manufacturing the ingredients for nerve gas. In addition, the CIA mounted a covert operation in collaboration with the famed Afghan guerrilla fighter, Ahmed Shah Massoud, designed to capture bin Laden, but to no avail.

Analysts in and out of the U.S. government who worked on counterterrorism were increasingly fearful of a terrorist attack on an American city with weapons of mass destruction. There were reports of bin Laden trainees working with chemical weapons and various kinds of poisons. An attack using anthrax seemed a serious threat. Specialists were also gravely concerned about Russian stockpiles of WMD that were poorly protected and might well be put up for sale. Knowledgeable Americans were uneasy and in response to raw intelligence warnings, there were frequent terrorist alerts and altered travel plans by officials. Clearly the initiative rested with bin Laden and his associates. Perhaps worst of all was awareness that even if bin Laden were captured or killed, even if al Qaeda was smashed, other men and women and other organizations of like purport, unhappy with the role of the United States in the world, and specifically in the Middle East, would pop up to take their place. It promised to be a long and violent struggle.

More immediately, the Clinton administration was confronted with a mounting crisis over North Korea's nuclear program. The Bush administration had succeeded in winning Pyongyang's assent to inspections by the International Atomic Energy Agency, but the process collapsed before Bush left the White House. The North Koreans attempted to conceal some of their plutonium holdings and continued provocations against South Korea. The South Koreans and the United States decided to resume joint military exercises in 1993. Clinton paid little attention and his National Security Council lacked any staff familiar with the problems of the Korean peninsula. In March 1993, the North Koreans gave notice of their intent to withdraw from the nuclear nonproliferation treaty regime they had accepted in 1985.

Reawakened to the danger, the United States attempted to revive some kind of diplomatic solution, offering the prospect of negotiations while threatening to ask the UN Security Council to impose economic sanctions on North Korea if it remained recalcitrant. Typically, Pyongyang denounced the United States and threatened to attack South Korea in retaliation for any UN sanctions.

Clinton, in East Asia for a Group of Eight (G8) meeting, stopped over in Seoul in July 1993, to reassure the South Koreans. In a speech he delivered there, he urged the North Koreans to halt their nuclear weapons program. He indicated that appropriate North Korean behavior might lead to an end to Pyongyang's diplomatic isolation and bring economic aid to a country where famine was rampant. The North Koreans agreed to negotiations and an American delegation arrived in Pyongyang to propose a roadmap to a resolution of the issue. But despite initial reports of progress, in August the North Koreans rescinded permission for IAEA inspections. The talks seemed to be going nowhere and some analysts in the United States proposed breaking the deadlock by canceling the joint U.S. South Korean exercise that seemed to enrage the North.

In December 1993, the discussion shifted to the UN where again hopes were raised of some kind of deal, perhaps cancellation of the exercise in exchange for North Korea permitting the IAEA inspectors to look at suspected nuclear waste sites. As the talks inched along, the North Koreans raising and then dashing hopes again and again, it appeared that they were stalling while continuing their efforts to develop nuclear weapons. Washington hesitated to press too hard, fearful of giving North Korea an excuse to withdraw from the nuclear nonproliferation regime. Coordination between the United States and its South Korean ally was minimal, alienating Seoul. No clear and consistent strategy emerged from Clinton and his advisers. There was no progress toward resolution of the issue. By the end of the year, the CIA estimated that the North Koreans had enough plutonium for nuclear weapons – at least one bomb, possibly two.

In the spring of 1994, apprehension about North Korea's nuclear program and possible weapons intensified. Criticism of the Clinton administration's ineffectiveness spread among East Asian specialists in the think tanks and universities. Former government officials, most notably Brent Scowcroft, demanded military action to eliminate the threat. At the Pentagon, plans to attack North Korea were reviewed and updated. The U.S. Air Force was prepared to turn North Korea into a "parking lot." Many experts argued, however, that there was no way to be certain that air strikes would take out underground or unknown sites. Many worried about what North Korea might do to South Korea in the process.

With the prospect of war drawing nearer, in June 1994, North Korea's "Great Leader," Kim Il Sung, invited former U.S. president Jimmy Carter to Pyongyang. Carter checked with the White House. Clinton and his advisers did not want Carter involved, but feared the domestic political ramifications of impeding a peace effort. Reluctantly, they acquiesced. Carter persuaded Kim to agree to an American condition to freeze his nuclear program before negotiations would begin. The North Koreans agreed not to refuel their Yongbyun reactor or to produce any more plutonium. In July 1994, instead of sending bombers, Clinton sent a delegation to Pyongyang to negotiate. Chalmers Johnson, a leading specialist on East Asian affairs called the breakthrough "a cardinal achievement of U.S. diplomacy and successful nuclear blackmail" (1995). Wisely, Washington determined to keep South Korea, China, Japan, and Russia closely informed.

The sudden death of Kim Il Sung as talks began unnerved observers around the world, but the work went on, resulting in what became known as the Agreed Framework. North Korea agreed to continue the freeze on its nuclear program and to dismantle it step-by-step. In return the United States pledged to assist North Korea in obtaining light-water reactors which provide energy, but could not easily be used to produce weapons-grade plutonium, and to provide fuel oil to replace energy lost when the existing reactors were shut down. The agreement provided for the creation of a multinational consortium, the Korean Energy Development Corporation (KEDO), to construct the light-water reactors; funding was to come from Japan and South Korea.

For the moment, the crisis passed, but the Agreed Framework was not without its critics. South Korean funding was essential and the Seoul government mistrusted Pyongyang – and was not confident that the Americans had kept it fully informed. At home, some analysts, especially those close to the Republican Party, charged the administration with having bribed a brutal and untrustworthy regime. And when the Republicans won control of both houses of Congress in the November 1994 elections, implementation of the agreement was in doubt. The light-water reactors were not built and Congress impeded the flow of promised economic assistance, especially of fuel oil. Calls for greater engagement with North Korea to encourage economic reforms went unheeded. It was merely a matter of time before the issue would reach the crisis point again. Only the late 1997 election of Kim Dae Jung, a long-time opposition leader and democratic reformer, a man committed to easing tension between Seoul and Pyongyang, as president of South Korea, provided a ray of hope for the future of the Korean peninsula.

One idea that seemed to be gaining traction in the mid-1990s was that of developing a strategic relationship with India. American leaders had long been indifferent to India, irritated by its Cold War neutralism that too often tilted in favor of the Soviets and contemptuous of the failures of its planned economy. India was indeed the world's largest democracy, but friendship between the two nations had never developed. As American analysts began to focus on the rising power of China, however, it was not much of a leap to imagine that India might prove useful in efforts to contain the Chinese. Other Americans, fearful of aggressive Islamic fundamentalism, imagined that the militant Hindus who had come to power in India might prove a valuable ally against that threat. And the Indian government of the 1990s had clearly abandoned Nehru's commitment to socialism, portending a stronger economy and new opportunities for American business.

One issue that remained troublesome was India's refusal to sign the Nuclear Nonproliferation Treaty. Although India had no nuclear weapons and was not guilty of providing materials for any other country's nuclear program, it was one of only four countries in the entire world that remained outside that nonproliferation regime. Nonetheless, the Clinton administration made overtures to India, confident on the basis of intelligence reports that the Indian government would refrain from developing nuclear weapons. In May 1998, the Americans were caught by surprise as India tested a nuclear weapon. Three weeks later, American pleas to the contrary notwithstanding, Pakistan tested its own nuclear device. The United States had failed to prevent either country from demonstrating its nuclear weapon's capacity.

American law mandated economic sanctions against India and Pakistan. Visions of a lucrative commercial relationship with India were put in abeyance. Efforts to improve relations with the two new nuclear powers were set back. In the UN Security Council, the Chinese, among the world's worst proliferators, largely responsible for Pakistan's program, were quick to assist in the American effort to obtain international sanctions against India. That was not the way things were supposed to work.

Clinton's notorious disengagement from foreign policy concerns did not apply, of course, to foreign economic policy. Globalization, especially the process of international economic integration, was a matter on which he could speak eloquently – and endlessly. But his commitment to "market democracy," his conviction that open markets would lead to open societies was not shared by many of the people who had elected him. Although economists could demonstrate that free trade was good for the economies of participating nations, the system unquestionably produced losers as well as winners. At the time of the struggle over NAFTA and in the years that followed, there was a growing sense among many Americans and others around the globe that the world economic system benefited capitalists at the expense of workers and the environment. Statistics revealed that imports and exports constituted an increasing percentage of the gross domestic product (GDP) of the United States – indeed 26% in 2000 – but that provided little satisfaction to the hundreds of thousands of Americans who had lost well-paying jobs in the manufacturing sector to low-wage workers abroad.

The collapse of the Mexican peso in 1994 did nothing to change the minds of the men and women who had been skeptical of NAFTA from the outset. Robert Rubin, who became secretary of the treasury early in 1995, took charge and concluded there was need for a $40 billion loan to stabilize the peso and the Mexican economy. He warned that failure to act would result in millions of additional illegal immigrants. The newly elected Republican-controlled Congress, unwilling to risk the taxpayer's money, refused the appropriation. Rubin, undeterred, persuaded Clinton to use $20 billion from an emergency account and found an additional $30 billion in international banking institutions – and the loan succeeded in stabilizing the Mexican economy. Within a year Mexico had registered a trade surplus and was able to begin paying off its debt. NAFTA survived the crisis and the Wall Street bankers, whose original loans to Mexico may have been exuberant, were bailed out as well.

In mid-1997, a financial crisis of enormous magnitude began in Asia, once again raising questions about the dark side of globalization and Washington's insistence on the free flow of capital as well as trade. It started with a speculative run on Thailand's currency, the baht. The Thai government allowed the baht to float against the dollar and it fell sharply. Thailand was in serious trouble, unable to pay off short-term loans to foreign banks. The International Monetary Fund came up with a stabilization loan package – to which the United States did not contribute directly, angering the Thais and the financial ministries of other Southeast Asian countries affected. Indonesia was soon in deep trouble and South Korea close behind.

From Washington came disparaging remarks about "crony capitalism." Unquestionably banking reform was needed throughout the region. None of these countries had regulatory institutions sufficiently strong to control the movement of capital in and out of their borders. The Indonesian economy was so depressed that the authoritarian Suharto government of more than 30 years was pushed aside. Not sorry to see Suharto go, the United States offered no help. The Americans did ride to the aid of Kim Dae Jung, determined to sustain his effort to bring democracy to South Korea.

Whatever the virtues of free trade, serious doubts about the wisdom of open capital markets were expressed by prominent economists. Even George Soros, a man who had gained great wealth as a currency speculator, pointed to the Asian financial crisis as evidence of the need for greater regulation of capital flows. Nonetheless, the United States, working through the IMF, continued to push for greater openness in Asia, part of the American mission to recreate the world in its own image. Asia managed to survive, but skepticism about Washington's approach intensified – and it was rejected outright by Malaysia.

Clinton also perceived greater opportunities for trade and investment in Africa and proposed the African Growth and Opportunity Act in his 1998 State of the Union address. The prospects for democracy had improved greatly on that diverse continent after South Africa put an end to apartheid and elected Nelson Mandela to lead the country. In Nigeria a military dictatorship had been overthrown and democratic processes restored. If greater democracy would bring greater stability, there would be benefits for American businessmen as well for the people of Africa. In 1998 Clinton flew to Africa for a ten day tour designed to build trade ties.

In South Africa, the American president accompanied Nelson Mandela to Robben Island, to see the cell where Mandela had been imprisoned for many years. In Senegal, Clinton paid homage to the slaves that been shipped to America from Goree Island. In Uganda, he apologized for the institution of slavery and, in Rwanda, for the failure of his administration to prevent the genocide of 1994. Although he accomplished little, he showed more interest in Africa than had any of his predecessors in the White House and he returned there briefly in September 2000.

There were two foreign countries whose affairs were followed closely by millions of Americans and often affected domestic politics: Ireland and Israel. These both had the president's attention. He was always aware of the importance of Irish and Jewish voters, presumably committed – perhaps blindly – to the goals of Irish nationalists in Northern Ireland and of Israeli visionaries dreaming of a Greater Israel.

In the presidential campaign of 1992, Clinton bid for Irish votes by promising to issue a visa to Gerry Adams, leader of Sinn Fein, the political arm of the Irish Republican Army (IRA) that sought to unify all of Ireland, and by criticizing Britain's human rights record in Northern Ireland. A Clinton administration would seek an active role in efforts to bring peace between Catholics and Protestants in that troubled part of the British empire. As president, he appointed Jean Kennedy Smith, sister of the late Irish Catholic president, John F. Kennedy, as ambassador to Ireland. There was no joy in London.

Nothing much happened for about a year and Clinton's campaign rhetoric began to fade from memory – just more empty talk. In December, however, the British government and the IRA reached an agreement on a cease-fire that would allow Sinn Fein to participate in negotiations over the future of Northern Ireland. Shortly afterward, Gerry Adams was invited to participate in a conference in the United States scheduled for early 1994. Clinton was confronted by a visa issue not unlike the one subsequently posed by the desire of Taiwan President Lee Teng-hui to visit the United States. Adams, too, had strong Congressional support, led by Senators Ted Kennedy (D-Massachusetts) and Pat Moynihan (D-New York). Clinton yielded quickly and Gerry Adams came to America, to the dismay of the British government and Sinn Fein's opposition, the Protestant Irish Unionists.

Over the next year, under pressure from the Irish-American lobby, the Clinton administration lifted a ban on official contacts with Sinn Fein and allowed Adams to meet with senior White House officials. Clinton appointed former senator George Mitchell as his special representative on the Northern Ireland issue. Mitchell spent much of the next three years chairing talks between Sinn Fein and the Unionists. As further gestures to Irish-Americans, the administration allowed Adams to set up an office in Washington and to raise funds openly in the United States. Adams was even invited to the White House for its annual St. Patrick's Day reception. There could hardly be any doubt of the legitimacy granted Sinn Fein in Clinton's America.

In April 1998, a precarious agreement on governing Northern Ireland was reached between Irish nationalists and unionists, in no small part due to Mitchell's efforts. Initially perceived as just another pro-nationalist American politician, he eventually won the trust of unionists. Despite frequently irritating London, Clinton's Irish policy was clearly a success. It solidified Irish-American support for his presidency and brought a significant promise of peace to Northern Ireland – although *precarious* would always be the key word. And the special relationship with Great Britain remained intact.

Coping with Israel and its hostile neighbors proved a more daunting challenge. Christopher traveled more than twenty times to Damascus in a vain attempt to broker peace between Syria and Israel. Yitzhak Rabin, the Israeli prime minister and military hero, offered to surrender the Golan Heights, taken from Syria in the 1967 "Six Day" war in exchange for a peace treaty, but Syrian president Hafez Assad showed no interest. He would not negotiate with Israel until after all his demands were met.

Israel's other immediate concern was the Palestinian *intifada,* an armed uprising of Palestinians in the occupied territories of Gaza and the West Bank, that had begun in December 1987. In August 1993, the Israelis and Palestinians astonished much of the world by announcing that in secret negotiations in Oslo, they had reached an agreement on principles for the resolution of their differences on the basis of land for peace. Israel would gradually turn over control of Gaza and the West Bank to a Palestinian Authority in exchange for an end to the *intifada*. At Israel's request, the signing ceremony was held in the United States, with Clinton standing alongside Rabin and Palestinian leader Yasir Arafat. The United States then cajoled 45 other countries to join it in pledging $2.5 billion in development aid for the Palestinians. In the months that followed, Israel succeeded in negotiating peace agreements with Jordan, Morocco, and Tunisia, always with the Clinton administration assisting in the process. Jordan, for example, received $200 million worth of military equipment from the United States and had $700 million in debt forgiven. Optimism about a comprehensive Arab-Israeli peace grew, despite Syrian President Assad's intransigence.

Then came one of those moments that force scholars to evaluate the role of the individual in history. In November 1995, Rabin, who had been vilified by the Israeli right, by those who opposed yielding any of the lands conquered in 1967, by those who had visions of a Greater Israel from which all Arabs would be expelled, was murdered by a right-wing Israeli Jew. His death proved to be an enormous setback for the peace process. In 1996, despite obvious American efforts to the contrary, Benjamin Netanyahu and his conservative Likud Party, opponents of the Oslo Accord, gained control of the Israeli government. Apprehension spread through the Arab world, through Washington and other capitals in the West. These fears proved to be justified. Deliberately heightening tensions, Palestinian radicals terrorized Israel with suicide bombings.

The Clinton administration did not stint in its pressure on Netanyahu to continue on the course Rabin had set. Netanyahu had no intention of withdrawing from the Golan Heights. He had no intention of working with Arafat's Palestinian Authority toward eventual Palestinian control of Gaza or the West Bank. But the Americans forced him to go through the motions, even to meet with Arafat. Of course Arafat, aware of American eagerness to force an accommodation, demanded new concessions. Ultimately, Netanyahu knew he could count on the Israeli lobby and supporters in the U.S. Congress to prevent the Clinton administration from punishing him – and the peace process came to a halt. Throughout the Arab world, the United States, as Israel's principal backer, was held responsible for Netanyahu's intransigence.

By 1997, the hopes that had been stimulated by the Oslo Accord, had evaporated. Some American analysts, such as Henry Kissinger, argued that the gradual approach envisioned at Oslo had failed. It was time, they contended, for "final status" talks, time to arrange for the creation of a Palestinian state, determine its borders, and resolve the question of who would control what parts of Jerusalem. But a Palestinian state was anathema to the Likud Party and its sympathizers all over the world. Netanyahu would not budge. Indeed, he perceived a threat from his right, from the yet more belligerent Ariel Sharon. Among Palestinians, radical groups such as Hamas and Islamic Jihad, led by men who considered Arafat too accommodating, came to the fore. In the summer of 1997, the Palestinians resumed suicide bombings against Israeli civilians.

The Clinton administration pushed harder, risking the alienation of the strong support it had hitherto received from the American Jewish community. Despite the efforts of Israeli lobbyists, Albright and Berger, himself Jewish, realized that many American Jews preferred Rabin's approach to that of Netanyahu. The president's wife, Hillary Rodham Clinton, went so far as to speak publicly of the need for a Palestinian state. Somehow they succeeded in reviving the peace process, in getting Netanyahu to agree to turn much of the West Bank over to the Palestinians in any final settlement. Clinton managed to get Netanyahu and Arafat to come to the United States in late 1998 and "persuaded" Netanyahu to agree to give the Palestinians yet another slice of the West Bank at some future date. But on the ground, conditions did not change.

There could be no doubt that Clinton was engaged in efforts to end the Israeli-Palestinian conflict – and ultimately the tensions between Israel and all of its neighbors. Unfortunately, cooperation from the principal parties to the conflict was minimal. The Israelis begrudged the Palestinians every inch of land claimed by the Palestinians and too many Palestinians would never be satisfied as long as the state of Israel existed. The Israelis continued to build settlements in the West Bank and the Palestinians persisted in acts of violence against Israelis.

A wisp of hope reemerged in May 1999 when the Israeli electorate turned against Likud and allowed Ehud Barak, the Labor Party candidate, to become prime minister. Barak seemed to be cut of the same cloth as Rabin, a tough military man likely to pursue less ideological policies than had Netanyahu. Urged on by Albright and Berger, Clinton pressed Israelis and Palestinians to resolve the issues that continued to divide them. At some point, Clinton decided that peace in the Middle East would be the foreign policy legacy of his administration, a great diplomatic triumph that would cap his presidency. Barak proved to be accommodating, but it was clear that Clinton was more eager for negotiations than either the Israelis or the Palestinians.

By July 2000, sufficient progress had been made by American diplomats shuttling between Barak and Arafat to attempt a Camp David meeting of the two men with Clinton. Talks began July 12 and word of progress leaked to the press. But after two weeks, the negotiations failed, ostensibly over arrangements for Jerusalem. Grudgingly and at great risk to himself physically as well as politically, Barak accepted an American proposal to give the Palestinians authority over some Jerusalem neighborhoods. It was not enough of a concession for Arafat who needed much more to compensate for concessions he would be required to make on the Palestinian right of return – the right of those who fled or were driven out of Palestine in 1948 to return to what was now Israel.

Clinton was devastated by the breakdown of the talks, angry at Arafat for having rejected terms the Clinton team had worked so hard to extract from the Israelis. Doggedly, he persisted in his efforts, a full court press to win peace in the Middle East before he left office in January. A second *intifada*, provoked by Sharon, began in September. Clinton was still trying in late December 2000, but both Israelis and Palestinians turned down an American proposal on December 30. For Clinton, the game was over.

The Israelis and Palestinians resumed talks in late January 2001, on the eve of Israeli elections. Again, despite reports of progress, the talks failed. A few days later, Barak's Labor Party was badly defeated and the man most dreaded by Palestinians and most feared by peace advocates the world over, Ariel Sharon, was Israel's new prime minister. Clinton had certainly applied himself heroically, but he accomplished nothing toward a final settlement of the Israeli-Palestinian conflict.

There were several other marks on Clinton's scorecard worthy of mention before his overall record on foreign policy is assessed. One important achievement of his first term was the establishment of diplomatic relations with Vietnam. The Carter administration had been moving in that direction in the late 1970s, just a few years after war ended in that unfortunate country. Complications arising out of simultaneous efforts to normalize relations with China – which was about to go to war with Vietnam – forced Carter to put off the plan until his second term, an opportunity the American people denied him. Reagan had shown no interest in the idea, to which many of his supporters were hostile. Bush was preoccupied with closing out the Cold War and beginning the new world order by teaching Iraq that aggression did not pay. But there were good economic and strategic reasons for resolving any remaining issues with Vietnam and establishing a working relationship between Hanoi and Washington.

In 1993, there remained domestic political opposition to opening relations with Vietnam, especially because of the festering POW/MIA issue – the demand of many Americans that Vietnam account for GIs whose death in the war had never been verified. Some people suspected that the Vietnamese were still holding Americans prisoners, 20 years after U.S. forces withdrew. It was an especially difficult problem for Clinton to tackle because of the widespread conviction he had dodged the draft during the war.

From Hanoi came clear signals of willingness to assist in efforts to account for missing Americans. As long as the Vietnamese cooperated, Clinton could move, however gingerly, toward normalization. In 1993, the United States encouraged international financial support for economic development in Vietnam. Clinton took a riskier step by lifting the trade embargo in 1994, with support from the business community. In the same year, each country established a liaison office in the capital of the other, justified by new commercial contacts. To take the last big step of official recognition of the Hanoi regime and full diplomatic relations, Clinton needed political cover. He was fortunate to get that from prominent Vietnam War heroes, most importantly Senator John McCain (R-Arizona), who had spent more time in Vietnamese prisons than any other living American. In July 1995, Clinton acted. The two countries exchanged ambassadors and American businessmen pressed for opportunities in the communist country. In November 2000, Clinton became the first American president to visit Vietnam, accompanied by a delegation of corporate executives. Vietnam was about to be integrated into the global economic system.

Normalization of relations with Vietnam eliminated one post-Cold War anomaly, but another, Cuba, proved to be untouchable, a third rail in American foreign relations. The problem, of course, was the heavy concentration of Cuban-Americans in Miami and the power of the intensely anti-Castro Cuban-American National Foundation (CANF). Clinton had pandered to Cuban-American voters in the 1992 campaign and he was careful not to alienate them during his presidency. Relations with Cuba were probably worse at the conclusion of his years in office than they had been at the outset – although Castro unquestionably shared responsibility.

Cuba was in serious economic trouble at the end of the Cold War. Gorbachev's Soviet Union could not afford the subsidies, especially cheap oil, which had been provided since the days of Nikita Khrushchev. Yeltsin's Russia was even less interested in helping. In fact, Yeltsin had ties to CANF, which opened an office in Moscow. And help did not come from the Eastern European states that cast off their Communist regimes. Obviously, commerce with the United States could have been of enormous help, but the embargo on exports to Cuba that dated back to the closing days of the Eisenhower administration remained in place and efforts were made to expand it in hope of forcing the rapid collapse of Castro's government.

In the early 1990s, Cubans struggled in what Castro called a "Special Period," in which the quality of life for most Cubans deteriorated sharply. The regime tried to relieve the pressure by encouraging emigration to the United States, but the U.S. government reneged on an agreement to issue 20,000 visas a year to Cubans. The Americans had no interest in easing Castro's problems. However, the U.S. automatically granted asylum to any Cuban refugee who reached its shores as a presumed victim of a tyrannical communist regime. The effect was to encourage large-scale illegal immigration, Cubans on boats and rafts, risking their lives to reach Florida.

In 1994, Clinton was forced to announce a new policy toward Cuban boat people intercepted enroute to the United States. They would no longer be allowed to enter the country. Instead they would be taken to the U.S. naval base at Guantanamo Bay in eastern Cuba and advised to go home and apply for a visa in Havana. In addition, Clinton decreed an end to remittances from Cubans in America to their relatives in Cuba – an important source of hard currency for Castro's regime. He ordered a reduction in flights between Miami and Havana and an increase in anti-Castro broadcasts aimed at Cuba. All of these steps came after consultations with CANF leaders at the White House. After all, 1994 was an election year.

None of Clinton's measures proved effective. Castro did not fall. Cubans in America evaded restrictions on remittances and eventually demanded restoration of flights to Havana. With the base at Guantanamo overflowing with refugees, additional space for them had to be established in Panama. The Clinton administration decided it was wiser to negotiate a new arrangement with Cuba. Castro agreed to resume restrictions on illegal departures in exchange for an American agreement to issue more visas. And the Americans decided to admit all the migrants in the temporary camps into the United States.

Thanks to the exodus of thousands of discontented Cubans, continued remittances, and a new emphasis on and increase in tourism, living conditions in Cuba improved slightly in 1995. Christopher and his staff perceived evidence that Castro was moderating some of his repressive policies as well as opening his economy a little. The American business community was eager to get into Cuba, offering the standard argument of how increased commercial relations would lead ultimately to a more open Cuban society, perhaps even to a democratic Cuba. Members of the United Nations voted 101 to 2 in support of a resolution criticizing the American embargo. Public opinion seemed to be changing in the United States, even among Cuban-Americans who began drifting away from CANF's hard line.

Any dreams of rapprochement between Washington and Havana were blasted in February 1996, when Cuban fighter planes shot down two unarmed aircraft flown by members of Brothers to the Rescue, a Cuban exile group that tried to assist Cubans risking their lives on boats and rafts as they attempted to enter the United States illegally. CANF was invigorated and the outcry in the United States led to Congress passing the Helms-Burton Act, extending the embargo by punishing foreign companies that traded with Cuba. Helms-Burton was similar in purport to an amendment President Bush had vetoed in 1992, unwilling to provoke America's allies. Clinton, up for reelection in 1996, signed the bill into law, although in classic Clinton fashion, he found a way to avoid enforcing it.

In the United States, debate over policy toward Cuba persisted. It was evident that hard-liners in America and Castro enjoyed a symbiotic relationship. Owen Harries, a leading conservative analyst, noted (1996) that whenever Castro was in trouble, he manipulated a crisis that provoked a tough American response – which enabled him to blame Cuba's troubles on Washington (or Miami) and rally his people behind him. American policy had failed. It was time for a change. Separating himself from his more ideological fellow conservatives, Harries dismissed Castro as a "squalid local tyrant," no longer capable of harming U.S. interests – and called for an end to efforts to isolate Cuba. He thought it likely that depriving Castro of an American threat would force him to open Cuban society, ultimately losing control of the momentum for reform.

There is ample evidence that Clinton's foreign policy team wanted to follow Harries' advice, but it lacked the political courage. Albright, who succeeded Christopher as secretary of state in 1997, was busily cultivating Helms, trying to keep him from obstructing policy toward what she considered more compelling issues. Doubtless, easing of restrictions on commerce with Cuba would be a red flag to Helms and many other members of Congress, including some Democrats – many of whom were infuriated by the administration's decision to let the Baltimore Orioles play in Cuba. So the administration held back. The Pope's visit to Cuba in 1998 and his condemnation of the embargo provided an opportunity for Clinton to make a bold gesture, but he was unwilling to do battle with Helms and CANF.

In 1999, the arrival of an eight-year-old Cuban boy in Miami put Cuban-American relations on the front pages again. A raft carrying illegal immigrants capsized before it reached Florida. The boy's mother died, but the boy, Elian Gonzalez, survived. An epic battle then began between the mother's relatives in Miami determined to keep the boy with them, while his father, in Cuba, demanded the return of his son. The case became a great national issue in Cuba. Castro launched a major campaign for the boy's return. Cuban-Americans insisted that Elian, having reached American shores, was entitled to American citizenship and the benefits of freedom that came with it.

The courts – and American public opinion – sided with the father. To many Americans it was simply wrong to allow politics to keep a child from his parent. But the Cuban-American community in Miami rallied around Elian's mother's family, supporting its refusal to give him up, and blocking efforts by the authorities to return him. Finally, in April 2000, Attorney-General Janet Reno ordered that he be seized by force – probably damaging her political future in her native state of Florida. Once back in Cuba, Elian became a national hero.

Returning Elian was the largest step the Clinton administration took toward improving relations with Cuba. In the 1990s, relations between Cuba and the United States were never perceived as being of great strategic or economic importance. Clinton saw little to be gained and much to be lost by antagonizing Castro's enemies in the United States. Some day Helms would retire. Some day the indifference of young Cuban-Americans would prevail over the hatred their parents bore toward the Castro regime, And some day, Castro would die. There was no compelling reason to take political risks.

On one other major issue of the policy debate that followed the end of the Cold War, the Clinton administration record was ambivalent. In its unipolar moment, would the United States assert itself unilaterally in pursuit of its goals? Would it take this opportunity to maximize its interests? Or would it behave unlike any other hegemonic power, deferring to the broader interests of the world community, perhaps as represented in the United Nations? Richard Holbrooke subsequently contended that the administration chose to act "multilateral when it can, unilateral only if it must," a pattern he saw as consistent from the days of Franklin Roosevelt through the year 2000. Albright called it "assertive multilateralism."

Certainly George Bush had demonstrated in the Persian Gulf War that the United States could pursue its interests in tandem with other countries – a coalition of the willing – and with due regard for world opinion demonstrated by the request for an enabling resolution from the UN. Rhetorically, the Clinton administration promised to do no less – and it frequently turned to the UN before taking action. But when the UN posed obstacles to what Clinton and his advisers perceived as the appropriate course for the United States, the UN was bypassed. And, as demonstrated in the case of Rwanda, Washington was capable of preventing the UN from taking action UN administrators perceived as essential to stop genocide.

In fairness, it must be noted that support for the United Nations among the American people had diminished over the previous several decades. In the early years of the Cold War, when the UN seemed to function as an extension of American power, when the organization was dominated by the United States, it allies, and nations dependent on American largesse, it had been popular with the public. In the 1960s, when the membership of the UN was greatly enlarged by the admission of newly emergent states, most of which appeared more sympathetic to the Soviet Union than to the United States, American opinion began to shift. The vote of the General Assembly to equate Zionism with racism in 1975 alienated Jewish-Americans and further eroded support among a segment of the population generally internationalist in outlook. Gradually the UN began to appear to be an organization dominated by countries that that did not share the purposes of the United States or the values of the American people.

Congress historically had reflected more parochial interests than the executive branch, especially in its reluctance to appropriate funds for the use of foreigners or foreign organizations that did not clearly and unquestionably serve the interests of the United States. As more and more members of the UN seemed to behave in questionable ways, either supporting the Soviets or failing to give adequate support to the United States, Congress became increasingly reluctant to pay the country's membership dues. Complaints were heard in Washington about the management of the organization, about the quality of its international civil servants, about the excessive influence of Third World countries that contributed little to the UN's finances. Ultimately, the Congress rejected pleas from Presidents Reagan and Bush to pay America's dues in full.

With the end of the Cold War, special interest groups, especially opponents of abortion, were able to press their domestic agendas at the expense of the UN, demanding assurances no money would be used for population control or family planning. When, in 1998, congressmen succeeded in attaching an antiabortion amendment to a bill designed to pay what the United States owed to the UN, Clinton, under pressure from family planning organizations and women's groups, vetoed the bill. Both Congress and the White House demonstrated that domestic concerns outranked the UN in importance.

Of course, no American president could be expected to subordinate American interests to prove its commitment to any international organization. But especially after the Republicans won control of Congress in the 1994 election, Clinton was restrained by the hostility Republican leaders evinced toward the UN and multilateral activities and agreements generally. They were not easily persuaded that a "decent regard for the opinion of mankind" was in the nation's long term interest.

To appease critics of the United Nations, the Clinton administration, led by its ambassador to the UN, Madeline Albright, struck at Boutros Boutros-Ghali, the organization's secretary-general. She and her colleagues blamed him for the debacle in Somalia in 1993. They were displeased by his reluctance to step aside and allow NATO to bypass the Security Council when it undertook airstrikes against Bosnian Serbs or tackled Milosevic in Kosovo. In his unwillingness to serve as a compliant tool of American foreign policy, he had come to symbolize all that was wrong with the UN. Boutros-Ghali's term as secretary-general ended in 1996 and as was customary, he was expected to be re-elected for a second term. All other members of the Security Council agreed to his reelection – but it was vetoed by the United States.

Toward the end of 1999, the United States was on the verge of losing its vote in the UN General Assembly because of its failure to pay its dues. Albright, by then secretary of state, and Holbrooke, her successor at the UN, persuaded Clinton and the Congress to compromise. Clinton agreed to accept a modified version of the amendment restricting abortions, but was allowed to waive the restriction. Congress agreed to appropriate the funds for UN dues, but with provision to reduce the funding each time Clinton used the waiver. We will never know if Clinton would have been willing to sacrifice the UN rather than compromise on abortion restriction if he had been running for re-election in 2000.

The administration's record on several other important issues of multi-lateralism was mixed. Clinton deserves credit for his one success, the Chemical Weapons Convention of 1997. Blame for his several failures, however, can reasonably be directed at Congress. The Convention, banning the production, storage, or use of poison gas had been signed by President Bush in January 1993, after 10 years of negotiations. Clinton made no effort to achieve ratification in his first two years as president – when his party controlled Congress. Inattention rather than politics was probably the cause of the delay. After the Republicans obtained a majority in the Senate and Jessie Helms became chair of the Senate Foreign Relations Committee, the convention was in trouble. Clinton needed substantial Republican support for ratification and that would require some political capital.

An effort to ratify the convention in 1996 failed when Senator Robert Dole (R-Kansas), Republican presidential nominee, opposed it and the administration withdrew it from consideration. After the election, Dole reversed himself, opening the door for another try. Helms and his supporters argued that the United States should not ratify before Iraq, Syria, and North Korea. Ultimately, that tactic failed and after Clinton made several inconsequential bargains with Senator Trent Lott (R-MS), the new Senate majority leader, Lott and 28 other Republicans joined all Democratic senators to provide the votes necessary for ratification.

In 1994, Clinton called for an international ban on the use of antipersonnel mines that were killing and maiming thousands of innocent civilians in various parts of the world – mines often remaining from wars long past. Strong international support was generated by nongovernmental organizations and at a conference in Geneva in 1996, 121 countries signed an agreement to prohibit the use of land mines. The United States was not one of them, largely because of objections voiced by the Pentagon. Antipersonnel mines were viewed by the American military as an essential weapon in the defense of South Korea. The opposition of the Pentagon almost certainly precluded acceptance of the agreement by the Congress and promised to create political problems for Clinton at home. In 1997, the United States announced it would not sign the agreement, to the disgust of participants in the antimine movement worldwide.

Also in 1997, the Clinton administration sent representatives to the Kyoto summit conference on global warming. The urgency of reducing carbon dioxide emissions had been stressed by Clinton in his presidential campaign in 1992 and he attempted, unsuccessfully, to act on his campaign promises. In the United States, industry was opposed, labor was opposed, and the public was not sufficiently concerned to be willing to absorb any costs that might be passed on to it by factories forced to comply with clean air standards. And there were always fringe scientists to argue that global warming was a myth. Internationally, there was broad recognition of the threat to the environment and of the need to act, but the American political context was not promising. In 1995, the Senate passed a resolution unanimously (95 to 0) opposing any binding treaty requiring the United States to reduce emissions that did not apply to developing countries.

In 1997, the American delegation at Kyoto hoped to negotiate concessions with developing countries such as China that would get them to accept limitations on their emerging industries. The Americans failed in that effort, but signed the treaty nonetheless. It never had a chance of approval in the U.S. Senate and Clinton never submitted it for ratification. Global warming was an issue that seemed to engage the president and environmental issues generally had captured the imagination of Vice President Al Gore, but it would require a sea change in American politics before the United States would take the necessary action. Doubtless the administration could have managed the issue better, but success in the effort to ratify an agreement such as that reached at Kyoto was inconceivable given the strength of conservative Republicans in the Senate.

Another Clinton initiative that failed and angered allies and friends across the world was the president's call in 1995 for an international criminal court to try crimes against humanity, to try as war criminals those responsible for horrors such as occurred in Yugoslavia and Rwanda. In 1997, the United States asked the UN General Assembly to create such a tribunal – and it did. When the protocol came up for a vote, however, and was approved 120 to 7, the United States joined several rogue states and Israel in opposition. Again, the Pentagon was critical, fearing American forces might be unjustly accused and forced to stand trial. Controversial American political leaders, such as Henry Kissinger, a hero to most Americans, a war criminal to a handful, feared being brought up on charges. European diplomats worked frantically to meet American concerns, yielding on point after point, but when the treaty to establish the International Criminal Court was presented in 1998, the Clinton administration refused to sign, angering much of the world. On December 31, 2000, as he prepared to leave the White House, Clinton did in fact sign the treaty, but with a proviso that it would not be submitted to the Senate for ratification until all American objections were met. It was not a pretty performance.

One treaty that gained popular support in the United States was the Comprehensive Test Ban Treaty (CTBT) that meant to put an end to all testing of nuclear weapons. Helms refused to hold hearings on the treaty, convinced it was flawed, and prevented a vote as a means of blackmailing the administration into making concessions to him on other issues. In this instance, Lott proved unwilling to circumvent Helms.

Clinton had signed the treaty in September 1996 and in September 1997 submitted it to the Senate – where Helms kept it bottled up for two years. In 1999, Senator Jon Kyl (R-AZ), organized a group of conservative Republicans who realized they had enough votes to prevent ratification. And then the games began. Kyl proposed that Helms allow the treaty to come up for a vote, but Helms wanted more negative votes to deliver a crushing defeat of the treaty and repudiation of Clinton. Senate Democrats mistakenly believed they could get enough Republican votes to win ratification and challenged Lott, threatening to block the Senate's calendar if he refused to allow a vote. When the Republican caucus was certain it could count on a majority against the treaty, Lott sandbagged the Democrats and agreed to a floor vote.

Belatedly the White House realized what was happening and tried to stop Kyl and Helms, but they and their followers torpedoed efforts by the Republican leadership to reach a compromise. The vote was held and the treaty was defeated, 51 to 48. The next day, in a front page story in the *New York Times,* R.W. Apple, comparing the event to the defeat of the Treaty of Versailles, called the vote "the most explicit repudiation of a major international agreement in 80 years" and declared that "it further weakened the already shaky standing of the United States as a global moral leader" (1991).

Defeat of the CTBT manifested all of the problems of Clinton's foreign policy. The administration managed the campaign for ratification poorly, energized only after it was too late. Partisan bitterness on both sides allowed domestic politics to prevail over a major foreign policy issue. Intensely nationalistic ideologues such as Helms and Kyl would yield nothing to world opinion or the importance other national leaders attributed to international cooperation. And many Republican Senators were so hostile to Clinton that they placed repudiation of him above a long-standing security interest of the United States – an end to the testing of nuclear weapons. And so the United States never ratified the treaty.

Writing at about the time of the defeat of the CTBT, one analyst assessed the sum of Clinton's foreign policy as bad but not disastrous – an assessment that is hard to fault. At the conclusion of his term in office, American security was about what it had been when he began, American power seemed greater as a result of economic growth, and the public seemed content with his performance.

The president and his foreign policy advisers did not lack a vision: they were determined to expand the community of free market democracies. But Clinton, despite his degree from the Georgetown University School of Foreign Service and his youthful internship with the Senate Foreign Relations Committee, kept his campaign promise to focus on domestic affairs. His election in 1992 and the election of a nativist Congress in 1994, riddled with men who proudly advertised that they had no passports and had never traveled abroad, demonstrated that with the end of the Cold War, little desire for an activist foreign policy remained among the American people – never known for a deep interest in foreign affairs.

The critical problem with the Clinton administration's foreign policy was the lack of presidential leadership. His appointment of Christopher as secretary of state and Lake as national security adviser compounded the problem. Both were highly intelligent, experienced and able, but neither had the charismatic personality that might have allowed them to compensate for a disengaged president. Their successors, Albright and Berger, proved to be only a marginal improvement. In fairness to Christopher, Lake, Albright, and Berger, it probably would have taken someone as forceful as Dean Acheson or Henry Kissinger to fill the gap.

The other principal – and related – criticism of Clinton's management of foreign policy, levied by friends and foe alike, was of his consistent pandering to public opinion, his constant subordination of international political considerations to domestic politics. His handling of trade policy, humanitarian interventions, NATO expansion, and relations with China were all tainted by his calculations as to what action would win him political advantage. In defense of his approach, one could argue that in a democracy the will of the people should weigh heavily in presidential decisions. But on foreign policy issues in particular, the public is generally uninformed and America's greatest presidents have taught them and led them and occasionally gotten out in front of them in pursuit of the national interest. They were leaders, but in foreign affairs, Bill Clinton was not.

Of course, it could get worse.

6

THE VULCANS TAKE CHARGE

As Bill Clinton left the White House in January 2001, the United States was riding high as the world's only superpower – or "hyperpower" as a French critic called it. The American economy was in superb condition, serving as the engine that drove growth in the world economy. Democracy was established firmly in most of Eastern Europe, in South Africa, and surging again in Latin America. No immediate threats to the security of the nation appeared on the horizon, although conservatives dissatisfied with Clinton's post-Cold War defense budget warned of a rising China, a danger looming in the not too distant future. North Korea's nuclear weapons program was worrisome, but it was difficult to imagine its unfathomable government launching an attack on the United States. Saddam Hussein's Iraq was a constant annoyance and a potential threat to American interests in the Middle East, but for the moment containment seemed to be working, although challenges to the UN sanctions program were mounting in Europe. Iran was troublesome, both because of its nuclear program and because it was known to support terrorism. However, the election of Khatami as president and indications of the growing strength of moderates in Tehran allowed for a degree of complacency.

Clinton had invested enormous effort in 2000 to brokering a peaceful resolution of the Israeli-Palestinian conflict. He failed, but few faulted him. He had pushed the Israelis to offer greater concessions than they had ever considered before, perhaps more than Israeli Prime Minister Barak could deliver, but it was not enough to satisfy the aspirations of the Palestinian people.

One other concern that had emerged in the 1990s resulted from the terrorist attacks on American embassies in Kenya and Tanzania and on the American destroyer, the *U.S.S. Cole*, as it sat in a Yemeni port. There was no evidence that Iran or any other state in the region was behind the attacks.

It became increasingly apparent that the United States was confronting nonstate terrorism, against which retaliation was difficult. Gradually American intelligence accumulated evidence pointing to a shadowy organization called al Qaeda, led by the wealthy Saudi, Osama bin Laden. An effort to seize bin Laden when he was residing in Sudan was botched. An attempt to kill him with a cruise missile attack on an al Qaeda facility in Afghanistan missed. Coping with this new threat to American interests in the Middle East proved extremely difficult. Worst of all was the possibility that the 1993 bombing of the World Trade Center in New York was linked to al Qaeda – and that other attacks on American soil might be forthcoming.

All of these concerns were passed on to members of the incoming administration of George W. Bush. Bush and his foreign policy team had been sharply critical of Clinton's management of international affairs and were disinclined to give credence to his priorities. They held him responsible for the alleged decline of American military power and pledged to rebuild it. They were contemptuous of humanitarian interventions in general and in Haiti in particular. Nation-building was anathema to them. Clinton had been foolish, they suggested, to waste his energy and risk American credibility trying to resolve the intractable Israeli-Palestinian conflict. They ridiculed his "pin-prick" retaliations against Iraqi transgressions and insisted that China was a strategic "competitor," not the strategic partner Clinton had blessed. Taiwan was worthy of more support than he had offered. They portrayed the Agreed Framework with which Clinton's staff had attempted to stop North Korea's nuclear weapons program as nothing more than bribery, submission to blackmail.

Clinton's policies toward Russia were found wanting by the Bush team. He had been too cozy with the recently departed Boris Yeltsin and had not been sufficiently aggressive in pressing American interests, specifically the need to abrogate the Antiballistic Missile Treaty that obstructed the missile defense system to which the Republicans were committed. Several key Bush advisers were intensely skeptical of the Clinton administration's efforts to work through the United Nations and to participate in international agreements that limited America's freedom of action.

Insofar as they were concerned about terrorism – and they were – the incoming Bush administration was fixated on state-supported terrorism and determined to deal with rogue states, especially those that were believed to possess or to be developing weapons of mass destruction. Al Qaeda was not considered by Bush or any of his principal advisers to be a high priority concern, despite the urgency perceived by holdover specialists on counterterrorism at the National Security Council and the CIA.

Bush's highest priority was to define himself as not Clinton, to differentiate himself from his predecessor and the policies of the previous administration. But foreign policy was no more his passion than it had been Clinton's and he had shown little interest in world affairs prior to becoming his party's candidate for the presidency. Conceivably, disinterest in foreign policy was a way of distinguishing himself from his father. Unlike his father, *xiao* (little) Bush – as the Chinese called him – did have a vision for America's role in the postwar world. It could be called Wilsonian in the sense that he was determined to use the power of the United States to promote American values as well as interests, to spread democracy around the world. Bush, however, did not share Wilson's perception of the importance of international institutions in accomplishing the Wilsonian mission. He was very much an assertive nationalist, determined to shed restraints on the use of American power.

If any voters had been troubled by Bush's ignorance of world affairs, they would have been reassured by the superb, highly experienced team of foreign policy specialists he had assembled to advise him. Of these, Colin Powell was the most widely respected. Among the many important posts he had held were national security adviser to the president and chairman of the Joint Chiefs of Staff. Had he chosen to run for office, he might well have been a nominee of either party for president or vice president. Knowing that Powell was in the Bush camp and likely to serve as secretary of state in a Bush administration provided assurance that foreign affairs would be in safe hands should the Texas governor be elected president. Largely unnoticed was the fact that Powell was not a member of Bush's inner circle, very obviously not one of the close-knit group of advisers who called themselves the "Vulcans." Doubtless unforeseen was the general inability of Powell to direct the course of policy in the years that followed.

The central figure among the Vulcans was Condoleezza Rice, a specialist in Soviet affairs who had served under Brent Scowcroft on the National Security Council during the administration of the elder Bush and gone on to serve as the youngest provost in the history of Stanford University. There were early indications that she was the foreign policy adviser with whom the president-to-be was the most comfortable and it was evident that she would be his national security adviser with an office in the White House and ready access to the president. After Bush took office, she spent many weekends with the Bush family at the Camp David presidential retreat. An exceptionally able analyst and articulator of administration policy, it was soon apparent that she was unable to harness the rest of the president's team, least of all Donald Rumsfeld, a late choice for secretary of defense, and his protégé, the vice president, Dick Cheney. One commentator referred to her as "a marble caught between two elephants."

Another Vulcan was the widely admired Paul Wolfowitz, then dean of the Johns Hopkins School of Advanced International Studies, a man with a distinguished career of service in both the Department of State and the Department of Defense. He had a reputation as both an indifferent administrator and a brilliant analyst and planner. His administrative shortcomings denied him the top post at the Pentagon, but he was named deputy secretary of defense. Although he had been involved in East Asian affairs for much of his career, his writings in the 1990s left little doubt but that his focus in the Bush administration would be the Middle East. He had been gravely disappointed by the survival of Saddam Hussein and his government in 1991 and determined to bring about change in Iraq. He argued that deposing Hussein and replacing his tyrannical regime with a friendly democratic state would be the answer to the region's woes. He seemed convinced that democracy would spread to nearby states, thus serving the interests of the United States and its friends in the Middle East. It was an argument enormously attractive to the neoconservative intellectuals with whom he was often identified.

In 1999, long before Bush's presidential campaign formally began, Rice and Wolfowitz pulled together a group of men with whom they had worked during the Reagan or Bush administrations, both to brief the candidate and to map strategy for his administration. Among them was Richard Armitage, perhaps Powell's closest friend, a man best known for his ability to bench-press 500 pounds. Armitage was a Vietnam veteran who had consistently demonstrated fearless initiative and an ability to get the job done, whether it was rescuing Vietnamese refugees or, as assistant secretary of defense, implementing the Reagan administration's plans for supporting rebels against leftist regimes in the Third World. He was especially well-informed about the affairs of East Asia. Powell had hoped Armitage would be deputy secretary of defense, increasing the likelihood that State and Defense would be able to work in tandem – and protecting Powell's influence from efforts by Defense to control policy. When Wolfowitz was named to that post, Armitage accepted the post as deputy secretary of state.

A less widely admired member of the team was Richard Perle, known among the foreign policy elite in New York and Washington as the "Prince of Darkness." He was considered a leading neoconservative ideologue and an aggressive supporter of the Israeli Right. He and Wolfowitz had worked together on and off for three decades. As an aide to Senator Henry Jackson (D-WA), Perle had been intensely hostile to the Soviet Union, constantly harping on the Soviet threat to American security. He had been a staunch supporter of antiballistic missile systems since the late 1960s and an equally staunch opponent of arms control agreements with the Soviets. Always outspoken and abrasive, he generally worked as a Senate staffer, but also served as assistant secretary of defense during the Reagan years, focusing on Soviet affairs. He would not hold a post in the administration, except to serve as chairman of the Defense Policy Board, an unofficial group that advised the secretary of defense. In the absence of his Soviet bete noire, Perle focused on the Middle East and the threat he perceived from Iraq and Iran. In 2002, he emerged as a leading advocate of war with Iraq.

Ultimately, it was not Powell or any of the Vulcans who dominated the foreign policy agenda of President Bush, but rather Dick Cheney, the man he selected as his running-mate in the 2000 election. Cheney was the consummate Washington insider. He had served in Congress, as White House chief of staff, and as secretary of defense – where his relationship with Powell had been cool. He knew where all the levers of power were and how to use them. As vice president he was more involved in the foreign policy process than any of his predecessors. He immediately set up his own national security council, headed by a Wolfowitz protégé. Men associated with him filled many of the key positions in the national security bureaucracy.

Cheney had been among the last American leaders to concede that the Cold War was over and no one surpassed him in conceiving of justifications for increasing American military power. And he had little use for the United Nations or any other multilateral organizations that might restrict America's freedom to act as it chose to anywhere on the globe. Like the president he served, he was very much an assertive nationalist, but he seemed less committed to the vision of spreading democracy that the president had come to share with the neoconservatives. For Cheney, it would be enough to crush any state or organization that obstructed pursuit of the interests of the United States or threatened its security.

Bush and his foreign policy team wasted little time demonstrating that it would embrace wholeheartedly the unilateralist approach to the world that Washington had adopted after the Cold War. Unlike Clinton, Bush was never embarrassed when he chose to ignore the opinions of the rest of the world's leaders. His administration never attempted to blame congressional restraints or pressure from the Pentagon for its blatantly self-interested approach. An early signal was the appointment, at the insistence of the White House, of John Bolton as undersecretary of state for arms control and international security. Bolton was notorious for his contempt for international law and international treaties and he lived up to his reputation.

One agreement that outraged Bolton was the Agreed Framework that the Clinton administration had designed in 1994 to halt North Korea's nuclear program. In March 2001, Powell indicated that the Bush administration would continue on the course set by Clinton, but Bolton and those of like mind in the White House had no such intention. The day after Powell spoke, Bush undermined him by telling Kim Dae Jung, the South Korean president, that he did not trust the North Koreans and had no intention of talking to them. He was dismissive of Kim's "Sunshine policy," designed to seek accommodation with the North. Pyongyang could yield to American demands for verification of its promises or the United States would wait until the North Korean regime was replaced by a regime more to Washington's liking. Not only were Koreans, both North and South, put on notice of a change in American policy, but Powell, too, received a message: the White House and not the secretary of state would make policy.

In the same month, Bush reneged on a campaign promise to take action to lower carbon dioxide emissions from American power plants. Lobbyists for the industry did their work well. Shortly afterward, the White House spokesman stated flatly that the United States would withdraw from the Kyoto Protocol of 1997, the international agreement to reduce CO_2, methane, and other emissions contributing to global warming. Aware of Senate opposition, Clinton had never submitted the Protocol for ratification, but there remained a modicum of hope that a compromise of some sort could be negotiated. Bush had never hidden his disapproval, but his blunt rejection provoked outrage in European capitals. When he traveled to Europe in June, he professed to listen to the objections European leaders raised to his decision, but they were immediately aware that he was merely going through the motions of consulting: his decision was irreversible. The remaining signatories to the Protocol, led by Japan and America's European allies, went ahead without the United States and moved to put the Protocol into effect in 2002. (Russian machinations, withholding ratification while bargaining for trade concessions, delayed implementation for several more years.) Bush doubtless could have achieved the same result by simply neglecting to submit the protocol to the Senate, but that was not to be his style. He much preferred to risk being perceived abroad as arrogant, provided he was viewed at home as decisive and in charge.

Similarly, the administration – not including Powell – was dismissive of arms control treaties. The Comprehensive Test Ban Treaty and efforts to strengthen the Biological Weapons Convention were rejected. The basic philosophy to which Bush adhered was that the terms of treaties like these were observed only by countries such as the United States and its friends. Rogue states that signed could not be trusted to meet their commitments. The result was to produce a false sense of security among Americans. It made no sense to tie the hands of the "good" states while those the president perceived as evil acted as they pleased.

Shortly before he left office, Clinton had agreed to American membership in the International Criminal Court. His administration had handled the negotiations poorly, unnerved by opposition from the Republican-controlled Congress and the Pentagon. Clinton and Albright, unwilling to be lumped with Libya and Iraq in opposition to the Court, won what modifications they could and signed on, but the agreement was not submitted to the Senate. Bush left no doubt that he would never submit it for ratification, but he went further, demanding that the signatories agree that they would never turn an American over to the court. No American could stand trial for war crimes, for crimes against humanity. The Bush administration then bullied its allies, insisting they sign bilateral agreements to exempt Americans from prosecution. The administration cut off military assistance to countries that hesitated and threatened to veto UN peacekeeping missions if the United States did not get its way. No friends were made in the process and many lost, but the American public, ignorant of foreign reactions, was unperturbed. Bush and most of his advisers demonstrated to the world that the United States was law unto itself.

The members of the Bush team had hardly settled into their new offices when the first crisis hit – triggered by the collision between an American spy plane (EP-3) and a Chinese interceptor off the coast of China on April 1, 2001. With the usual arrogance of an incoming administration, Bush and his advisors were confident that they had a better approach to managing the Chinese-American relationship than Clinton had. They would confront the Chinese early, leave them with no doubt of their intent to strengthen Taiwan, and act as necessary to demonstrate that the United States would not allow China to challenge American influence in East Asia or American pre-eminence in the world. They would remind Beijing that the United States looked to Japan and South Korea as its true strategic partners across the Pacific. The new approach was signaled immediately when Bush deliberately excluded Chinese President Jiang Zemin from the list of leaders to whom he placed courtesy calls upon moving into the Oval Office.

In the collision, the Chinese plane fell into the sea and the pilot was never recovered. The American plane made an emergency landing on China's Hainan Island. To the astonishment of the U.S. government, the Chinese detained the crew members and demanded a formal apology from the United States. The instinctive response from the White House was to attempt to intimidate China. In Congress and across the country there was talk of war or other means of forcing the Chinese to comply. The Bush team seemed surprised that the Chinese did not immediately come to heel. Indeed, no senior Chinese official would take calls from Washington or meet with the American ambassador in Beijing.

Fortunately, each government was well represented in the other's capital and their respective ambassadors met with officials authorized to negotiate – Armitage for the United States. After a few days the Chinese accepted an American expression of regret for the loss of their pilot and for the failure of the American crew to obtain clearance before they landed on Chinese territory, although the United States avoided issuing an actual apology for either the EP-3 surveillance mission or the collision. The crisis passed and Bush learned valuable lessons: China was too strong, too important to American business interests to be ignored, and too proud to be dictated to by the American superpower. A little of the humility Bush had promised during the election campaign proved necessary.

For all the attention the Clinton administration had lavished on Boris Yeltsin's Russia, the policy it left to its successor has been described as "benign neglect." As Yeltsin self-destructed in Moscow, Talbott and others concerned with Russian affairs despaired of their efforts to move Russia toward free-market democracy. They were wary of Yeltsin's anointed successor, the erstwhile KGB operative, Vladimir Putin. They backed off and watched.

Russia was, of course, still very important. It had thousands of nuclear weapons, a veto in the United Nations, and, sprawled across the Eurasian continent, its role in Eastern Europe, Central and East Asia, and the Middle East remained significant. Of Bush's advisers, Rice was obviously the most knowledgeable about Russia. She still saw Russia as a potential threat. Cheney had only grudgingly conceded that the Cold War was over. The consensus in the Bush administration was that this was the moment to take advantage of America's overwhelming power to force Moscow to accept decisions that would be unpopular in Russia.

Conservative activists in the United States had demanded a national missile defense (NMD) system since Ronald Reagan had first proposed one in the mid-1980s. The Clinton administration had never indicated comparable enthusiasm for the very expensive project, considered by many scientists to be of questionable feasibility. Bush was committed to build NMD, despite objections from the Russians and Chinese who perceived the system as designed to undermine their nuclear deterrents, giving the United States a first-strike capability to which they might not be able to respond. There was also the issue of an antiballistic missile (ABM) treaty limiting the ABM systems each side could build that the United States had entered into with Moscow during the Cold War – and which appeared to preclude NMD.

The other policy the Bush administration was prepared to press was the continuation of NATO enlargement begun by Clinton. One after another, members of the former Soviet bloc, were inducted into NATO. Even the Baltic states – Latvia, Lithuania, and Estonia – once constituent members of the Union of Soviet Socialist Republics, were in line to join NATO. The Russian minister of defense had been an outspoken opponent of NATO enlargement, demanding to know why NATO was still necessary after the Cold War. He was critical of the use of NATO military power in Yugoslavia in the 1990s. There was no doubt that he perceived enlargement as a threat to Russia's security. His views were widely shared by Russia's foreign policy elite, including many men and women who had welcomed the end of the Cold War and the prospects for Russian-American cooperation.

Bush and Putin met in June 2001 and the meeting went exceptionally well. The two men appeared to like each other and Bush was effusive in praise of his new friend. Putin had played his cards well. He understood that he was powerless to prevent the United States from abrogating the ABM treaty, from building a national missile defense system, or going forward with NATO enlargement. Confronted with American intentions, he yielded gracefully, winning Bush's respect and admiration.

However, on the matter of Russian assistance to Iran's nuclear program, an issue on which he could easily resist Washington's pressure, Putin gave no ground. The sale of Russian nuclear technology to Iran was an important source of income. Putin gently suggested that the hostile policy of the United States toward Iran was counterproductive and that a change might facilitate Russian-American cooperation to monitor Iran's program. A related matter that profoundly troubled American specialists in nuclear affairs, the insecurity of Russian nuclear materials, does not appear to have been raised by Bush or to have been of great concern to his administration. Indeed, after the successful meeting with Putin, Russia dropped off the administration's agenda.

Forced to allow the United States a relatively free hand, Russian leaders were greatly troubled by American unilateralism and explored opportunities to build coalitions that might resist U.S. primacy. Putin found sympathetic audiences in Beijing and several Western European capitals where even American allies longed for a multipolar world in which the United States could be restrained, but although some agreements were reached, they were without substance. Russia would have to accept American hegemony for the foreseeable future.

Problems with China and Russia disposed of for the moment, the president, troubled by the decline in his approval ratings, focused his attention on domestic affairs. His foreign policy team planned its strategy for challenging rogue states, specifically Iraq, Iran, and North Korea. In August 2001, Richard Clarke, the National Security Council's specialist on counterterrorism, a career bureaucrat with a reputation for being abrasively insistent, sent a memorandum to his superiors warning that Osama bin Laden and his al Qaeda operatives were planning to attack the United States. Clarke was convinced that the threat of terrorism was urgent and worthy of the highest priority. Rice and Bush's other advisers were not persuaded. Al Qaeda did not rank high on their agenda. The president felt no sense of urgency. He was much more concerned with Saddam Hussein who, after all, had tried to kill his father.

Of course, all that changed on September 11, 2001. America's view of the world was altered inexorably. American complacency came crashing down with the twin towers of New York's World Trade Center as Osama bin Laden's men, seizing control of airliners departing from Boston and Washington, flew suicide missions against the symbol of U.S. economic power in New York, against the Pentagon, symbolic of the nation's military might. A fourth attack, thwarted over Pennsylvania, had probably targeted either Capitol Hill or the White House. Bin Laden had succeeded in demonstrating the vulnerability of the most powerful country the world had ever known, killing approximately three thousand people in the process.

When the dust had settled and it was deemed safe for the president to return to Washington from the undisclosed location to which he had been flown as the attacks unfolded, he met with his advisers to determine America's response. Rumsfeld and Cheney urged him to invade Iraq. Wolfowitz contended that Iraq was likely to have been involved in the terrorist attacks. An invasion of Iraq would take months of preparation, however, and Bush wanted to act quickly. He understood that the American people wanted immediate retribution against those responsible for the attacks and all available intelligence pointed to bin Laden. Iraq could wait: the president ordered the military to prepare to go after bin Laden, then living in Afghanistan under the protection of the Taliban, a radical Islamist group that controlled most of the country. There would be no more of the timid responses Bush attributed to Clinton. He would demonstrate to bin Laden and the world that the United States could not be attacked with impunity. He would not distinguish between terrorists and states such as Afghanistan that protected them. The Yanks were coming.

Whatever reservations various countries had about the way the Americans had used their power prior to September 11 were put aside as leaders around the world, including Russia's Putin and China's Jiang, expressed their solidarity with Washington. Support was widespread. The United Nations condemned the terrorist attacks. NATO invoked its mutual defense clause for the first time. Many nations offered to help. Whatever reservations members of Congress had had regarding Bush's leadership were put aside. Opposition Democrats joined Republican stalwarts to give the president a free hand to fight the war he had declared on terrorism. His popularity with the American people soared.

After two weeks of diplomatic efforts to persuade the Taliban to turn bin Laden over to the Americans failed, the United States went to war against the Taliban regime with a mandate from the UN. British troops went in alongside the Americans. Indeed, British Prime Minister Tony Blair, once closely associated with Bill Clinton, proved to be a staunch ally of Bush as well. Powell gained the essential support of Pakistan, principal backer of the Taliban regime. But in general, offers of assistance from others were brushed aside. Once the Pentagon devised a plan for the attack, Rumsfeld rejected the idea of building a broad coalition. He wanted no interference with the implementation of the plan. He would not be bothered consulting allies. The United States would act and the rest of the world was expected to follow its lead. Bush's secretary of defense had no interest in encouraging expectations of multilateralism. Acting on behalf of the president, he would direct the war and serve the interests of the country as he saw fit. Increasingly, Rumsfeld would demonstrate utter indifference to the opinions of the leaders or publics of other nations.

The Pentagon's war plan stressed the use of advanced technology rather than American combat troops. Military leaders remained casualty adverse. Special Forces and CIA operatives set the stage, spreading $100 bills among potentially friendly Afghans. When, as has proven so often the case, air power and high tech devices proved insufficient, the United States recruited the troops of the Northern Alliance, Afghan forces hostile to the Taliban, to fight on the ground. The Taliban was routed quickly, but its leaders and al Qaeda leaders escaped into the mountains of Tora Bora. At this point, American tactics proved disastrous. U.S. forces were insufficient to cut off escape routes into Pakistan and American commanders were reluctant to assign their own troops to the deadly dangerous task of pursuing Taliban and al Qaeda fighters into the caves and passes they had chosen for their last stand. The troops of Afghan warlords upon whom the Americans depended, satisfied at driving the Taliban out of the territories they coveted, had little interest in risking their lives to avenge the attacks on the United States. Bin Laden and Mullah Omar, the Taliban leader, disappeared, presumably into the wilds of the Pakistani-Afghan borderlands.

And then, as it had when the Soviets were driven out of Afghanistan more than ten years earlier, the United States all but abandoned the country. The Bush administration had consistently declared its disinterest in peacekeeping and nation-building. Bush, Cheney, and Rumsfeld returned their attention to Iraq. Funds that might have been used for the reconstruction of Afghanistan, to stabilize that war ravaged country, were earmarked instead for an attack against Saddam Hussein. In the years that followed, Afghanistan slid slowly toward anarchy as the American-backed central government proved unable to assert its authority outside of Kabul. Regional warlords, once driven out by the Taliban, ruled much of the country – and stepped up opium production. Gradually Taliban and al Qaeda fighters came out of hiding to attack the American troops remaining in the country, other peacekeepers (who came under NATO command in 2003), foreign aid workers, and government outposts. It appeared that before long, Afghanistan would rejoin the ranks of failed states, breeders of terrorism. The American victory over the Taliban had been easy, but it was by no means certain that anything enduring had been accomplished. Certainly little progress had been made in the war against terrorism. Only in the period immediately preceding the presidential election of 2004 were American troops in Afghanistan reinforced and ordered to resume the hunt for bin Laden.

In the months that followed the horrors of the September 11 suicide attacks in New York and Washington, the Bush administration blithely alienated a world that had been largely sympathetic and supportive in response to the disaster. It initially brushed aside most offers of assistance. It perceived the war in Afghanistan as an American war when it could easily have assembled a broad coalition of states that recognized terrorism was a threat to all societies, not just American, not just Western. Its refusal to treat captives as prisoners of war, entitled to the safeguards of the Geneva Conventions, troubled people everywhere. Insisting that the Afghans and Arabs who fought the invasion were "illegal enemy combatants," many were shipped back to the American naval base at Guantanamo Bay, Cuba, where they were denied legal counsel and where some claim to have been mistreated. The president's chief legal aide advised him that the Geneva Conventions were antiquated and presumably could be ignored or modified unilaterally by the United States. In the view of the president and his advisers, no international agreement needed to be observed if it prevented the United States from acting as it deemed necessary to preserve its security. Sympathy for the United States dissipated rapidly across the world and fears rose that the only remaining superpower was led by – as a columnist for the *Financial Times* later phrased it – "a unilateral bully."

Further evidence of the Bush administration's indifference to the opinion of its allies came in the president's first State of the Union address to Congress in January, 2002. In it, Bush redirected the nation's focus in the war on terror from al Qaeda and other terrorist groups to the need for regime change in rogue states, specifically Iraq, Iran, and North Korea, which he labeled the "axis of evil." He warned that these countries were seeking weapons of mass destruction that they might make available to terrorists. The United States had to take the offensive and prevent that from happening. American power would be used to remake the world in America's image, a world of presumably democratic, peace-loving nations. The allies of the United States were not consulted or forewarned of the details of the speech. The French and German foreign ministers and the spokesman for the European Union, convinced American policy toward Iran was needlessly belligerent, complained of being treated like satellites. The Japanese and South Koreans, engaged in delicate negotiations with the North Koreans were stunned. But Bush was playing to a domestic audience and preparing it for war against Saddam Hussein.

The Bush foreign policy team had concluded that the policies of containment and deterrence used successfully during the Cold War were no longer applicable. Terrorism could not be contained or deterred. In the course of the year, they would lay out their conception of a new approach, beginning with the president's commencement speech at West Point in June 2002. He called upon the young men and women before him to be ready for pre-emptive action. The United States would not stand by and wait for the next terrorist attack. If it perceived an imminent attack or in some way felt threatened, it would strike first. Presumably, the United States, like other states, always, albeit quietly, had reserved the right to pre-empt an attack. But American public rhetoric had stressed that war was legitimate only in self defense – an argument Washington had repeated ever since it negotiated the Paris Peace Pact of 1928 outlawing the use of force as an instrument of national policy.

Bush did not stop with his declaration of America's right to act pre-emptively when an attack on it was imminent or even *preventively* when it suspected a *potential* problem. He also told his audience that the world's most powerful nation intended to remain the world's most powerful nation in perpetuity, acting as necessary to stifle any conceivable challenge. And he backed his rhetoric with dramatically increased military spending. Let the Chinese or any combination of competing states beware!

Three months later, as required by Congress, the Bush administration issued its statement on *National Security Strategy,* underlining the points Bush had made in his commencement address and taking them a step further. The United States would not hesitate to act pre-emptively against terrorists, even if it had to act alone. It was and intended to remain the unchallengeable superpower. And as grist for the neoconservative mill, the document declared that the United States would use its power to promote its democratic values worldwide. Not since Woodrow Wilson had an American president or his administration committed itself to the mission of remaking the world – and Wilson never imagined that the United States would use its military forces unilaterally. In the minds of many commentators, it was a revolution in American foreign policy.

Although the administration hoped to intimidate the three states named as the "axis of evil" and the three others jokingly referred to as the "junior varsity axis," Syria, Libya, and Cuba, its principal target remained Iraq. Tormenting the Castro regime in Cuba was a tactic with significant domestic political value in Florida, where the bulk of the Cuban exile community lived, but Cuba was a low value target. Most of Bush's advisers assumed that Syria and Libya would fall into line quickly once the United States demonstrated its resolve in the Middle East. Iran and North Korea posed far more complicated problems, not least of which was the fact that neither was as vulnerable to American power as was Iraq.

The development of policy toward Iran was hampered by deep divisions within the administration. Rice, Powell, and Armitage, supported by important elder statesmen such as Scowcroft and Thomas Pickering, a distinguished former career diplomat, favored engagement with the Khatami regime. Tehran was clearly interested in rapprochement. Cheney and Rumsfeld, however, insisted that regime change should be the goal of the United States and they were supported by prominent neoconservatives, especially those such as Perle with strong ties to the Israeli Right. Ariel Sharon, Israel's prime minister, insisted Iran was the major threat to the peace and security of the Middle East and there was no question but that the Iranian government supported anti-Israeli terrorists. Indeed, the U.S. Department of State labeled Iran the world's most active sponsor of terrorism.

As troublesome as Tehran's support for terrorism and quest for nuclear weapons was, there remained the fact that it was probably the most important power in the region, as had been evident to American leaders before the Islamic revolution overthrew the Shah, widely perceived as Washington's surrogate in the Middle East. In addition, Iran shared American distaste for the Taliban in Afghanistan and was equally eager to destroy Saddam Hussein's regime in Iraq. Iran conceivably could be of great assistance to the United States.

When al Qaeda struck in New York and Washington on September 11, 2001, Iranian leaders, conservatives as well as reformers, condemned the attacks. In the months that followed, Iran seized several al Qaeda operatives and facilitated American-led coalition operations in Afghanistan. Behind the scenes talks between Iranian and American diplomats indicated that further cooperation between the two countries was possible, that years of enmity that began with the Islamic revolutionaries' seizure of the American embassy in 1979 and subsequent mistreatment of its staff might soon come to an end.

But Cheney and Rumsfeld prevailed in the policy debate and in January 2002 Bush declared Iran to be a member of the axis of evil. The policy of the United States was to encourage revolt in Iran in hope of destroying the Islamic Republic. The effect of the speech was to weaken Iranian reformers, as conservative clerics tightened their grip on the country. The response in Tehran was two-fold. First, to protect Iran against a possible American attack, the Iranians stepped up their efforts to obtain a nuclear deterrent. Second, at the same time, Tehran intensified its efforts toward rapprochement with the United States, offering a roadmap of continued engagement. Unfortunately, the Bush administration was no longer interested.

Similar tensions over policy toward North Korea fractured Bush's foreign policy team along familiar lines. Cheney and Rumsfeld opposed engagement and favored a military solution if Pyongyang did not comply with American demands. Powell and Armitage had argued for a continuation of Clinton's approach, but failed to persuade the president. Bush refused to reaffirm the No Hostile Intent declaration the Clinton administration had offered the North Koreans in 2000 and openly expressed his contempt for Kim Jong Il, who had succeeded his father, Kim Il Sung and was known as the "Dear Leader" of the North Korean regime. The South Koreans, Japanese, and Chinese waited in vain for some kind of constructive approach from Washington.

Finding the Bush administration markedly unfriendly, the North Koreans intensified their nuclear weapons development program. With help from Pakistan they built a Highly Enriched Uranium (HEU) plant to supplement their existing and presumably dormant nuclear facilities and probably produced several nuclear bombs. American intelligence analysts reported on this new activity in November 2001, but Bush and his advisers were preoccupied with Afghanistan – and plans for war against Iraq. Unable to resolve differences within the administration, they simply allowed the North Korean situation to fester.

People knowledgeable about North Korea, both inside and outside the government, argued that there was an urgent need for the United States to resume a dialogue with Pyongyang. Many believed that North Korea's nuclear program posed a grave threat to American interests in East Asia, perhaps to the American people. Its economy was a shambles and its major source of income was the sale of weapons, especially missiles, to any country that could pay for them. The possibility of Pyongyang selling nuclear materials to bin Laden or other terrorists, of becoming the arsenal of terrorism, loomed large. Indeed, evidence later emerged that North Korea had sold uranium to Libya. It seemed a more immediate threat than Iraq.

It took nearly two years, but Powell and Armitage succeeded in winning Bush's approval of a mission to determine what it would take to persuade North Korea to give up its nuclear weapons program. Cheney, Rumsfeld, and Bolton were opposed to the mission, unconvinced that the United States should do anything but wait for the collapse of Kim Jong Il's regime. But the vice president and the secretary of defense were focused on planning the invasion of Iraq. Powell's acquiescence was useful to them. Grudgingly, they were willing to allow the department of state to undertake what they considered a hopeless diplomatic effort – provided Powell's emissary was not authorized to do much more than tell the North Koreans that the United States knew they were in violation of the 1994 Agreed Framework and demand that they dismantle their program.

Talks began in Pyongyang in October 2002. The North Koreans not only did not deny the existence of the HEU program, but declared that they were entitled to have nuclear weapons. The Bush administration now faced an awkward dilemma: how could it justify its plans to attack Iraq on the grounds that it *might* have a nuclear weapons program and at the same time do nothing about North Korea which had an advanced program and probably already had several nuclear bombs?

The initial administration tactic was to conceal the message from Pyongyang from the American people. After the story leaked out, Powell and others insisted there was no crisis, that little had changed. The option of fighting a preventive war against North Korea, of overthrowing Kim Jong Il's government before it could damage American interests or attack the United States, was often considered, but the risks were far too great. North Korea had an enormous army and countless missile launchers within range of Seoul. If attacked, North Korea could easily devastate South Korea. It could strike at Japan. Conceivably, it could launch a missile attack on the United States. In the absence of any perceptible military solution, in a rush to invade Iraq, the Bush team was resigned to leaving the North Korean problem to the diplomats, hoping, perhaps praying, that the Japanese or the Chinese would persuade Pyongyang to back down. But a serious effort by the United States to reach an accommodation with the North Koreans remained unacceptable – and Bolton did everything he could to undermine those who thought otherwise. More immediately, the United States persuaded its allies to cut off fuel supplies to North Korea.

The Chinese and Russians, as well as the South Koreans and Japanese, all fearful of provoking a desperate military action by the North Koreans, insisted that the United States stop increasing the pressure on Pyongyang. Washington called for the IAEA to declare North Korea in violation of inspection agreements and to forward the case to the UN Security Council for disciplinary action. The IAEA stopped short of going to the UN and the Bush administration floundered. As they moved toward war with Iraq, Bush and his advisers did not want a crisis with North Korea.

Kim Jong Il, however, confident of isolating the United States, clearly wanted to generate a crisis. On New Year's Eve, Pyongyang threw out the IAEA inspectors. Shortly afterward, American satellite photographs revealed intense activity at the Yongbyon reactor. Without any effort to disguise their actions, the North Koreans were taking nuclear fuel rods out of the storage to which they had been consigned by the Agreed Framework. There was no reason to doubt that they were determined to produce bombs as quickly as they could to have a credible nuclear deterrent in hand when the Americans finished with Iraq and prepared to move on to their next target.

In mid-January 2003, Bush signaled a major policy shift. He declared publicly that the United States had no intention of attacking North Korea. The United States would consider offering economic assistance and a security agreement to Pyongyang if it would dismantle its nuclear program. The Americans were even willing to talk to the North Koreans, as they were being urged to do by Tokyo and Seoul. On the eve of war with Iraq, the administration – with great reluctance – attempted to play down the crisis. The North Koreans responded by restarting the Yongbyon reactor. Critics at home charged the Bush team with adopting a Clintonesque policy of doing nothing and hoping the evil regime of Kim Jong Il would fade away. But the president was determined to keep the focus on Iraq and received strong support from like-minded neoconservatives.

There was one other issue that begged resolution before the United States invaded a Muslim nation in the Middle East: the Israeli-Palestinian conflict.

Whatever progress had been made through Clinton's efforts in 2000 and the Israeli-Palestinian negotiations in January 2001, vanished in the wake of the election of Ariel Sharon as Israeli premier in February. Probably no Israeli was more feared and hated by the Palestinians and few matched Sharon's contempt for the Palestinians. The second *intifada* intensified and terrorist attacks against Israelis increased.

Given the apparent disinclination of either Arafat or Sharon to work toward a peaceful settlement, the Bush administration saw no point in launching a major American effort to resolve the conflict. The problem seemed intractable and politically dangerous. Eventually, Israel would have to return much of the West Bank and Gaza strip captured in 1967, and accept a viable Palestinian state. Sharon was unlikely to make such concessions voluntarily and American pressure on the Israelis would be unpopular with American Jews, Christian evangelicals among whom Bush had found religious salvation, and other friends of Israel in the United States. Bush was not eager to jump into the fray. He surely remembered that his father had been hurt by his effort to stop new Israeli settlements in the West Bank. And so Palestinians and Israelis went on killing each other in numbers that Washington, at least, found tolerable.

The al Qaeda attacks on the United States in September 2001, forced the administration to assign all of the Middle East a higher priority. As Americans tried to understand why they had been targeted, many analysts pointed to Arab dissatisfaction with persistent American support for Israel and argued that the most useful response to the terrorist attacks would be to re-engage in the Israeli-Palestinian peace process. Others, eager to eliminate Saddam Hussein's regime, contended that the prerequisite to peace in the Middle East was the creation of a democratic Iraq. All of Bush's advisers understood that the Israeli-Palestinian conflict was an essential part of the politics of the Middle East in general and the Persian Gulf region in particular, but they were uncertain as to how to proceed.

Instinctively, the president equated Arab terrorist attacks on the United States with Arab terrorist attacks against Israel. He had no trouble understanding Sharon's retaliatory strikes against the Palestinians. Israeli fears that the horrors of September 11 would undermine American support proved unfounded. Although the U.S.-Israeli relationship grew stronger, Bush, in late September, appealed to Arab opinion by becoming the first American president to support explicitly the creation of a Palestinian state.

But Bush's first priority in the fall of 2001 was to go after bin Laden in Afghanistan – for which he needed support from Pakistan, Uzbekistan, Iran and other states in that region. Before his administration could focus on Israel and the Palestinians, Arafat reinforced Bush's conviction that the Palestinian leader was not interested in peace. In December a new round of bloodshed began, triggered by Palestinian suicide attacks. In January 2002, the Israelis intercepted a ship loaded with weapons and explosives being smuggled into Gaza by the Palestinian Authority for use in the uprising against Israel. Arafat's promise to attempt to curb violence seemed worthless.

In March, Cheney traveled to the Middle East in quest of Arab support for regime change in Iraq, next on Cheney's agenda. Arab leaders with whom he spoke were sympathetic to the idea of ridding the region of Saddam Hussein, but he found them reluctant to align with the United States against an Arab country while the Americans supported Israel's suppression of the Palestinians. Indeed, despite the ruthlessness with which Sharon responded to terrorist atrocities, Bush had labeled him a man of peace. It was evident to the president's advisers that a greater effort to reduce the conflict was essential, if only to demonstrate to the Arab street that the Americans were trying to ease the misery of the Palestinian people. But neither Arafat nor Sharon proved cooperative and Cheney failed to make any progress.

In April, Powell went to Israel to see if he could persuade Arafat to use what limited power he had to stop terrorist acts and to persuade Sharon to stop building Israeli settlements in the West Bank and Gaza, to pull back from the occupied territories, and allow Palestinians who worked in Israel to return. His chances for success were minimal because he lacked any backing in Washington to put pressure on Sharon. He was in no position to be a neutral mediator when Rumsfeld and Wolfowitz insisted that Sharon's crackdown on the Palestinians was a legitimate response to terrorism – and when Cheney and Bush and their domestic political advisers were aware that it was an election year in the United States with nothing to be gained and much to be lost if they appeared the least anti-Israel. Thousands of supporters of Israel had already organized for a demonstration in Washington. Suicide bombings increased in Israel and Sharon seemed more worried by Israeli critics on his right than about any pressure from the United States. Powell returned to Washington more pessimistic than ever about the prospects for peace.

The administration's Middle East initiative of early 2002 failed to restart the peace process and confirmed the majority view on Bush's foreign policy team that it was a hopeless cause. In June, Bush called for a new Palestinian leadership, untainted by support for terrorism. The United States would

not support statehood for the Palestinians until they had a new and democratic leadership. No longer would it waste time and energy trying to work
with Arafat. In addition to abandoning Arafat, the president abandoned
Powell's attempt at being even-handed. The first concessions would have to
come from the Palestinians. And the planning for war with Iraq went on,
despite mounting Arab anger at the American approach to the Israeli-
Palestinian conflict.

★ 7 ★

ONCE UPON AN EMPIRE

In the spring of 1991, after Iraqi forces had been driven out of Kuwait, some idealists, in and out of the U.S. government, urged the elder President Bush to send American troops into Iraq to depose Saddam Hussein and to establish a democratic regime in Baghdad. They envisioned a democratic Iraq becoming the cornerstone of a democratic Middle East. To the relief of analysts who considered themselves realists, the president resisted the temptation for "mission creep." Having liberated Kuwait, he had achieved his purpose.

When, contrary to expectations, Saddam retained power after his defeat, and massacred those who rose against him, Bush was criticized for having ended the war too soon. Various members of his administration then and in the years that followed rose to his defense. In February 1992, the then Secretary of Defense Dick Cheney warned against being "overly fixated on Saddam." Asking how many American lives were worth losing to be rid of Saddam, his own answer was "not very damn many."

Richard Haass, who had served as special assistant to the president and as senior director on the National Security Council during the Persian Gulf War, was one of several former administration officials who defended the president's decision. Writing a few years later in a book designed to advise when American military force should be used in the post-Cold War world, he explained that years of occupation would probably have been necessary to bring about an enduring change in Iraq's political system. He doubted if such an occupation would have been sustainable "in the face of modern media coverage, national and religious sentiments in Iraq, and domestic and international perceptions" (1999). He expressed skepticism as to whether even an extended American presence could bring democracy to Iraq. When Powell became secretary of state in 2001, he chose Haass to direct his Policy Planning Staff.

Even Wolfowitz, usually portrayed as the driving force behind the war on Iraq, in 1997 had offered a prescient defense of the decision not to send American troops to Baghdad to overthrow Saddam's regime. To be sure, he had wanted to continue the fighting beyond the point that it ended so as to weaken the Iraqi military further, but that was to improve the prospects for an uprising. If the Americans did the job, the new government would be the responsibility of the United States. It would require a long occupation that inevitably would be resented.

By 2001, however, frustration with Saddam's games and erosion of the sanctions regime designed to contain him had made the idea of regime change popular across the American political spectrum. His atrocities committed against Iraqi Shiites and Kurds and against any Iraqis unresponsive to his whims or those of his brutal sons rallied human rights advocates to the cause of intervention. And it was increasingly apparent that there was no force in Iraq capable of overthrowing him.

After 9/11, after the Bush administration girded itself for war in Afghanistan and declared itself at war with terrorism, Iraq seemed the obvious next step to several key players. Wolfowitz suspected Saddam was complicit in the al Qaeda attack – although no evidence to support the idea ever emerged. At the president's request, the Pentagon prepared the necessary plans, and in his State of the Union message, in his notorious reference to the "axis of evil," Bush targeted Iraq and threw in Iran and North Korea as well. The administration began a major review of policy toward Iraq with Perle, ostensibly an outsider, making the public case for war. The principal opposition appears to have come from key players in the *elder* Bush's foreign policy team: Brent Scowcroft, James Baker, and Larry Eagleburger. The Democratic Party opposition seemed cowed by the president's soaring popularity after 9/11 and fearful of being perceived as hindering the fight against terrorism.

As the months passed, it became increasingly evident that the administration was determined to overthrow Saddam. The internal debate was no longer over whether to invade but over when to go in, how to attack, what to with Iraq after deposing Saddam, and whether to try to involve the UN. By mid-year, the argument that the most urgent requirement in the Middle East, prerequisite to going after Saddam, was resolution of the Israeli-Palestinian conflict, was brushed aside. The vision of creating a democratic Iraq from which American values would radiate through the region captured the president's imagination. In July, Rice told Haass that the decision for war against Iraq had been made.

Cheney emerged as the most strident advocate for war. In late August, in a speech before the Veterans of Foreign Wars (VFW), he insisted that

Saddam had weapons of mass destruction (WMD) and that he was preparing to use them against the United States and its friends. There was no alternative but to overthrow his regime before he used those weapons. Cheney's growing obsession with the idea of war against Iraq appears to have been triggered by intelligence provided by Ahmed Chalabi's exile group, the Iraqi National Congress, an organization strongly supported by American conservatives, members of Cheney's staff, the civilian leadership at the Pentagon, and perhaps most vociferously of all, Richard Perle. The Defense Department's own Defense Intelligence Agency (DIA) and the State Department's Bureau of Intelligence and Research (INR) were skeptical of Chalabi's sources, but Cheney and Rumsfeld brushed them aside. They set up a competing intelligence unit in the Pentagon which confirmed Chalabi's warnings.

The most highly regarded outside analyst of Iraqi WMD and conventional military capability was Kenneth Pollack, who had been tasked to watch Saddam's military when serving with the CIA and NSC in both the elder Bush and Clinton administrations. In 2002, Pollack was with the Brookings Institution, a generally centrist Washington think tank, probably the most respected in the city. In articles, public appearances, and ultimately in a book published in September 2002, he offered a very nuanced argument for war with Iraq, insisting Saddam had to be overthrown before his regime obtained nuclear weapons. Containment had eroded and deterrence would not be effective against Saddam. But Pollack insisted there was no connection between al Qaeda and Iraq – and that the destruction of al Qaeda had to come first. He feared that the campaign against Iraq might cause a break with allies whose support was needed against bin Laden. There was no rush: he thought Saddam was several years away from having nuclear weapons.

Within the administration, Cheney was also the strongest advocate of unilateral action by the United States and of ignoring the U.S. Congress as well as the UN. He insisted on a broad interpretation of presidential power that precluded the necessity of legislative consent in matters of foreign affairs. He was also opposed vehemently to seeking authorization for war from the UN Security Council, unwilling to risk restraints on the use of American power and insisting that the United States did not require international approval to defend itself. He lost on these two issues to Powell and others who were less enamored of the idea of the imperial presidency and who thought it important at least to attempt to win international support for the use of force against Saddam. At minimum, public support for war would surely be stronger if Congress and the UN approved.

Other issues that emerged involved the number of ground troops needed to overthrow the Iraqi government and planning for what to do after that was accomplished – and who would pay for the postwar reconstruction of Iraq. Pollack called for 200–300,000 soldiers, conceivably all American, to defeat Saddam's forces in one month. He disparaged plans for relying on air power, whatever forces the Iraqi National Congress could raise, and a relatively small American contingent. General Eric Shinseki, Army Chief of Staff, thought he would need several hundred thousand to stabilize the country at war's end. Powell, of course, was author of the doctrine that called for the commitment of overwhelming force. But Cheney, Rumsfeld, and Wolfowitz, perhaps deluded by Chalabi's sources, were convinced that Saddam's army could be defeated with relatively few Americans, perhaps 150,000 at most. Rumsfeld was contemptuous of the Powell Doctrine, pushed Shinseki aside, and argued persuasively that with new technologies and the use of Special Forces, the smaller number would be sufficient.

The peak of self-deception was the conviction expressed most strikingly by Cheney that the Iraqis would welcome American troops as liberators. Elaborate plans prepared by the State Department for postwar Iraq were brushed aside. Management of the war and its aftermath were left to Rumsfeld, who apparently shared Cheney's assumptions as to how U.S. forces would be received and that Iraqis would quietly await the arrival of Chalabi to run the country. Chalabi would install a democratic government in Iraq which would establish friendly relations with Israel and invite the United States to use Iraqi territory for bases from which to intimidate supporters of terrorism in Syria and Iran. Pollack joined those who argued the Pentagon was not prepared for victory in Iraq and, unfortunately, they were proven correct by events.

The several participants in the process of reaching the decision to launch a preventive war against Iraq each had his or her own reasons. Some were genuinely fearful of Saddam's alleged weapons of mass destruction. Some were eager to spread American power and values in the Middle East. Control of Iraqi oil does not appear to have been a high priority for any of them, but all were aware that it would be a useful side effect of the conquest of Iraq. Certainly the intensity of American interest in Iraq and its neighbors had always been rooted in awareness of the importance of access to the region's oil for the industrial and military power of the United States.

Humanitarian concerns were also secondary, but there can be no doubt that they were sincere: Saddam was a brutal tyrant and his people would benefit enormously from his departure. Ultimately, the decision for war was made by the president. He heard all the arguments for war and found them persuasive. But most of all, he was taken by the Wilsonian vision of spreading democracy through the Middle East. Aware that many foreign affairs analysts and leading Republican conservatives such as Kissinger and Scowcroft would prefer a policy more immediately related to American interests, the administration chose the WMD issue as the rationale for war to be presented to the public.

On September 12, 2002, one day after the first anniversary of the terrorist attacks on New York and Washington, President Bush addressed the United Nations General Assembly. His focus, however, was not bin Laden and the war on terrorism, but rather the need for the United Nations to take action against Iraq. The danger that concerned him was Saddam Hussein's possession of weapons of mass destruction that Bush contended were meant to be used against the United States and its allies. Iraq's conduct, its expulsion of UN inspectors, constituted a threat to the authority of the United Nations and to the peace of the world. The United States would ask the Security Council for a new resolution demanding the resumption of inspections. To Americans – and others – uneasy about the administration's unilateralist approach to world affairs, it was comforting to hear his appeal to the international community.

Next, Bush turned to the U.S. Congress and requested authorization to use force against Iraq. The rationale was slightly different from that used with the UN. Again, the administration focused on WMD, arguing that Saddam had used such weapons before and would not hesitate to use them again. Perhaps worst of all, he might give biological, chemical, or nuclear weapons to terrorists. Strong congressional support would demonstrate to UN members and the peoples of the world that the Bush administration had the backing of the American people and would strengthen its hand at the UN and in its overall diplomatic efforts. The president assured Congress that there had been no decision for war. On October 10, the House voted to give the president the authorization he requested and the Senate followed suit the next day, despite strong opposition from many Senate Democrats. All of the Democrats with presidential aspirations – Richard Gephardt (Indiana), the House Minority Leader, Senators John Edwards (North Carolina), John Kerry (Massachusetts), and Joe Lieberman (Connecticut) – voted in favor of the resolution. The debate in the United States was over. But several of America's traditional allies in Europe, most notably France and Germany, remained unpersuaded of the wisdom of Bush's course.

Throughout the fall, thousands of American troops were deployed openly to the vicinity of Iraq, mostly in Kuwait. The Iraqi government took note and suddenly announced that the UN inspectors were welcome to return. Hans Blix, the chief inspector, and the foreign ministries of Europe perceived Saddam yielding to coercive diplomacy – without which the inspections would never have been allowed to resume. In Paris, Berlin, and Moscow, leaders imagined there would be no need for the actual use of force. In November, the Americans and the French crafted a compromise resolution demanding that Iraq surrender all weapons of mass destruction or be declared in "material breach" of UN resolutions. It did not provide the authorization to use force that the United States wanted, but the Bush administration was pleased when the resolution won the unanimous approval of the Security Council. The president believed that it was enough to give legitimacy to an invasion of Iraq and the removal of Saddam. In December, a massive deployment of American forces to the region began. On January 11, 2003, Rumsfeld told the Saudi ambassador that war was certain. Powell was informed subsequently.

Blix and his inspection team initially charged Baghdad with noncompliance, as anticipated by most of the Bush team. It was an opportunity to muster international support for American action, but the president rejected the British proposal for going to the Security Council for a resolution finding Iraq in violation of previous resolutions and thus justifying the use of force. The opportunity disappeared shortly afterward when, presumably in response to Blix's report, the Iraqis became more cooperative. Consistent with Cheney's fears, European leaders interpreted Iraqi actions as evidence that coercive diplomacy was working and that war was unnecessary.

In Washington, Saddam's cooperation with the inspectors was met with palpable disappointment. Still more troubling were indications that Blix's team was not finding evidence of WMD or programs to produce them. American forces were ready to invade and the Pentagon was eager to act before spring, before the high desert heat became a problem. Across Europe, however, it was evident that public opinion was strongly opposed to war. Tony Blair, the British prime minister, Bush's most reliable foreign supporter, pressed for a further effort to obtain UN support to meet his domestic political needs. Finally, in February, Powell introduced the second resolution.

Powell's presentation of the American case for the existence of WMD in Iraq was impressive and won over many skeptics in the United States and perhaps elsewhere for whom he had more credibility than anyone else in the administration. But the French were determined to deny the Americans the legitimization they wanted for their war with Iraq. The Germans, Russians, and Chinese also held out for further inspections, for giving Blix more time. Bush, Cheney, Rumsfeld, and Wolfowitz had no expectation of success with diplomacy, and did not see any need for UN approval for the pending invasion, but to help Blair, the president allowed Powell to keep trying. Even Powell's efforts seemed perfunctory and it was soon evident that the enabling resolution sought by the United States, Great Britain, and Spain had no chance for success – and the effort was abandoned.

By the eve of war, the administration had succeeded in persuading more than half of the American people that Saddam Hussein had been involved in the 9/11 suicide attacks on the United States. The time had come to wreak vengeance upon the alleged perpetrators. Congressional Democrats uneasy about their country acting unilaterally were intimidated by their loss of seats in the November election and either remained quiet or expressed their objections so subtly that few Americans noticed. And so, undeterred by massive antiwar demonstrations all over the world, the United States, the most powerful nation the world had ever known, equipped with the most extraordinary military technology, went to war with a Third World country possessed of a decrepit military armed with obsolete Soviet era weapons. Despite a last minute failure by the United States to obtain permission to operate out of bases in Turkey, the outcome was never in doubt.

On March 19, 2003, having received a report that Saddam would be at a home just outside of Baghdad, President Bush authorized a "decapitation" attack. Operation Iraqi Freedom began. The American military fired missiles at the house in which Saddam was believed to be, hoping to kill him at the outset of the war, perhaps resulting in a quick surrender by a leaderless Iraqi government. The house was destroyed, but Saddam lived on and his troops, with occasional success, resisted the invasion by American and British forces. Across the Middle East, Islamists – including several who had condemned the al Qaeda attacks on the United States – called upon their followers to launch a *jiha*d to defend Iraq against the Americans. Australia, Spain, Poland and a few American client states sent token forces to join the U.S.-led "coalition of the willing." The "bandwagon effect," the expectation of some of the Bush team that most other states would join the Americans once they demonstrated their power and will, was noticeably absent, as was international support for the war generally.

Despite a few tense moments in the early days of the invasion, it took "coalition" forces only three weeks to move into Baghdad and only three weeks more before President Bush, standing on the deck of the *U.S.S Abraham Lincoln*, declared victory. It was May 1, 2003. Unfortunately, it was already apparent that defeat of the Iraqi army had been easy compared to managing the postwar situation. American forces in Baghdad were unprepared for the chaos that followed the destruction of the Iraqi government, for which there was no immediate replacement. There were not enough troops to prevent widespread looting or to provide security for the people of the city. In the absence of any authority, thugs ran rampant through Baghdad. Hospitals, museums, libraries, public buildings generally – even sites believed to have held weapons of mass destruction – were left unprotected and were ransacked. People were robbed and women raped. Residents of Baghdad were left without basic necessities: water, electricity, jobs – and the mood quickly turned ugly. Many Iraqis were doubtless glad to be freed from the tyranny of Saddam's rule, but few could have anticipated the incompetence of their liberators. And Saddam and his sons were nowhere to be found.

The Pentagon had named Jay Garner, a retired general who had won many friends among Iraqi Kurds for his management of a refugee crisis in 1991, to run the new civilian administration. Garner and his team did not arrive in Baghdad until two weeks after the city had fallen to coalition forces and the looting had spun out of control. It quickly became apparent that Garner's team was not up to the task. It lacked the means for establishing law and order across the country and was overwhelmed by the situation. In the north, Kurds who had worked with the Americans and had enjoyed a large degree of independence in the years before the war, established control. In the south, the power vacuum was filled by Shiite religious leaders, some of whom commanded militia forces. As the majority sect in the country, the Shiites expected to lead Iraq after coalition forces left – which they hoped would be soon. But in Baghdad and central Iraq, in the area that came to be known as the Sunni Triangle, forces hostile to the United States and its allies continued to generate unrest. American "liberators" were being killed with increasing frequency. The American military, using its overwhelming firepower in an effort to crush the resistance, killed and wounded many civilians, turning more and more Iraqis against coalition forces.

In Washington, it was becoming apparent that the most optimistic scenario – a quick victory to be followed almost immediately by the assumption of authority in Iraq by an interim government of friendly Iraqis and a sharp reduction of American forces – was a fantasy. However much the Bush team despised the idea of nation-building, there was no alternative. The United States would have to accept responsibility for the occupation of Iraq until the security of its people could be assured and the reconstruction of the country could be put on a firm footing. This was not an assignment for Garner and the team he had assembled. They were shunted aside and Garner was replaced by L. Paul Bremer, a former diplomat and close associate of Henry Kissinger. Bremer became de facto dictator of Iraq for the year that followed – although many of his dictates had little impact outside of the compound in which his Coalition Provisional Authority (CPA) was housed.

Attacks on coalition forces continued to be a daily occurrence and by June at least one American was being killed every day. President Bush was contemptuous of the insurgents: he was quoted as saying "bring 'em on." And the violence escalated, reminding some Americans of the quagmire in which they had found themselves in Vietnam.

Bremer arrived in Baghdad May 12, 2003 and asserted himself immediately. He brushed aside Garner's plan to give significant authority to Iraqi opposition leaders by the end of May. He would not allow the formation of a national assembly. Before long he indicated that an extended occupation would be necessary to achieve stability and to prepare the country for democracy and a market economy. Chalabi and other members of his Iraqi National Congress were openly critical of Bremer's approach, but efforts by Iraqi politicians to appeal over Bremer's head to their sponsors in Washington failed. After a two month struggle, they grudgingly accepted Bremer's plan to create an Iraqi Governing Council, which would be composed of his slate of candidates, and have little power or authority.

The intensifying anti-American insurgency in the Sunni triangle and Shiite demonstrations demanding that the Americans go home forced Washington to reconsider its intent to draw down its forces in the fall. In June, Muqtada al-Sadr, a young Shiite cleric, son of a revered cleric killed by Saddam, raised his own militia to support his opposition to the occupation. The situation in Iraq was deteriorating rapidly. Analysts in the United States and abroad were contending that the Pentagon had greatly underestimated the number of troops necessary to maintain order after the overthrow of Saddam Hussein's regime. The Iraqi army had been disbanded precipitously and Iraqi police and security forces, whom some advocates of the war assumed would quickly return to work, simply vanished. The media began to portray an American government that was bewildered by the failure of its troops to be welcomed as liberators, a government that was stumbling and bumbling. Even Rumsfeld seemed less cocky, less sure of himself as the weeks passed. It was clear that achieving American goals in Iraq would require more time, more money, and more troops than anticipated – and more of everything than what the American public was prepared for and willing to accept.

The Bush administration was also in trouble at home because of its failure to find the weapons of mass destruction, the threat from which it had used to justify going to war. As soon as the Baghdad regime was overthrown, teams of American inspectors searched suspected sites – and found nothing. Interrogation of captured Iraqi officials led nowhere. By the end of May, Rumsfeld conceded that the alleged WMD might not exist, but President Bush vowed to find these weapons – although in June he began to refer to weapons "programs" rather than actual weapons. Questions arose in Great Britain and the United States about the quality of intelligence reports used to defend the decision to attack Iraq. In his State of the Union speech in January 2003, Bush had claimed that the Iraqis had attempted to buy uranium for nuclear weapons in Africa, but the allegation proved false. A scandal over "cooked intelligence" broke in London. In the United States charges that the Bush administration had "cherry-picked" intelligence to suit its preferred course of action were widespread. It was reasonably clear that WMD no longer existed in Iraq and probably had been destroyed years before in grudging compliance with UN demands. The administration would have to find a new rationale for its actions, especially after Wolfowitz admitted that the focus on WMD had been chosen as only the most likely to gain public acceptance.

New tensions between the United States and the UN and between Bremer's Coalition Provisional Authority (CPA) and Grand Ayatollah Ali Sistani, the leading and most revered Shiite cleric, emerged in July. The UN, troubled by Bremer's assertion that it would take one to two years to draft a constitution and hold elections before returning control of the country to the Iraqis, called for a swift transition to Iraqi rule. Sistani, fearful that the majority Shiites and their religious concerns would be slighted by a Bremer-appointed constitutional drafting committee, demanded that the committee be elected. Washington chose to ignore the UN and Bremer succeeded in gaining Sistani's grudging acquiescence to a compromise that fell short of an elected committee.

Toward the end of the month, the U.S. military in Iraq received a tip as to the whereabouts of Saddam's sons, Uday and Qusay, both of whom had reputations for being at least as vicious as their father. The two men were among those killed in the ensuing shoot-out, but if any Americans imagined their deaths would result in a lessening of violence, they were very much mistaken. In the course of the summer, the U.S. military had to acknowledge that it was facing intensified guerrilla warfare – and American casualties mounted. In addition to rocket, mortar, sniper, and roadside mine attacks, car bombs and suicide bombers appeared with increasing frequency. Although the occupation authorities were uncertain as to the numbers and whether they were integrated into the Iraqi insurgency, non-Iraqi *jihadis* had joined the fray. The American presence in Iraq had made it much easier for anti-American forces, al Qaeda-directed or others, to reach their targets. Intelligence reports indicated that volunteers for *jihad* were increasing across the Muslim world.

Symbolic of the inability of coalition forces to contain the insurgency was the tragic bombing of UN headquarters in Baghdad on August 19, 2003 –

including the death of the UN special representative, the greatly admired Brazilian diplomat, Sergio Vieira de Mello. The UN ordered the survivors of its mission to leave Iraq and refused to resume its presence in Baghdad until the security situation improved. The attack on the UN caused various countries and nongovernmental organizations to cancel or delay plans to send personnel to aid in the reconstruction of Iraq.

In Washington, the possibility that the United States would fail to stabilize Iraq or attain any of its more visionary goals there began to be discussed openly. The administration was unwilling to compromise on control of Iraq with either the UN or Iraqis clamoring for self-government. It could not anticipate significant help, military, political, or financial from anywhere. Even in Great Britain opposition to the war and criticism of Blair's support of Bush had soared. American neoconservatives attacked the administration for failing to devote sufficient resources to the cause of democratizing Iraq. Polls showed declining support for the war. Most troubling to the president and his closest advisers were polls that revealed that approval of his leadership was also declining.

Efforts by the US military in Iraq to smash the insurgency became desperate and heavy-handed, alienating more and more Iraqis. Searching for their elusive enemies, American troops forced their way into Iraqi homes, roughing up innocent civilians and terrifying children. They trashed some, perhaps most of the houses they entered. Attacks were launched against presumed hostile forces who turned out to be ordinary Iraqi citizens. By the end of September, the effort to pacify the country had failed, countless Iraqis died, and more Americans had been killed during the occupation than in the war itself. Only in the Kurdish-held areas in the north was there a semblance of security.

On October 3, David Kay, the lead American inspector searching for WMD reported to the House and Senate Intelligence Committees that he had found nothing. Perhaps, he speculated, Saddam had been bluffing, unwilling to reveal the absence of weapons that might deter an attack by the United States or Iran. Despite Cheney's persistent claim of a connection between Iraq and the 9/11 attacks on the United States, no evidence to sustain the claim could be found. Indeed, there was evidence that Saddam had rejected an overture for cooperation from Osama bin Laden. Slowly the administration backed away from using the alleged connection to justify the war. Increasingly, Bush stressed the undisputable fact that the United States had eliminated a brutal dictator, guilty of many atrocities against his own people and his neighbors – a man whose rule would always constitute a threat to the region. In place of Saddam's regime, the United States would enable the Iraqi people to enjoy freedom and democracy. In November, the administration promised to end the occupation, to transfer sovereignty to an Iraqi government on June 30, 2004, after a constitution had been prepared by the Iraqi Governing Council, a national assembly had been elected and had appointed a prime minister.

The insurgency continued. The offices of the International Red Cross were attacked. Italian military police, operating in support of the Coalition Provisional Authority, were attacked. Hotels in which foreign workers and journalists resided were attacked. Large numbers of Iraqi bystanders were killed and the Iraqi public blamed the occupation forces for their failure to stop the bombings and provide reasonable security. Tapes believed to carry the voice of Saddam, urging his people to fight against the invaders, kept appearing. One theory was that Saddam was directing the insurgency: catch him and it would peter out.

And on the evening of December 13, U.S. troops found Saddam, hiding in a "spider hole," a small pit dug into the ground on a farm near his home town of Tikrit. In Baghdad, jubilant Iraqis celebrated the news and praised Americans for the first time since the "liberation" turned sour in March. In the United States, delight was even more widespread. Bush declared that the capture of Saddam ended an era in Iraq, that the tyrant would face justice, and that the path to an independent democratic Iraq was clear. To many Americans it seemed that a corner had been turned in Iraq, that they could see the proverbial "light at the end of the tunnel." Polls confirmed the sense that the capture was a major victory for the administration. Bush's approval ratings rose and concern about the course of the occupation declined.

American military and intelligence analysts were less optimistic. They did not believe Saddam was directing the resistance and the setting in which he was found, specifically the absence of communications equipment, reinforced their views. They did not expect security to improve – and it did not. Attacks on coalition forces and Iraqis who appeared to be collaborating with the occupation authorities continued, even intensified. The American military commander in Iraq warned that his troops would likely remain in Iraq for at least another year or two. In the American media, fears of another Vietnam-like quagmire reappeared.

The plan for creating a transitional government and restoring a semblance of Iraqi sovereignty on June 30 ran into trouble on the ground. The Kurds, having enjoyed virtual autonomy since 1991, told Bremer point blank that they would not surrender the power and freedom they enjoyed to the new government. They received strong support in Washington, especially from military men grateful for the support Kurdish fighters (the *pesh merga*) had given them in the battles against Saddam's forces. Bremer was forced to back off and warned the Bush administration not to press the point. Bremer also ran into obstacles posed by some members of the Iraqi Governing Council, primarily former exiles, who were determined to retain power during and after the transition.

Ultimately it was neither the Kurds nor the Governing Council that forced major changes to the American approach, but rather Ayatollah Sistani. Sistani demanded that the proposed constitution be drafted by democratically elected Iraqis and he wanted assurance that nothing in it would violate Islamic law. To demonstrate his power, 100,000 Iraqis marched peacefully to demand elections. When Bremer tried to explain that elections would take time to organize, Sistani insisted that the UN be brought in to determine whether and when elections would be held. To the chagrin of Bush, Cheney, Rumsfeld, and others in the administration contemptuous of the UN, there was no choice but to beg UN secretary-general Kofi Annan to send a mission to Baghdad. In due course, after wringing assurances of protection for the mission and respect for its conclusions, Annan agreed and sent the former Algerian foreign minister, Lakhdar Brahimi as his special representative. The one issue on which the Bush administration was unyielding was the June 30 end of the occupation. 2004 was, after all, an election year, and the president wanted to campaign as a man who had returned self-rule to the Iraqis.

Before Brahimi reached Baghdad, the failure of Americans to find weapons of mass destruction in Iraq led to renewed criticism of the Bush administration and charges that the president and his foreign policy team had deceived Congress and the American people. Investigations of the intelligence failure were triggered by the resignation of David Kay, chief inspector, and his subsequent testimony before congressional committees. Efforts by the White House to deflect blame to the intelligence community were only marginally successful. The administration had implied there was an immediate threat from Iraq and that was clearly false. Dissatisfied with intelligence reports that could not be used to justify war in the early months of 2003, the administration had assembled an alternative group of analysts who provided precisely the kind of threat analysis the Bush team was looking for. Eventually, in June 2004, CIA director George Tenet resigned, but questions about the legitimacy of the war continued to be raised in the news media – largely a reflection of criticism from prominent political figures as the consensus within the foreign policy elite in support of the war evaporated. A previously docile American press was meeting White House attempts to manage the news with increasing skepticism.

Brahimi arrived in Iraq in mid-February 2004 and immediately supported Sistani's call for direct elections, dooming the American plan for assembly delegates to be selected by regional caucuses. He did concede, however, the validity of the American argument that preparation for elections would take time and Sistani proved amenable to the need for delay – provided the elections were held by the end of 2004, not 2005 as the Americans proposed. Brahimi also endorsed the June 30 date for the proposed turn over of authority from the CPA to an Iraqi interim government, to the relief of the Bush administration. His intention was to replace the CPA-appointed Iraqi Governing Council with a group of nonpolitical technocrats who presumably would not be candidates for elected office.

There remained the matter of the temporary constitution, scheduled to be in place by February 28. Problems had arisen within the Governing Council and both Ayatollah Sistani and the Kurds were taking strong stands that were not easily compromised. There were also questions to be addressed about the status of coalition forces in Iraq after the interim government was established. Bremer argued that the Iraqis would not be able to provide security for the country for some time to come, an indisputable argument – the failure of coalition forces to provide security in the eleven months of the occupation not withstanding. The Governing Council members seemed concerned primarily with retaining their own power after the turnover, fearful that they might be shunted aside or their power diluted by the promised elections. The Kurds were unwilling to surrender their autonomy and Sistani wanted Islamic law to be the foundation of the constitution and the primary source of any subsequent legislation. Both Kurds and Sistani had effective veto power.

Bremer succeeded in forcing essential compromises to get a document signed on March 1. The Kurds were promised broad autonomy, if not the veto power over legislation that they wanted. Islam was to be the official state religion, with guarantees of freedom of religion to others, and Islamic law would be *a* source of legislation – not the primary source. Sistani was assured that no laws contrary to Islamic law could be passed. Women, who had been promised 40 percent of the seats in the national assembly by Bremer and the Governing Council, would have to settle for 25 percent. All involved seemed content for the moment.

On March 2, insurgents made it abundantly clear that drafting a constitution and promising to transfer authority to a provisional government in four months would not bring peace to Iraq. Unknown attackers struck at Shiite mosques in Baghdad and Karbala killing nearly two hundred worshippers. American intelligence pointed to one Abu Musab Zarqari, a Jordanian-born *jihadi* as the mastermind behind the attack, but Shiites focused their anger at the United States for its failure to protect them. Less than two weeks later, terrorists bombed trains in Madrid, killing more than two hundred passengers. Three days later, the people of Spain voted to oust Jose Maria Aznar, the prime minister who had supported President Bush and sent 1,300 Spanish troops to Iraq. His victorious opponent, Jose Luis Rodriquez Zapatero, had campaigned on a promise to withdraw Spanish troops from Iraq and to align Spain with France and Germany, opponents of American policies. To the dismay of the Bush administration, he kept his word.

A year after Bush ordered American forces into action against the regime of Saddam Hussein, Saddam was imprisoned, his sons were dead, and his army was gone. Had overthrowing a tyrant been the principal rationale for the war – or the principal goal of the United States, Americans could have gone home and celebrated. But the war had been sold to the American people as an act essential to destroy Saddam's weapons of mass destruction before he could threaten the United States or its friends in the region or provide such weapons to terrorists. It was portrayed as part of the war on terror. It would bring democracy to Iraq which would then spread throughout the Middle East and enhance the security of Israel. In the event, there were no weapons of mass destruction. The war did nothing to reduce the threat of terrorism. It did not bring democracy to Iraq – although the possibility of democratic Iraq was surely far greater than it had been when Saddam roamed Baghdad.

One year after the war began, Iraqi civilians were being killed almost daily by suicide bombers and assassins. Hundreds of American troops had been killed and thousands more wounded in the months *after* Bush declared victory. Thousands of Iraqis had been killed and wounded by Americans, foreign *jihadis,* or indigenous insurgents. Hundreds of thousands of Iraqis were out of work, among them many of the 400,000 who had lost their jobs when the Americans disbanded the Iraqi army. Crime was rampant in the streets. Security hardly existed outside the compound of the occupation authorities. Even members of the Iraqi Governing Council fell victim to assassins. And the supply of electricity was still uncertain. For all of their suffering, the Iraqis blamed the Americans. Most were grateful to be rid of Saddam, but they had no love for their new "oppressors," the occupation forces of the coalition, and were equally eager to be rid of them.

For the Bush administration, a rapid exit from Iraq was no less desirable. The president had focused his re-election campaign on his leadership in the war on terror – and the fact that that war – as well as the forgotten one in Afghanistan – was going poorly was apparent every day in the front pages of the world's newspapers. It was time to declare victory and get out. Bush and his advisers hoped Brahimi could develop a credible exit plan for them. Perhaps after the nominal transfer of power to the provisional government on June 30, Iraq would disappear from headlines, at least in the United States. Until then, optimists in the administration hoped for evidence that the resistance had been broken and pessimists feared that worse was yet to come. The pessimists proved closer to the mark.

Several events in March and April of 2004 portended disaster for Bush's war in Iraq and its consequences at home. In Washington most of the damage was done by a pair of books. First, Richard Clarke, the top counterterrorism specialist on the National Security Council, a career bureaucrat who had served in several administrations including those of Clinton and Bush, published a volume that reopened the debate on why the United States attacked Iraq. Clarke claimed that Bush had failed to grasp the threat from al Qaeda before 9/11 and had pressed him to implicate Iraq in the attack. He alleged that Bush was fixated on Iraq and had taken the United States into an unnecessary and costly war there that had strengthened terrorism around the world. Clarke proved a credible witness before Congress and efforts by the administration to discredit him failed.

Before the brouhaha over Clarke's book had passed, Bob Woodward, the journalist whose work uncovering the Watergate scandal had made investigative reporting seem the world's most attractive career, published his second book on the Bush administration. Unlike the first one, widely considered uncritical, in *Plan of Attack* Woodward (2004) suggested that Bush was obsessed with Iraq and had decided to go war against Saddam's regime shortly after American forces commenced the attack on Afghanistan. He revealed that the administration had secretly – and probably – illegally diverted funds appropriated for Afghanistan to use for planning the war against Iraq.

Then, on the ground in Iraq, a gruesome atrocity reminded Americans of the inability of coalition forces to provide adequate security. On March 31, four American civilian security contractors were pulled from their car in Fallujah, in the heart of the Sunni triangle, murdered, and their bodies mutilated. TV footage showed hundreds of Iraqis joyously celebrating as the mutilated bodies were exhibited and burned. Coalition troops, specifically American marines, moved on Fallujah, hitting presumed insurgents hard with minimal regard for civilian casualties. Soon nearly all of Fallujah was up in arms against the Americans, who were ultimately forced to back off, lest they alienate the entire population.

At approximately the same time that the marines were engaged in a major confrontation in Fallujah, the CPA decided to attempt to arrest Muqtada al Sadr, the radical Shiite cleric, who had emerged as the spokesman for the Shia of the slums of Baghdad and who had raised a militia army. Bremer was unwilling to tolerate a rogue military force and Sadr was perceived as a thuggish troublemaker. Sadar's army revolted, seized control of the holy city of Najaf and succeeded in rallying many of the majority Shiites to his side. The policies of the occupation authorities were succeeding in uniting Sunnis and Shiites against the United States and the American presence in Iraq. Although coalition forces were able to contain the revolt, they were not able to capture Sadar. A settlement negotiated by moderate Shiite leaders brought a halt to most of the fighting, but left Sadar free to continue competing with Sistani for leadership of the Shiite community – and his forces in control of Najaf and Karbala.

All through Iraq, even in the Kurdish-controlled areas of the north, the level of violence rose. Although most of those killed by the attacks of the insurgents were Iraqis, foreigners were increasingly being kidnapped and murdered in an apparent effort to intimidate and drive out foreign reconstruction workers. The UN was gone, the Red Cross was gone, the NGO presence dwindled, and foreign contract workers became harder to recruit.

Bush insisted the United States would hold firm: its policies were just and it would not falter. By mid-April, however, he endorsed a plan to give the UN a larger role in Iraq. Brahimi rather than Bremer would appoint the interim body to succeed the Iraqi Governing Council on June 30 and the UN would oversee the election scheduled for January 2005. The United States officially conceded "a" central role to the UN, as the administration was forced to surrender to arguments that only the UN could bestow legitimacy on the interim government. With the polls indicating sharply diminishing support for American efforts in Iraq and the presidential election in the United States less than seven months away, the president and his advisers were desperately eager to find a face-saving way out.

Before the month ended, Americans would look far worse as the story broke of the horrors inflicted on Iraqi prisoners at Abu Ghraib by American guards. The photos of prisoners being tormented and humiliated, forced to simulate sexual acts, attacked by dogs, piled naked in human pyramids, beaten, were aired on CBS on the evening of April 28. Quickly the shocking pictures spread around the world: American soldiers, female as well as male, photographing each other grinning while abusing prisoners – souvenirs of their service in Iraq, bringing the blessings of democracy to the Middle East.

The administration could not escape responsibility for the shame Americans felt and the anger directed at the United States by the rest of the world. It was quickly apparent that the abuse had been reported months earlier and nothing had been done to stop it. Evidence emerged at congressional hearings or was dug out by investigative reporters revealing that the administration had deliberately evaded the requirements of the Geneva

Conventions prohibiting mistreatment of POWs in its quest for useful intelligence. So much for the American self-image: was it still possible to insist that Americans didn't do things like that? Could the United States still claim to be the world's foremost champion of human rights? Bush and Rumsfeld tried with minimal success to argue that blame could be limited to a few rogue elements in the military, but the scandal kept creeping up the chain of command. Revelation of the events at Abu Ghraib constituted a setback of enormous proportions.

By May an air of defeatism had settled over Washington. Neoconservatives such as William Kristol of the *Weekly Standard* remained convinced the United States could prevail in Iraq if it used sufficient power, but senior military officers warned the country was on the road to defeat. It might win all the battles – as it claimed in Vietnam – but lose the war nonetheless. American troops in Iraq were likely to suffer casualties for years to come without succeeding in establishing a free and democratic Iraq. And the uniformed military blamed Rumsfeld and Wolfowitz.

The level of violence in Iraq continued to increase, resulting in the deaths of thousands of Iraqis, sometimes scores in one day. On one June day more than a hundred Iraqis were killed by suicide bombers. In May the president of the Iraqi Governing Council was among the victims and the insurgents beheaded an American civilian who was trying to aid the country's reconstruction. In public, at least, President Bush remained confident of ultimate victory, but public approval for the war and for his job performance had dropped sharply. By mid-May a majority of those polled indicated that they disapproved of the way the president was doing his job.

The administration was panicked and in disarray. As Robert Kagan, a leading neoconservative intellectual, charged in late May, it was "clueless." It had no idea of how to get the violence in Iraq under control. It had no idea of how to achieve its goal of transforming Iraq into a democratic state with a free market economy. The dream of sparking democratic reform throughout the Middle East was all but forgotten.

Grudgingly the White House concluded that it had to get additional support from the United Nations to legitimize the Iraqi regime to which it would – at least nominally – turn over power on June 30. Much of the world perceived the heralded transfer of power as a charade. Few people expected the United States to surrender significant control, certainly not of the military forces it intended to keep in Iraq for months, perhaps years after the interim government was anointed. The UN Security Council was amenable to the Anglo-American request for a new resolution restoring sovereignty to Iraq, but it forced major concessions from Washington. Bush had to promise "full sovereignty" to the Iraqis, grant the Iraqi government sole authority to dispose of gas and oil revenues, and allow it control of its own forces – which could opt out of American-led operations. Finally, Washington conceded the right of the Iraqi interim government to order the withdrawal of coalition forces from the country.

Although the administration could claim it had achieved its goal with acceptance of the revised resolution, it suffered an embarrassing defeat in the UN two weeks later. In 2002 the United States had demanded and obtained a grant of immunity from prosecution from the International Criminal Court for American troops engaged in peacekeeping operations. That grant had been renewed in 2003 and the administration sought a further renewal in June 2004. On June 17, Kofi Annan angrily criticized the United States for seeking immunity for its troops. After the exposé of the abuse of prisoners at Abu Ghraib, the American position was untenable. It was clear that the nine votes needed for renewal could not be obtained and a few days later, the United States gave up the effort.

Brahimi's efforts to select the leaders of the new Iraqi interim government were minimally successful. Nor were the Americans able to dictate their choices. As May drew to a close, it became evident that the Iraqi Governing Council, composed largely of former exiles, had no intention of fading away. The men preferred by either Brahimi or Bremer were forced to step aside and the Governing Council selected, from within its ranks, Iyad Allawi as interim prime minister and Ghazi Masahal Al-Yawer for the ceremonial post of president. Most of the cabinet positions were also filled by members of the Governing Council.

All through the summer of 2004 the insurgents stepped up their attacks, focused primarily on Iraqis perceived to be collaborating with the occupation authorities. Foreign fighters linked to al Qaeda found Iraq hospitable terrain and flocked to the country. Nearly one thousand Americans soldiers had been killed in the course of the occupation – in addition, of course, to tens of thousands of Iraqis.

On June 28, in a move that caught Iraqis and the rest of the world by surprise, Paul Bremer, hoping to avoid a major attack on June 30, the date of the scheduled end of the occupation, transferred authority to the Iraqis early, and left the country. In his place came one of the most prominent diplomats in the U.S. government, John Negroponte, the new American ambassador, who would preside over the largest embassy in the world. And 130,000 American soldiers and marines (85 percent of coalition forces) and 20,000 American contractors remained on the ground in Iraq and the violence continued. On the same day, William F. Buckley, doyen of American conservatives, declared: "If I knew then what I know now about what kind of situation we would be in, I would have opposed the war" (in Kirkpatrick 2004). Polls showed that the majority of the American people agreed – and the president's approval ratings continued to sink.

By the time the occupation ended, June 28, 2004, Americans were forced to realize that the war in Iraq had been a war of choice and not of necessity. It was abundantly clear that at the time of President Bush's decision for war, Saddam Hussein no longer had weapons of mass destruction and that his regime, weakened by war and sanctions, no longer posed an imminent threat to the United States or any of its friends in the region. It was equally apparent that there had been no link between Iraq and the al Qaeda attack on the World Trade Center and the Pentagon September 11, 2001. Bush and his foreign policy team had deluded themselves on the issue of WMD and had misled the American people on Saddam's ties to Osama bin Laden. In March 2003, when the United States led coalition forces in an attack on Iraq, Iraq did not constitute a threat to the security of the United States nor would the defeat of Iraq do anything to diminish the menace of terrorism. The war was not necessary.

Did the Americans who gave their lives in Iraq die for nothing? No. Surely the overthrow of Saddam's brutal regime was a great blessing to the Iraqi people. Surely the world is better off with one less vicious tyrant. The defeat and capture of Saddam was a great victory for human rights. Of course, the Bush foreign policy team was composed largely of people who were contemptuous of humanitarian intervention. It seems unlikely that they would have chosen to spend scores of billions of dollars, as well as the lives of so many young Americans, in an effort to improve the human rights situation in Iraq; nor would they likely have found much congressional or public support for such a venture. Even the grand vision to which Bush succumbed, the neoconservative dream of creating a democratic Middle East, would not likely have been marketable in the United States without the illusion that there was an imminent threat to which even hard-nosed realists would respond.

The war to topple Saddam went well. Of that there had been little doubt. But Rumsfeld's rejection of Shinseki's insistence on the need for more troops proved disastrous – not for fighting the war, but for winning the peace. The immediate failure to provide security for the Iraqi people quickly erased their hopes for a better life. Most were surely glad to be freed of Saddam's reign, but they assumed the Americans would preserve and build on the existing infrastructure. When the "liberators" failed to provide normality, thugs took control of the streets of Baghdad and local militias rose to fill the security vacuum. People wanted electricity, clean water, jobs, and safe streets. The Americans provided little of any of that – and Bremer exacerbated the situation by disbanding the Iraqi army. Soon the Iraqis reprised their experience with the British empire in the 1920s and organized a resistance to rid their country of the occupation and gain control of their lives.

The insurgency grew stronger and more sophisticated with each passing month. The death of Saddam's sons and the capture of Saddam did nothing to improve the situation. Ordinary Iraqis, helpless to control their environment, condemned the Americans for failing to stop the misery. In June 2004, polls indicated that only 2 percent of the Iraqi people had a favorable view of the occupation. And then, on June 28, 2004, Bremer left precipitously and quietly. Officially, the occupation was over. Perhaps, indeed, Iraq would slip off the front pages of American newspapers and the Bush administration could claim success in setting the Iraqis on the path to freedom and democracy. But there was no apparent reason to share the administration's optimism. Resistance to the American occupiers continued unabated and *jihadis* from the Middle East, South Asia, and Africa found it easier to achieve martyrdom in Iraq than to find their way to the United States. The January 30, 2005, election allowed some to imagine that they saw the proverbial "light at the end of the tunnel," but the insurgency remained out of control and demand for an exit strategy mounted at home.

★ 8 ★

ALL THE REST – AND BUSH ASSESSED

After 9/11, President Bush focused sharply on his "war against terrorism." He defined himself as a "war president," and employed powers as commander-in-chief that Congress and the media might have challenged in less highly wrought times. By 2003 he had sent American forces to fight Islamic militants in approximately fifty countries across the world. This battle was central to his management of foreign affairs.

Before evaluating the policies of the Bush administration, it is essential to examine briefly the relations of the United States with the rest of the world while American attention was focused on Iraq. Some of Washington's activities were related to the war on terrorism, as in the Philippines where U.S. troops were deployed to help in the local battle against Muslim insurgents. The need for cooperation against terrorists led the United States to overlook the human rights transgressions of its friends in Central Asia, especially Uzbekistan, of the Russians in Chechnya, and the Chinese in Xinjiang. It had little choice but to cozy up to General Pervez Musharraf and the Pakistani military, condemned by Washington when they seized power from a democratically elected government in 1999.

Apparently in response to the American application of force in the Middle East, late in 2003, Libya, on Washington's list of nations that support terrorism, agreed to abandon its nuclear weapons program. Diplomatic ties with Qaddafi's regime were resumed in 2004. Syria, however, after an initial flutter of fear of American forces in neighboring Iraq, became an unrepentant conduit for *jihadi* enroute to engage those American forces.

Even less promising were efforts to maintain pressure on the remaining two members of Bush's "axis of evil," Iran and North Korea, both of which continued their nuclear programs, determined to have credible deterrents against the threat of an American pre-emptive strike. Advocates of regime change within the administration, led by Cheney, Rumsfeld, and Bolton, had succeeded in preventing negotiations with Pyongyang until it became evident that the North Koreans had started a second nuclear weapons program. The talks held in October 2002 were doomed from the outset because the American representative, Assistant Secretary of State James Kelly, lacked authority to negotiate. His mission was designed primarily to pacify Powell and the other concerned parties – China, Japan, South Korea, and Russia. Failing to obtain any American concessions, the North Koreans threw out the IAEA and openly resumed work at Yongbyon.

On the verge of war with Iraq, the administration denied the situation in North Korea constituted a crisis – despite the widespread assumption that the North Koreans already had nuclear weapons and could produce more quickly, perhaps a bomb every month or two. In mid-January 2003, Bush found it expedient to offer conciliatory gestures to Pyongyang, but his attention and energies were focused on Iraq. Once the war started, Kim Jong Il could not compete with Saddam Hussein for media coverage. Although it denied that it was doing so, the Bush administration chose to accept the fact that North Korea was a nuclear power. In response to concerns about Kim selling weapons to terrorists, the administration announced a plan to interdict shipments, hardly reassuring given the ease with which nuclear materials could be hidden and transported.

Into the vacuum created by the failure of the United States to address the crisis in any reasonable fashion, the Chinese stepped, much to the surprise of a world unaccustomed to Chinese initiatives in foreign policy. In April, they volunteered to hold three nation talks and the administration sent Kelly to Beijing, over the objections of Rumsfeld who first opposed participating and then tried to have Bolton substituted for Kelly. The North Koreans insisted on a private meeting, but Kelly was denied permission to meet separately with them. A personal request from the Chinese ambassador, virtually begging the Americans to allow the meeting, was brushed aside.

Using their leverage with Pyongyang, which relied on China for food and fuel supplies, the Chinese won North Korean assent to six nation talks – an American demand – and obtained an American agreement to meet one-on-one with the North Koreans – a North Korean demand – at the multilateral conference. Washington had given Beijing the opportunity to supplant American influence in Northeast Asia and the Chinese seized it. The meeting was convened in Beijing in late August 2003, amidst rumors that Bush was considering offering some concessions, despite opposition from the usual quarters. Bolton did what he could to sabotage the conference with intemperate remarks about North Korea, delivered in Seoul shortly before it convened, but the North Koreans merely denounced him as "human scum" and proceeded to Beijing.

In the private session between the American and North Korean representatives, Kelly was once again restrained from any diplomatic bargaining. He was allowed to suggest the possibility of a joint document, signed by all the participants, assuring Pyongyang that it would not be attacked. He was also allowed to indicate American willingness to offer economic incentives if the North Koreans agreed to the complete, verifiable, irreversible, dismantling (CVID) of their nuclear weapons programs. The administration would go no further, given the preference of the dominant figures in Washington for regime change. The other participants in the meeting saw little prospect for progress when the Americans were so vague in their offerings and so rigid in their demands.

The Chinese refused to give up. Ending the impasse was enormously important to Beijing. A nuclear-armed North Korea had no appeal to them and violence on the Korean peninsula would constitute a threat to their vital interests. They put intense pressure on Pyongyang, winning agreement for further talks in December. In Washington, the Bush administration was torn between the perceived need to respond to criticism that its unwillingness to negotiate was heightening the danger – and the determination of Cheney, Rumsfeld, and Bolton to make no concessions to the North Koreans, at least not before they surrendered to the maximum American demands. As the moment for the December talks approached, Cheney succeeded in getting the president to rebuff Chinese compromise efforts. The North Koreans rejected the Cheney-Rumsfeld-Bolton plan and the talks were postponed to sometime in 2004, an election year in which posturing by the president and Democratic candidates to replace him was assured.

Once the political campaign began, the administration's principal concern was to avoid a crisis over Pyongyang's nuclear weapons. Senator John F. Kerry of Massachusetts, who emerged from the primaries as presumptive Democratic presidential nominee, quickly focused on the refusal to hold direct talks with North Koreans as part of his criticism of Bush's foreign policy. From the perspective of the White House, the issue had to be pushed aside until after the election. Some analysts believed Kim Jong Il also preferred to wait until after the election, hoping that a Kerry administration might be more forthcoming. The Bush team recognized the need at least to appear more flexible, more willing to reach a negotiated settlement.

The Chinese convened another six-nation meeting in February and the Americans went through the motions again. The talks went nowhere and a joint statement implying progress was put aside when the North Koreans backed out unexpectedly. Nonetheless, all parties agreed to meet again in

June. By May the pressure on the Bush administration to show good faith was irresistible. American intelligence estimated the North Koreans now had enough nuclear material for eight bombs. Perhaps even more worrisome was evidence that they had sold uranium material needed to build warheads to Pakistan. North Korea was also assumed to be the source of similar material Libya had obtained on the "black market." Fears that Pyongyang would sell nuclear bomb-making material to anyone able to pay the price grew. Some progress was reported from "mid-level" talks held in Beijing in mid-May and finally, in preparation for the June meeting, Bush changed course.

It was apparent that South Korea and Japan were no longer willing to support the American position. Bush had little choice but to accept their intent to offer to provide fuel oil if North Korea agreed merely to freeze its weapons program. The United States, he announced, would offer "provisional" assurance that it would not attack if North Korea in turn would agree to dismantle its nuclear weapons facilities. North Korea would have three months to shut down these operations and then to admit inspectors to verify their actions. In the interim the United States would be willing to discuss lifting economic sanctions. In other words, Washington would not insist on complete, verifiable, irreversible dismantling as a precondition. Indeed, the Bush administration indicated that it would consider different wording to achieve the same goal.

When the six parties met in June, the North Koreans also showed rare flexibility. They called the new American proposal "constructive" and agreed to meet again in September. Soon afterward, they rejected the three-month timetable, but declared that they believed progress was being made toward a settlement. Efforts by Powell to sweeten the American offer were blocked by Rumsfeld whose mistrust of Pyongyang prevailed. Most analysts anticipated further stalling by both Kim and Bush until after the November elections. Much might depend on how the two men interpreted polling data in September.

And then there was Iran, the remaining member of Bush's "axis of evil." In fact, the Bush administration had no strategy for dealing with Iran. Fantasies of forcing regime change in Tehran as soon as Saddam Hussein was overthrown vanished once the realities of postwar turmoil in Iraq were confronted. As on so many issues, the administration was badly divided on policy toward Iran. Now it was too exhausted by the situation in Iraq and efforts to respond to North Korean provocations to resolve internal differences. So it did virtually nothing and hoped the Europeans or the IAEA or Iranian reformers – somebody – would make the danger go away.

Iran actually posed greater problems than Iraq had. Tehran was relent-
lessly pursuing ballistic missile and nuclear weapons programs – with assistance from Russia. The State Department had labeled Iran the "most active"
state sponsor of terrorism. It supported Hezbollah in its fight against Israel
and Iranian diplomats were believed to have masterminded a major terrorist attack on the Jewish community in Argentina. Iran was opposed to
the peace process in the Middle East. The real power in Iran, Ayatollah Ali
Khameni, was intensely anti-American as well as anti-Israel.

However, Iran had been surprisingly supportive of the United States in
the immediate aftermath of 9/11. The attacks on the World Trade Center
and the Pentagon were denounced by so-called hardliners as well as reformers. Iran cooperated with the Americans in Afghanistan. It, too, was hostile
to the Taliban. The Iranians arrested some al Qaeda operatives and even
permitted the U.S. military to conduct search and rescue operations on
Iranian territory. There were hints coming out of Tehran that it was prepared to reach further toward a rapprochement with the United States.

Bush's "axis of evil" speech stalled efforts to improve relations with Iran
and undermined Iranian reformers. For the moment, contacts were broken
off, to the delight of Cheney and Rumsfeld – and leading neoconservatives
such as Perle and Kristol. Perle considered Iran to be the most dangerous
country in the Middle East. All of these men understood that after
Afghanistan the administration would attack Saddam, but they perceived
Iran as the next target. Of course, the Iranian government also perceived
itself as high on the American hit list.

Washington's demands on Iran had been consistent ever since the end of
the Cold War. The United States insisted that Iran stop posing obstacles to
the Israeli-Palestinian peace process, stop supporting terrorism, and stop
trying to develop nuclear weapons. The Iranians had been unresponsive
throughout the 1990s and the Americans lacked leverage to persuade them.
Its European allies considered U.S. efforts to isolate Iran impractical and
certainly unprofitable. They would not cooperate. The Russians and
Chinese found Iran a wonderful market for their weapons and the Russians, with relatively little to export, were also pushing the sale of nuclear
reactors. In the absence of a strategy for coping with Iran, the administration called on the Iranian people to carry out the regime change the Americans could not accomplish for them.

In May 2003, after victory over Saddam, but before it was evident that
the postwar situation would be a disaster, the Bush foreign policy team was
startled by a new Iranian initiative. Tehran proposed ending its support to
militant Palestinian groups such as Hamas and Islamic Jihad and convert-
ing Hezbollah into a strictly social and political organization. It would be

willing to recognize Israel and a separate Palestinian state. Ali Khameni's representative, who delivered the offer, left unclear Iran's intentions toward its nuclear energy program (Iran had never admitted to a nuclear weapons program). In return, they expected the United States to guarantee Iran's security and to remove economic sanctions.

Once again the administration was immobilized by division. From the sidelines, Brent Scowcroft urged taking up the offer and engaging the Iranians in discussion of all of the issues between the two countries. Within the administration, Powell, Armitage, and Rice responded favorably to engagement. Once again, Cheney and Rumsfeld prevailed. They and their neoconservative supporters wanted regime change in Iran to be the announced policy of the U.S. government and they were convinced of the imminent collapse of the Islamic Republic. They were confident that a new generation of Iranians would transform their country and spark reform throughout the Islamic world — just as they were confident that the overthrow of Saddam would bring democracy to Iraq and spread throughout the Islamic world.

Unable to strike a deal with Washington, Iran accelerated its nuclear weapons program. By the fall of 2003, even the Russians, who were openly supplying nuclear technology, were uneasy. Under pressure from the United States, the IAEA demanded that Iran give a full explanation of its nuclear activities, suspend its uranium enrichment program, and sign an additional protocol to the Nuclear Nonproliferation Treaty that would strengthen safeguards against the production of nuclear weapons — including surprise inspections. The Iranians resisted until less than two weeks from the October 31 deadline. A visit by the foreign ministers of France, Germany, and Great Britain and public pressure from Moscow persuaded the Iranians to comply. Fear of isolation, of sanctions, and of an invasion by U.S. forces contributed to the decision. The United States, conscious of loopholes that would allow Iran to continue to develop weapons, remained suspicious and concerned, but grudgingly endorsed the agreement. For the Americans, the alternative would be another divisive battle with France and Germany.

In the months that followed, the IAEA found increasing evidence that the Iranian government was lying to the inspectors and the international community. In February, 2004 the inspectors found hidden blueprints for a device to enrich uranium. Iran failed to ratify the "additional protocol." In June, the IAEA charged Tehran with cheating on its promise to suspend uranium enrichment and continuing to conceal elements of its nuclear program. Analysts all over the world assumed Iran had every intention of producing nuclear weapons and the ballistic missiles to launch them. It seemed evident that the Iranians would ignore their obligations under the nonproliferation treaty and the promises they had made the previous October.

Tehran's audacity can be explained in part by the astonishing remarks of the Iranian ambassador to the UN at a meeting at the Brookings Institution in Washington in May 2004. Noting the extraordinary difficulty confronting the American occupation forces in Iraq, he said simply that Iran could make life easier for the Americans in Iraq if the Americans would give Iran a pass on its nuclear program. Just as the apparent success of coalition forces in the invasion of Iraq gave pause to some Iranian leaders who feared intransigence would result in an American attack upon Iran, the failure of the occupation assured Ayatollah Khameni that the Americans had no stomach for further military adventures. Iran could safely go nuclear without fear of retaliation. The Middle East was about to become more dangerous than ever.

Of course, for most Arabs and the Iranian leadership, the Israeli-Palestinian conflict was a major concern. Many Muslims viewed the United States through the prism of its policies in support of Israel. The contrast between the American effort in Iraq and Washington's virtual disengagement from the Israeli-Palestinian strife exacerbated Muslim anti-Americanism.

In Israel and in the territories it occupied the violence continued. The Israeli settlements grew and Palestinian gunmen attacked settlers. Israelis carried out "targeted assassinations" against leading militants. Palestinian suicide bombers continued to kill innocent Israelis, and Israeli retaliatory raids killed even more innocent Palestinians. The Americans came to realize that Arafat's Palestinian Authority lacked the power and/or the will to dismantle terrorist groups in the areas over which it presumed to rule. It seemed evident that neither Arafat nor Sharon was interested in a reasonable solution, that peace probably would not come until both men were off the stage – if then.

The Israelis began to build a security barrier to separate Arabs and Israelis on the West Bank. They hoped to be able to protect themselves against suicide attacks, but the barrier would cut Arabs off from some of their lands and constitute a major obstacle for those who sought work in Israel. Washington expressed unhappiness about the barrier and applied some modest pressure on Sharon's government, but to no avail. Sharon and his advisors were confident that they could ignore the Americans without suffering any significant consequences. After all, they knew George Bush would be running for re-election in 2004 and he would not want to alienate Israel's American supporters, both Christian Evangelical and Jewish Zionists.

In November 2003, groups of moderate Israelis and Palestinians holding no government positions announced that they had signed a "Geneva Accord" after approximately two years of negotiations. They agreed to the creation of a Palestinian state, to the dismantling of most Israeli settlements on the West Bank and in Gaza, and the sharing of Jerusalem. They agreed that Israel should have the authority to limit the "right of return" of Palestinians who fled or were driven out of Israel during the Arab-Israeli war of 1948. The accord was similar to the outcome many independent analysts had long argued was the only possible road to peace, but, unfortunately, those who signed it had no authority either in Israel or in Palestinian-controlled areas. It was rejected immediately by Sharon. Secretary of State Powell thought it praiseworthy and agreed to meet with the primary signatories, but the president and the rest of the administration kept their distance.

In December, Sharon surprised the world – including his own Likud Party – by announcing his intention to withdraw unilaterally from the Gaza strip and parts of the West Bank. He would not negotiate with Arafat and because no other Palestinian official could negotiate without Arafat, he would draw the lines where he pleased and retreat behind them. Settlements on the other side of the line would be abandoned, an idea that infuriated Israeli settlers and most members of Likud. Sharon's map meant that part of the West Bank would be annexed to Israel, outraging many Palestinians and their supporters in the Arab world and Europe. In Washington, however, Sharon won the endorsement of President Bush.

A few weeks later, the Likud Party voted against Sharon's plan. Sharon modified it slightly, reshuffled his cabinet to achieve a majority in favor of unilateral withdrawal, and plowed ahead. He had much more trouble with his own party than with Israelis generally – or with the United States. In April 2004, Bush announced a major shift in American policy. For the first time since the Six Day War in 1967, the American government stated that it did not expect Israel to return to its pre-1967 borders and it approved Israel's policy of denying Palestinian refugees the right of return. The administration did urge Sharon to begin dismantling the West Bank settlements and continued to press the point gently in the months that followed. Sharon was unresponsive to Washington's complaints about the barrier's impact on Palestinians, but in June, the Israeli Supreme Court ruled that the path of the barrier had to be redrawn – that security concerns had to be balanced against the hardships being imposed.

Barring extraordinary developments in Israel, the occupied territories, or the United States, it was evident that the Bush administration would do nothing to attempt to resolve the Israeli-Palestinian conflict before the

November presidential election. Both Democratic and Republican politicians pledged their undying support for Israel and there was less questioning of Israeli policy in the United States than there was in Israel.

However, the administration was eager to see elections in Afghanistan before November, to demonstrate the success of its policies there. There was some progress toward the reconstruction of the country and large sums of money became available in 2004, from international donors as well as from the United States. But the Taliban and al Qaeda were determined to prevent the election and mounted a campaign of intimidation against potential voters.

The critical issue in Afghanistan remained the lack of security. Hamid Karzai, the American-backed Afghan president, and his tiny national army had little control of areas outside Kabul. The small NATO-led International Security Force also stayed close to Kabul. Warlord armies outnumbered Karzai's troops by a ratio of more than 10 : 1. And the warlords were overseeing an enormous increase in poppy cultivation, financing their armies by expanding the drug trade. In much of the country, people lived in fear of banditry as well as of the politically and religiously motivated Taliban. The carnage was not as relentless as in Iraq, but Afghan and American troops were constantly under attack by Taliban raiders – and frequently killed. The Taliban also targeted provincial officials and aid workers. Humanitarian organizations, unable to protect their workers, left the country. Many women complained that they had been safer under Taliban rule.

Nonetheless, there was a sliver of hope. Refugees were returning, suggesting that life in Afghanistan looked better than it had before the overthrow of the Taliban. Many Afghans seemed genuinely fascinated by the prospect of voting and attracted by what they understood of democracy. Much would depend on whether the United States, which still had approximately 10,000 troops there in 2004, and other NATO countries would continue to work toward providing security and on the reconstruction of the country.

Much also depended on developments in Pakistan. Pakistan had been the principal supporter of the Taliban prior to 9/11 and the Pakistani military was facilitating terrorist operations in Indian-controlled Kashmir. Afghanistan was considered a client-state that provided Pakistan with strategic depth in its unending struggle against India. After al Qaeda's attack on the United States, however, President Musharraf reversed course. When Washington demanded that he choose sides, he aligned Pakistan with the American cause in Afghanistan. But Musharraf's control of his country was tenuous. Among the Pakistani people, overwhelmingly Muslim, the majority were sympathetic to the Taliban and al Qaeda. In the regions closest to Afghanistan, the dominant local authorities were more likely to provide refuge to bin Laden and Taliban leaders than to turn them over to the Americans. Allying with the United States put Musharraf's life at risk and there were several attempts to assassinate him. There was always the danger that he would be killed or overthrown and the possibility that Pakistan would dissolve into chaos. His was a high-wire act that facilitated American operations in Afghanistan, aided in the apprehension of al Qaeda leaders in Pakistan, but refrained from actions that would trigger open revolt.

Perhaps the greatest American fear regarding Pakistan was that its government would lose control of its nuclear arsenal. Pakistan had never signed the Nuclear Nonproliferation Treaty and in 1998 had tested its weapons and become a declared nuclear power. American intelligence had long suspected Pakistan of being involved with China, Iran, and North Korea in the exchange of plans and materials for the development of nuclear weapons. In February 2004, Abdul Qadeer Khan, the scientist considered by Pakistanis to be a national hero for making their country a nuclear power, confessed to having assisted Libya, Iran, and North Korea in their programs. After a public apology, he was pardoned immediately by Musharraf. The obvious point − that he could not have carried out his operations without the complicity of the Pakistani military and almost certainly Musharraf himself − was not addressed.

Washington accepted the Khan saga as interpreted by Musharraf. In exchange, Musharraf allowed American Special Forces to operate in the mountainous border region abutting Afghanistan − where bin Laden was believed to be hiding. Capturing bin Laden before the president faced the voters in November was a very high administration priority. Thousands of Pakistani troops were sent to the area for the purpose of driving al Qaeda leaders who might be there into the arms of the Americans. There was a vigorous spurt of fighting, but no one of significance was killed or captured and the offensive petered out. The fighting captured headlines in the United States for a few days and then Pakistan, never a major feature of American news coverage, disappeared from the media. Fear of terrorists obtaining nuclear materials did not disappear from the minds of specialists in nonproliferation issues who continued to view Pakistan as the most dangerous country in the world.

The possibility of Pakistan provoking a pre-emptive strike by India also troubled the administration. Musharraf would not or could not stop Islamic terrorists, most with ties to Pakistani military intelligence, from raiding Indian-controlled Kashmir. Twice in the year following 9/11, Pakistan and

India, both armed with nuclear weapons, came close to going to war. The Indian government was losing patience. Washington successfully urged restraint.

Relations between the United States and India were among the few bright spots in American foreign affairs in the early years of the twenty-first century. Throughout the Cold War, India had been an irritating critic of the United States and, although officially neutral, had developed close ties to the Soviet Union. In the 1990s, however, India began to change. Some of its differences with the Americans remained, but they were managed more diplomatically. Of greater importance was India's retreat from the socialist inclinations of its leaders during the first four decades of its existence as an independent state. Major reforms to liberalize its economy were undertaken in 1991.

In the closing years of the Clinton administration, American policies in support of India against Pakistan convinced New Delhi that rapprochement with the United States was in India's national interest. Improvement in relations between the world's two largest democracies was also facilitated by the lobbying activity of the U.S.-India Political Action Committee and the fact that nearly two million Indians were resident in the United States. In March 2000, Clinton traveled to India where he spent five days – compared to a five hour stopover in Pakistan. The message could not have been clearer.

The Bush administration was no less interested in nurturing Indian-American relations. The two countries shared a common interest in fighting against Islamic terrorists. Trade relations soared as did American investment after the Indians opened up their economy and their society became more productive – albeit possibly less equitable than ever. India, with a well-educated, low-wage, English-speaking population, became a major receptor for the outsourcing of American work. Perhaps most striking was the scarcely noted military cooperation between the two countries. Their special forces conducted joint training exercises on Indian and American territory and their navies jointly patrolled the Straits of Malacca and cooperated in the Indian Ocean to keep the sea lanes open for the flow of oil. U.S. warships refueled in Indian ports on both sides of the subcontinent.

The record in Latin America was mixed as that part of the world rarely succeeded in gaining Washington's attention, despite President Bush's interest in Mexico. With the Cold War over, and preoccupied with its war on terrorism generally and on Iraq in particular, the administration made little effort to prevent the election of a leftist government in Brazil. It seemed indifferent to the economic collapse of Argentina. Pandering to the Cuban vote in Florida, however, required actions presumably aimed at the overthrow of Fidel Castro's communist government. Similarly, the democratically elected government of Hugo Chavez in Venezuela became a target of the Bush administration, in large part because of Chavez's overt economic nationalism and his affinity for Castro. Fear of another wave of Haitian boat people to Florida forced Bush to intervene against President Aristide – never a favorite of American conservatives. The major American activity in the region was in Colombia, source of most of the cocaine Americans used and the primary target of the war on drugs.

Outside of Afghanistan and the Middle East, Colombia was the top recipient of security assistance from the United States. Under Plan Colombia, its predecessors and successors, the United States spent billions in what Congress called "The War on Drugs and Thugs." Several hundred American soldiers, several hundred civilian contractors, and scores of helicopters were sent to the country to assist it in suppressing both antigovernment insurgents and the "narco-terrorists" from whom they were not always distinguished. Reports to Congress from the administration and Colombian officials forever reported progress, but the violence within the country continued and the drug traffic to meet American demand barely slowed. Critics in the United States and Colombia complained that too much emphasis was put on a military solution, but suggestions that development aid might be more effective were ignored. The argument that reduction of demand for drugs in the United States was urgent always received polite agreement, but no action.

In return for substantial American aid, Colombia became the only country in South America to join the "coalition of the willing" in support of the Bush administration's war on Iraq. This did not stop the administration from withholding part of the aid for 2003 and threatening to cut it severely or completely in 2004 when Colombia hesitated to grant Americans in Colombia immunity from prosecution by the ICC (International Criminal Court). The threat was effective and Colombia signed the necessary bilateral agreement with the United States.

American policy toward Cuba appalled most analysts but pleased the older generation of Cuban exiles in Miami to whose taste it was presumably tailored. Cuban-Americans contended that they had provided the margin that allowed Bush to claim victory in Florida and win the election in 2000. In return they wanted policy toward Cuba stiffened. They wanted Bush to enforce provisions of the Helms-Burton act that Clinton had waived. They wanted Cuba condemned by the UN Human Rights Commission. They wanted restrictions on travel to Cuba tighted.

Bush understood the importance of appeasing the Miami Cubans, but he was also being pressed by other supporters in the business community and big agriculture to ease sanctions, to allow trade with Cuba. Initially, he gave the Cubans little more than rhetoric and symbolic gestures. He nominated Cuban-born Otto Reich, a great favorite among anti-Castro activists, to be assistant secretary of state for hemispheric affairs, but there was little chance of Reich being confirmed by the Senate. He hosted a huge party at the White House to celebrate Cuba's independence day and told Cuban-Americans he opposed lifting sanctions. Polls, however, showed that the public, including Florida Hispanics, supported Congressional efforts to ease sanctions. Bush's first major act relating to Cuba was to follow Clinton's practice of waiving the provisions of Helms-Burton that would have created problems in relations with most of the friends and allies of the United States.

In the summer of 2001, the administration succeeded in preventing a House vote to lift the ban on travel to Cuba from becoming law. To demonstrate its resolve, it intensified government efforts to crack down on illegal travel. Of the 200,000 Americans who visited Cuba every year, approximately a third did not fall into permitted categories: they were not visiting relatives; they were not journalists; they were not licensed to travel by the Treasury Department. Many simply flew to Cuba from Canada, Mexico, or the Bahamas and entered Cuba without having their passports stamped by Cuban authorities. Over the years little effort had been made to crack down: it simply wasn't worth the bother. But Bush had to demonstrate his bona fides with his Cuban-American supporters.

In November, when Cuba was hit hard by a hurricane, the administration allowed the sale of $30 million in food supplies, presumably as a humanitarian gesture – that also pleased American exporters of agricultural products. Anti-Castro activists begrudged the gesture and were increasingly disappointed with Bush's policies. Certainly in the immediate aftermath of the 9/11 attacks, regime change in Cuba was not a high priority in Washington.

For the next several years, Congress and Bush's domestic political advisers waged a tug of war over the decades-old sanctions that had failed to end Castro's rule. In May 2002, Jimmy Carter visited Cuba and called for lifting the trade embargo. Bush flew to Miami the following week to give a harsh anti-Castro speech, assuring his audience that he would not lift the embargo and would veto any legislation to ease restrictions on trade with or travel to Cuba. The House and Senate at various times passed bills to eliminate travel restrictions and business interests pressed for opportunities. Numerous speakers and analysts argued that the best chance for democracy to emerge in Cuba was to expand trade and to allow more travel between the two countries, but Bush feared alienating Castro's enemies in Florida – and losing the state in the 2004 election.

In 2004, the administration put into effect new travel restrictions that severely limited intellectual and cultural exchanges and, in July, instituted travel restrictions that prevented Cuban-Americans from visiting relatives more than once every three years. The limits on travel to the island by Cuban exiles appeared to divide the Cuban-American community, pleasing Castro's most vocal opponents, but angering others with aging or needy relatives still on the island. It was evident that attitudes among Cuban exiles were changing as those who had fled communism in Cuba in the 1960s began to pass from the scene and a younger generation expressed a willingness to move on to other issues, confident that Castro's days were numbered no matter what American policy might be.

Problems with Haiti continued, long after the Clinton administration restored Aristide to power. His presidency proved to be as disappointing as his most vociferous American critics had anticipated. He was guilty of demagoguery and his administration provided little improvement in the lives of his people. Haiti came no closer to good government or satisfactory economic development. Part of Haiti's problems, however, can be linked to the failure of the United States to provide aid promised by the Clinton administration. Led by Jessie Helms, Congressional Republicans hostile to Aristide blocked the appropriation of funds. It is at least questionable whether the money would have been used wisely and improved conditions in Haiti, but without it, there was virtually no chance that Aristide would succeed.

Aristide's term as the first democratically elected president of Haiti expired in 1996 and he stepped down, to be succeeded by one of his followers. In 2000, there was a disputed election to the Haitian Senate followed by Aristide's unopposed re-election in November. The legitimacy of his government was challenged by his opponents at home and in Washington. The Bush administration was unfriendly from the outset and lobbyists connected to the administration encouraged Aristide's opponents to resist his rule. Initially, Aristide's populist proclivities kept the masses of Haitians on his side against the business elite toward which the Bush administration inclined. But as conditions worsened, Aristide's policies and practices became more erratic and less defensible. His support eroded and before the end of 2003, it was evident that political violence was increasing and civil war or rebellion was likely. Calls for Aristide's resignation were sounded, but he insisted he would stay in office until his term expired in 2006.

By February 2004, armed rebellion was spreading in the country, looting was widespread, and Aristide's government was in danger of being overthrown. Fearing the violence would lead to a flood of Haitian boat people to Florida – with negative political consequences for Bush – the administration sprang to life. Colin Powell flew to Haiti and persuaded Aristide to leave the country, which he did on February 29. He claimed subsequently he had been forced to leave by the Americans and there is surely substance to his complaint. The next day the UN authorized a peacekeeping operation for Haiti and American and French troops moved in to maintain a semblance of order. It seemed unlikely, however, that international forces would remain long enough and international donors would be generous enough to set Haiti on the road to democracy and economic development.

Perhaps the most disappointing of the Bush administration's relationships in Latin American was with Mexico. Initially, Bush and Mexican president Vicente Fox seemed extraordinarily close. Bush's first foreign visit was to Mexico where he and Fox cavorted in their cowboy boots. Fox was the first foreign leader invited to the White House, early in September 2001. Mexico, often an irritant to American leaders in the past, was realigning its foreign policy to be more supportive of the United States. Fox's government cooperated with the United States in its efforts in Colombia. Although its policy toward Cuba was radically different from that of the United States, Mexico became less tolerant of the human rights violations of the Castro regime. Thanks to NAFTA, Mexico had become the second largest trading partner of the United States and there were expectations that it might overtake Canada as number one.

Fox's major request of the Bush administration was for immigration reform, to allow much larger numbers of Mexicans to enter the United States legally. An estimated eight million undocumented Mexicans were believed to be living in the United States. The northward march of Mexican workers was an important safety valve for Mexico, which could not yet provide employment for millions of its people. Bush was sympathetic: many of his supporters were eager to have a source of cheap labor. But others opposed the influx of Spanish-speakers, fearing they would dilute the imagined Anglo-Saxon identity of the American people. It was a tricky political issue that would not have been resolved easily under any circumstances but became nearly impossible after 9/11. Once homeland security became the focus of Washington's attention, every effort was made to raise the barriers against entry to the United States − and no exception was made for Mexicans.

Fox was bitterly disappointed by his inability to win any concessions for Mexican emigrants and he found himself unable to gain the attention of the White House, much as he tried. He was scheduled to meet Bush at the president's Texas ranch in August 2002, but canceled his visit abruptly after Texas executed a Mexican national, notwithstanding a personal plea from Fox to Bush. It was clear that the Bush administration cared little for his priorities and relations between Mexico and the United States cooled appreciably.

Bush's determination to go to war with Iraq created further tensions between Washington and Mexico City. In October 2002, its concerns having been neglected by its northern neighbor, Mexico refused to support the United States in the UN Security Council. In January 2003, the Mexican foreign minister resigned, complaining of his inability to be heard in Washington. To the astonishment of the Bush team, Mexico refused to support the Anglo-American resolution in the Security Council designed to legitimize the invasion. Mexican-American relations were the chilliest they had been in years.

Both Bush and Fox had an interest in repairing their relationship. Bush would need the Latino vote in the 2004 election and Fox was under pressure from Mexico's business community, fearful of some sort of economic reprisal. Fox made the first gesture, firing his ambassador to the UN, a man notable for his outspoken criticism of the policies of the Bush administration. A few months later, in January 2004, Bush announced a broad immigration reform policy that would give undocumented workers "guest worker cards" and allow them to stay in the United States for at least three years. His plan was denounced by advocates for illegal immigrants and nativist organizations alike, but almost everyone saw it as an election ploy that would not get Congressional attention in an election year. Fox, however, professed to see the plan as a useful start and the two men drew closer at a Summit of the Americas meeting in Mexico later that month. In March, Fox visited Bush at his Texas ranch and public relations specialists for both announced that they had agreed to let bygones be bygones. But the political fortunes of Bush and Fox appeared to be in sharp decline with the meeting likely to gain little political benefit for either.

In July 2003, when the adventure in Iraq had turned sour and much of the world seemed hostile to Bush, the president traveled to Africa, ostensibly to boost the fight against the AIDs epidemic that was ravaging the continent. Africa had little strategic value to the United States after the Cold War, but was increasingly an important source of oil. At the time of the Bush visit Africa – primarily Nigeria and Angola – was providing between 15 and 20 percent of American oil imports, a figure expected to rise to 25 percent over the next decade. American businessmen had invested tens of billions of dollars in Nigeria and elsewhere in West Africa. The president was persuaded that it would be useful to show the flag – and to demonstrate humanitarian as well as economic concerns.

While Bush was in Africa, a brutal civil war raged in Liberia, a nation with links to the United States that dated back to the early nineteenth century, when American black nationalists had established a colony there. For much of its subsequent history, the country had been ruled by Liberians of American descent. In the 1920s, the Firestone corporation had invested in rubber plantations there. During the Cold War, especially during the Reagan administration, the United States had provided substantial aid to the Liberian government, although American-Liberians had lost control and the various regimes in Monrovia were undemocratic, often vicious. After the Cold War, Washington lost interest in Liberia and withdrew support abruptly. It had no commodity of importance to the United States, no useful bases. The country's weak economy grew worse, its government best described as kleptocratic. Beginning in 2000 a rebellion took root and brought extraordinary misery to the Liberian people. By July 2003, the country undeniably had become a humanitarian disaster.

Bush had expressed concern for the well-being of the people of Africa and pressure began to build for the United States to do something to stop the carnage in Liberia. Colin Powell spoke of the historical ties between the two countries and the obligation of the world's most powerful nation to help. But American forces were already stretched thin in Iraq and Afghanistan. Not unreasonably, Washington chose to leave the task to West African, primarily Nigerian, troops who moved into Liberia as peacekeepers. Unwilling to look unconcerned or helpless, the Bush administration sent 2,000 American marines to the coast of Liberia, to provide support for the peacekeepers. It would not lead and it would not send troops ashore. Happily for all concerned, the war wound down in August as Charles Taylor, the troublesome Liberian president, resigned and accepted exile in Nigeria.

Although the administration was similarly unwilling to use American power in 2004 to stop ethnic cleansing in Sudan, its performance compared credibly with that of the rest of the developed world. Civil strife between the primarily Arab Muslim north and the largely black Christian south had begun in Sudan on the eve of independence in 1955. In the 1990s, American evangelicals, horrified by the deaths of nearly two million Christians in the fighting, had raised money to help victims and they won support in Congress for their efforts to stop the fighting. Clinton was never engaged, but Bush took up the cause in on the eve of 9/11. He sent a highly respected former Missouri senator, John Dansforth, to Sudan to press for peace talks between the Arab Muslim dominated government and the black Christian rebels of southern Sudan. Dansforth met with success in bringing north and south together late in 2003, but the government, as it eased its raids in the south, began bombing its people in Darfur, in western Sudan. In addition, the regime armed Arab tribesmen, called *janjaweed*, to raid the villages of Darfur, killing the men, raping the women, stealing everything that could be moved, and destroying the rest. The people of Darfur were almost all Muslims, but they, too, were black, and viewed with contempt by Arab Muslims. The government's intention was to drive them out of the country – and few people in the rest of the world seemed concerned.

It was March, 2004, before the UN humanitarian coordinator called events in Darfur "ethnic cleansing." President Bush was quick to condemn the attacks and demanded that Khartoum stop abetting them. His own officials warned that even if there were a substantial increase in world aid, three hundred thousand people would die before the year was out. Without that additional aid, a million lives might be lost. Powell joined Kofi Annan in asking the Sudanese government to stop the massacres, but there was no follow up. In the spring and summer of 2004, the American media began to publicize the atrocities and in July, a Congressional resolution labeled the killings "genocide." The Bush administration contributed nearly two hundred million dollars in relief aid to the refugees from Darfur and tried unsuccessfully to get the UN Human Rights Commission to issue a strong denunciation of the atrocities. It received virtually no support from Europe. France refused to contribute to the UN's relief program and Germany gave but one million dollars. Hostile to the Bush team for its past unilateralism and self-righteousness, the world's other major powers did not rally to America's side, even in so worthy a cause. Bush had forfeited Washington's right to lead – and the people of Darfur were paying the price.

After 9/11, Russia faded from the view of the Bush administration, despite Condoleezza Rice's specialized knowledge of and interest in the country. No senior official had comparable interest in or knowledge of Chinese affairs, but the need for China's help in coping with North Korea, and the simmering tensions in the Taiwan Strait compelled occasional attention to Beijing's concerns. Moreover, while Russia was arguably a declining power, China, with its extraordinary economic growth, most obviously was not.

Putin had opposed the American invasion of Iraq and the Russians were clearly uneasy about Washington's unilateralism and Bush's doctrine of preventive war. They were profoundly displeased by the continued expansion of NATO, including acceptance of the Baltic states. They foresaw and warned against the movement of NATO's bases eastward, toward Russia, questioning why NATO even needed to exist after the Cold War. Russian complaints were ignored by the Bush administration.

A major American interest in the 1990s had been promotion of democracy in Russia. By 2004 it was evident that efforts in that direction had failed. Although the Bush administration professed that fostering democracy was its central goal in Iraq and the Middle East, only Colin Powell expressed unhappiness with the fact that Putin and his comrades from the former KGB were eliminating opposition and silencing critics in Russia. It was not Soviet-style totalitarianism, but Putin's authoritarian rule was surely reminiscent of Tsarist Russia. And an American government that countenanced the horrors of Abu Ghraib had lost the moral authority to criticize Russian brutality in Chechnya.

China's surging power forced Washington to treat it with increasing respect and, on occasion, even deference. China had become the engine of economic growth in East Asia, supplanting Japan, and it was poised to challenge American political and strategic influence in the region. Chinese foreign policy was less passive and its diplomats were becoming increasingly skillful. China's leaders and foreign policy intellectuals were transcending the victim mentality so prominent in the last half of the twentieth century and beginning to accept for their country the role of a great power. The changes were most apparent in China's dominant role in the effort to resolve the North Korean nuclear crisis.

Fortunately, the tensions that arose out of the spy plane incident in April 2001, had begun to ease before 9/11. Bush had learned that although tough anti-Chinese rhetoric played well with some of his constituents, it was not in the national interest. Talk of China as a strategic competitor disappeared, replaced with emphasis on the constructive and cooperative nature of the relationship. The Chinese, although uncomfortable with the new American military presence in Central Asia, portrayed themselves as united with the Americans in opposition to global terrorism. Similarly, the Chinese did not allow their unease about American unilateralism in general and the war in Iraq in particular to roil the bilateral relationship.

Most of the issues between the two countries proved manageable. Knowledgeable Americans remained troubled by human rights violations in China and the refusal of the Beijing government to tell its people the truth about the Tiananmen massacres of 1989, but for the most part, the Bush administration muted its criticism – even to the point of dropping efforts to have China condemned by the UN Human Rights Commission until 2004.

Concerns that increased about the erosion of the freedoms promised to the people of Hong Kong also were expressed quietly, to the disappointment of Bush's neoconservative supporters.

Similarly, American irritation with China's continuing role as a proliferator of missile and nuclear technology did not generate any crises. The Chinese continued to sell dual-use materials to Pakistan and Iran and Washington continued to complain. Occasionally, specific Chinese companies were hit with sanctions. Chinese protests were pro forma. Occasionally, Congress pressed the administration to do something about the imbalance in trade between the two countries and the secretary of the treasury or some lesser official would ask the Chinese to do something about it. As they always did when caught proliferating or pirating movies and CDs, they responded with empty promises.

Of course, the one major flashpoint, the Taiwan Strait, allowed for no such complacency, if for no other reason than that it was not a bilateral issue. As often as not, it was the Taipei government that stirred the pot. Initially, troubled by the PLA's modernization program and preparations for attacking Taiwan – and the missile buildup in China across the Strait from Taiwan – Bush had warned that the United States would defend the island against an unprovoked attack. "Unprovoked," however, was subject to interpretation and Taiwan's President Chen Shui-bian, leader of the pro-independence Democratic People's Party, kept trying Beijing's patience with gestures and rhetoric designed to win more international space for Taiwan.

The Chinese contended that American arms sales encouraged Chen's troublesome behavior. Bush was caught in an exceptionally difficult position: he needed a good working relationship with China for a host of very important reasons, but he could not allow himself to be perceived as betraying the interests of democratic Taiwan. In December 2003, to the dismay of Taiwan's leaders and the American friends of Taiwan, Bush publicly warned Taipei against taking unilateral action toward independence. Most shocking was his decision to issue the warning in the company of Chinese Premier Wen Jiabao.

There was little doubt that Beijing and Washington both hoped to see Chen defeated in Taiwan's March presidential election. The Kuomintang Party, the party of the late Chiang Kai-shek and Chiang Ching-kuo, was perceived as less likely to be provocative, more willing to accept the one-China principle considered the best hope for an eventual peaceful resolution of the perennial Strait crises. But Chen won a narrow, disputed victory, trimmed his sails a bit, and both the Bush administration and the government of China's new president, Hu Jintao, swallowed their disappointment and waited for Chen's next provocation. Washington continued to counsel

China to be patient and did what little it could to rein in Chen. Beijing, of course, never thought the Americans were doing enough.

The foreign policy team Bush assembled for his first term easily constituted the equal of John F. Kennedy's "best and the brightest." Its members were all highly intelligent, experienced, and thoughtful – and like Kennedy's team the policies they advised took the nation to the brink of disaster. They brushed aside warnings about bin Laden and al Qaeda and focused on the threat they perceived from rogue states, precluding any possibility of averting the 9/11 attacks and the devastation those caused. Even after 9/11, they directed most of the nation's power and energy toward the overthrow of Saddam Hussein. In the course of their obsessive pursuit of war with Iraq they alienated many of America's friends in the world and generated enormous resentment against perceived bullying by the United States. As a result of their delusions about what would happen in Iraq, they mired the American army in a quagmire of their own creation. At the conclusion of Bush's first term in 2004, the American people were less safe than they had been at any time in the post-Cold War world and the United States was held in lower esteem by other nations and peoples than at any time in the twentieth century.

Iraq was the prism through which the Bush administration's foreign policy was examined and found wanting. To its credit, it had rid the Iraqi people of the scourge of a brutal dictator – surely a worthwhile accomplishment. It was, however, guilty of criminal neglect for its failure to plan adequately for the aftermath of the war. Again, there had been warnings from within the bureaucracy and from senior aides of the president's father, but the president, the vice president, the secretary of defense, and those they relied on for advice ignored the warnings and imagined a quick handover of power to a pro-American democratic Iraqi government that would finance its own reconstruction with its oil revenues. The contrast between their vision and reality was so enormous as to be laughable – were it not for the ensuing suffering of the Iraqi people, the loss of American lives, and the price the American people would be condemned to pay for years to come.

With its military bogged down in Iraq and most of the rest of the world mistrustful of American claims and motives, the Bush administration was unable to cope with the more serious nuclear weapons programs of Iran and North Korea. The president's bluster about the "axis of evil" and the need for regime change had convinced Pyongyang and Tehran of the need to continue their programs for producing a nuclear deterrent. Despite fantasies about what the United States, the sole superpower, could accomplish unilaterally, the Bush team was forced to concede that it could not confront Iran or North Korea alone. Pre-emption or preventive war was not a feasible option. In the case of Iran, the United States had little choice but to defer to the European Union and the IAEA preference for negotiation and to pray that Iran would be responsive. Refusing to negotiate with North Korea, the Bush team left the future of North Korea's nuclear weapons largely in China's hands, apparently willing to surrender longstanding American strategic dominance in the region.

Less immediately damaging to the security of the United States was the unwillingness of the Bush administration to confront long-term threats to the environment or to use American wealth and power to ameliorate miseries such as the spread of AIDS, especially in Africa. The president made reasonable promises, but they were never kept. On the environmental issues, the administration consistently catered to the interest of domestic constituencies that opposed regulation, especially if it resulted from international agreements premised on the assumption that clean air, clean water, or other environmental protection measures are a public good. Only a fraction of the funding the president offered to help combat AIDS was forthcoming.

Across the world, the actions and rhetoric of the Bush administration turned opinion against the United States. Perhaps the starkest example was Indonesia where attitudes that had been 75 percent positive in 2000 became 83 percent negative in 2003. Resentment against the United States was strongest in Muslim countries, not because of American values but because of administration policies. Muslims were angered by Washington's indifference to the plight of Palestinians as evidenced by Bush's reference to Sharon as a man of peace. They were outraged by the invasion of Iraq, especially in the absence of the stockpiles of weapons of mass destruction whose alleged existence had been used by the Bush team to justify the attack. But the growing hostility toward the United States was not specific to the Middle East: public opinion polls virtually everywhere indicated the widespread perception that the United States was itself the greatest threat to world peace. Despite the end of the Cold War, American defense spending remained enormous and there seemed to be no force on earth that could restrain Washington's use of its military. There was an extraordinary erosion of the "soft power," the admiration for American values and what America had once stood for.

What had gone wrong? In the United States and among political elites elsewhere in the West, the neoconservatives were held responsible. To be sure, Richard Perle and others like him will have much to explain when they meet their maker, but none of them were guilty of anything other than providing rationalizations for the action the two men who dominated the policy process, Dick Cheney and Don Rumsfeld, wanted to take. Cheney and Rumsfeld were not neoconservatives. They were simply old-fashioned nationalists determined to exercise American power without restraint. They were eager to punish America's enemies and maximize American interests. There was a temporary congruence of their goals and those of the neoconservatives, but nation-building and the expansion of democracy had never been high on their list of priorities. The postwar situation in Iraq was a result of their disinterest in the ultimate concern of the neoconservatives – as indicated by the complaints of neoconservative icons such as William Kristol and Robert Kagan.

Of course, as Harry Truman, once said, "The buck stops here." It was the man in the Oval Office who made the final decisions and gave the orders. Historians of American foreign relations will not be kind to him.

REFERENCES AND SUGGESTIONS FOR ADDITIONAL READING

REFERENCES

Introduction: Cold War as History

Kennedy, Paul *Rise and Fall of the Great Powers*, New York: Random House, (1987).

Chapter Two: In Search of a Compass

Bandow, Doug "Avoiding War," *Foreign Policy*, 89 (Winter 1992–3), 156–74

Carpenter, Ted Galen in Symposium, "America's Purpose Now," *National Interest*, 21 (Fall 1990), 26–61

Carpenter, Ted Galen "The New World Disorder," *Foreign Policy*, 84 (Fall 1991), 24–39

Fukuyama, Francis *The End of History and the Last Man*, London: Hamish Hamilton, (1992)

Harries, Owen "Of Unstable Disposition," *National Interest*, 22 (Winter 1990/91), 100–4

Harrison, Selig and Prestowitz, Clyde "Pacific Agenda: Defense or Economics," *Foreign Policy*, 79 (Summer 1990), 56–76

Hendrikson, David "The Renovation of American Foreign Policy," *Foreign Affairs*, 71 (Spring 1992), 48–63

Hormats, Robert "The Roots of American Power," *Foreign Affairs*, 70 (Summer 1991), 132–49

Indyk, Martin "Beyond the Balance of Power: America's Choice in the Middle East," *National Interest*, 26 (Winter 1991–2), 33–43

Joffe, Josef in Symposium, "America's Purpose Now," *National Interest*, 21 (Fall 1990), 26–61

Krauthammer, Charles "The Unipolar Moment," *Foreign Affairs*, 70 (1991), 23–33

Kristol, Irving "Defining Our National Interest," *National Interest*, 21 (Fall 1990), 16–25

Maynes, William "America without the Cold War," *Foreign Policy*, 78 (Spring 1990), 3–25

Nye, Joseph, *Bound to Lead*, New York: Basic Books (1990)

Nye, Joseph "Soft Power," *Foreign Policy*, 80 (Fall 1990), 3–13

Pfaff, William "Redefining World Power," *Foreign Affairs*, 70 (1991), 34–48

Russett, Bruce & Sutterlein, James "The U.N. in a New World Order," *Foreign Affairs*, 70 (Spring 1991), 69–83

Stedman, Stephen John "The New Interventionists," *Foreign Affairs*, 72 (1993), 1–16

Chapter Three: Clinton and Humanitarian Intervention

Huntington, Samuel "Why International Primacy Matters," *International Security*, 17 (Spring 1993), 68–83

Power, Samantha *"A Problem From Hell": America and the Age of Genocide*, New York: Basic Books, (2002)

Record, Jeffrey *Making War, Thinking History: Munich, Vietnam, and Presidential Uses of Force from Korea to Kosovo*, Annapolis: Naval Institute Press, (2002)

Chapter Five: The Clinton Years Assessed

Apple, R.W. *New York Times*, October 14, (1999), 1

Harries, Owen "An Offer Castro Couldn't Refuse – or Survive," *National Interest*, 44 (Summer 1996), 126–8

Johnson, Chalmers "Korea and Our Asia Policy," *National Interest*, 41 (Fall 1995)

Mandelbaum, Michael "Foreign Policy as Social Work," *Foreign Affairs*, 75 (January/February 1996), 16–32

Chapter 7

Clarke, Richard A. *Against All Enemies*, New York: Free Press, (2004)

Haass, Richard N. *Intervention: The Use of American Military Force in the Post-Cold War World*, rev. edn., Washington, D.C., Brookings Institution Press, (1999)

Kirkpatrick, David D. *New York Times*, June 29, (2004), 18

Woodward, Bob *Plan of Attack*, New York: Simon and Schuster, (2004)

ADDITIONAL READINGS

The student of America's role in recent world affairs will find several periodicals of exceptional value. They are *Foreign Affairs, Foreign Policy, Inter-*

national Security, National Interest, and Survival. There is no issue discussed in this book that is not raised and debated in those journals – to which policymakers, past and present, as well as scholars, contribute.

Introduction: Cold War as History

The most accessible surveys are Warren I. Cohen, *America in the Age of Soviet Power, 1945–1991* (Cambridge: Cambridge University Press, 1993) and Walter LaFeber, *America, Russia, and the Cold War, 1945–2002* (New York: McGraw-Hill, 2002). The ninth edition of LaFeber's classic includes a brief discussion of the decade after the end of the Cold War.

Chapter One: The End of the Cold War International System

The best place to start is with the perspective of President George H.W. Bush in George Bush and Brent Scowcroft, *A World Transformed* (New York: Alfred A. Knopf, 1998).

Other administration memoirs of value are James A. Baker III, *The Politics of Diplomacy: Revolution, War, and Peace, 1989 – 1992* (New York: G.P. Putnam's Sons, 1995); Robert M. Gates, *From the Shadows: The Ultimate Insider's Story of Five Presidents and How They Won the Cold War* (New York: Simon & Schuster, 1996); Colin Powell, *American Journey* (New York: Random House, 1995). See also essays in Seweryn Bialer, *Politics, Society, and Nationality Inside Gorbachev's* Russia (Boulder: Westview Press, 1989), Jack F. Matlock, *Autopsy on an Empire: The American Ambassador's Account of the Collapse of the Soviet Union* (New York: Random House, 1995), and Archie Brown, *The Gorbachev Factor* (Oxford: Oxford University Press, 1997) for insights into developments in the Soviet Union. Lawrence Freedman and Efraim Karsh, *The Gulf Conflict, 1990–91: Diplomacy and War in the New World Order* (Princeton: Princeton University Press, 1993) and the relevant chapters in Gary R. Hess, *Presidential Decisions for War* (Baltimore: Johns Hopkins University Press, 2001) are excellent on the Gulf War. For a brief discussion of Bush's mishandling of the Tiananmen massacre, see Warren I. Cohen, *America's Response to China*, 4th edn., (New York: Columbia University Press, 2000).

Chapter Two: In Search of a Compass

The journals noted above contain all of the articles discussed in this chapter. The conservative (sometimes neoconservative) *National Interest* is easily the most stimulating, especially for the years when it was edited by Owen

Harries. See also Ronald Steel's thoughtful *Temptations of a Superpower* (Cambridge: Harvard University Press, 1995)

Chapter Three: Clinton and Humanitarian Intervention

Warren Christopher's *Chances of a Lifetime* (New York: Scribner, 2001) is the memoir of Clinton's first secretary of state, indicating his priorities 1993–6. Thomas Lippman, *Madeline Albright and the New American Diplomacy* (Boulder: Westview Press, 2000) is a generally sympathetic biography of the first woman to serve as secretary of state and is useful for Clinton's first term when she served as ambassador to the UN. Albright tells the story her way in *Madam Secretary: A Memoir* (New York: Mirimax, 2003). David Halberstam's *War in a Time of Peace* is twice as long as it needed to be, but as in all of his work, filled with useful information and character sketches. William G. Hyland, *Clinton's World: Remaking American Foreign Policy* (Westport, C.T.: Praeger, 1999) is an unflattering analysis. There are useful articles on Somalia and Haiti in Demetrios James Caraley (ed.), *The New American Interventionism: Essays From Political Science Quarterly* (New York: Columbia University Press, 1999). Samantha Power, *"A Problem From Hell" America and the Age of Genocide* (New York: Basic Books, 2002), has superb accounts of events in Rwanda, Bosnia, and Kosovo.

Chapter Four: Managing the Great Powers

The memoirs and biographies suggested for Chapter Three are useful for Russian-American and Chinese-American relations as well. See also James M. Goldgeier, *Not Whether But When* (Washington, D.C.: Brookings Institution, 1999) on NATO expansion. Excellent access to the Russian side is provided by Michael Mandelbaum (ed.), *The New Russian Foreign Policy* (New York: Council on Foreign relations, 1998), Lilia Shevtsova, *Yeltsin's Russia: Myths and Reality* (Washington, D.C.: Carnegie Endowment for International Peace, 1999) and Archie Brown and Lilia Shevtsova (ed.), *Gorbachev, Yeltsin, Putin: Political Leadership in Russia's Transition* (Washington, D.C.: Carnegie Endowment for International Peace, 2001). Gail Lapidus, "Transforming Russia: American Policy in the 1990s," in Robert J. Lieber, *Eagle Rules?:Foreign Policy and American Primacy in the Twenty-First Century* (Upper Saddle River, NJ: Prentice Hall, 2002) is the best short discussion of its subject. For relations with China, see David M. Lampton, *Same Bed, Different Dreams* (Berkeley: University of California Press, 2001) and Robert Suettinger, *Beyond Tiananmen: The Politics of*

U.S.-Chinese Relations, 1989–2000 (Washington, D.C.: Brookings Institution, 2003). Frances G. Burwell and Ivo H. Daalder (ed.), *The United Sates and Europe in the World Arena* (New York: St. Martin's Press, 1999) is useful on the 1990s. The last chapter and epilogue of Michael J. Green's, *Arming Japan: Defense Production, Alliance Politics, and the Postwar Search for Autonomy* (New York: Columbia University Press, 1995) covers the initial Clinton administration approach to Japan. See also Michael H. Armacost, *Friends or Rivals: The Insider's Account of U.S. Japan Relations* (New York: Columbia University Press, 1996).

Chapter Five: The Clinton Years Assessed

Previously mentioned books by Hyland and Lippman are useful for Clinton's efforts to deal with Iraq. Material on Iran is less accessible. See Zbigniew Brzezinski, Brent Scowcroft, and Richard Murphy, "Differentiated Containment," in *Foreign Affairs*, 76 (May/June 1997) and Mark N. Katz, "The Khatemi Factor: How Much Does it Matter?" *National Interest*, 51 (Spring, 1998). Christopher discusses problem of coping with terrorism in his memoir. See also articles by Richard K. Betts, Bernard Lewis, and Ashton Carter, John Deutch, and Philip Zelikow in *Foreign Affairs*, 77 (1998). The Clinton administration's approach to North Korea and its nuclear weapons program is explained superbly by Joel S. Wit, Daniel B. Poneman, and Robert L. Gallucci in *Going Critical: The First North Korean Nuclear Crisis* (Washington, D.C.: Brookings Institution, 2004). For India, see Strobe Talbott's *Engaging India: Diplomacy, Democracy, and the Bomb* (Washington, D.C.: Brookings Institution, 2004). The relevant sections of Alfred E. Eckes, Jr. and Thomas W. Zeiler, *Globalization and the American Century* (Cambridge: Cambridge University Press, 2003) are helpful in understanding the meaning of globalization, its flaws, and Clinton's commitment to the concept. Christopher and Lippman discuss relations with Israel.

Chapter Six: The Vulcans Take Charge

The essential book on the backdrop to the Bush presidency and the Bush administration's foreign policy is James Mann, *Rise of the Vulcans: The History of Bush's War Cabinet* (New York: Viking, 2004). Also very useful is the volume by Ivo H. Daalder and James M. Lindsay, *America Unbound: The Bush Revolution in Foreign Policy* (Washington, D.C. Brookings Institution, 2003). An extreme statement of neoconservative positions can be found in David Frum and Richard Perle, *An End to Evil: How to Win the*

War on Terror (New York: Random House, 2004). There are several intriguing conservative critiques of neoconservative influences on Bush's policies, of which the most temperate is Stefan Halper and Jonathan Clarke, *America Alone: The Neoconservatives and the Global Order* (Cambridge: Cambridge University Press, 2004). The issues facing the Bush team – and its inability to confront them – are indicated in Michael O'Hanlon and Mike Mochizuki, *Crisis on the Korean Peninsula*, (New York: McGraw-Hill, 2003). Some insight into the administration's approach to the Middle East can be found in Tom Clancy and Tony Zinni, *Battle Ready* (New York: Putnam, 2004).

Chapter Seven: Once Upon an Empire

The literature on the American invasion and occupation of Iraq consists largely of journalistic accounts of daily events. To understand why so many members of the foreign policy elite accepted the decision to attack Iraq, start with Kenneth Pollack, *The Threatening Storm: The Case for Invading Iraq* (New York: Random House, 2002). John Newhouse, *Imperial America: The Bush Assault on the World Order* (New York: Knopf, 2003) is highly critical of the administration's contempt for its friends and the UN on the road to Iraq. Mann, Daalder and Lindsay, and Halper and Clarke mentioned above also have useful information on the war. See also Bob Woodward, *Plan of Attack* (New York: Simon and Schuster, 2004).

Chapter Eight: All the Rest and Bush Assessed

Again, accounts of other issues confronted by the Bush administration are provided primarily by journalists and in the journals mentioned above. A final assessment of the Bush team's approach to the world may be premature.

INDEX